GANDHI, BOSE, NEHRU

Gandhi, Bose, Nehru

*and the Making of the
Modern Indian Mind*

REBA SOM

PENGUIN

VIKING

An imprint of Penguin Random House

VIKING

USA | Canada | UK | Ireland | Australia
New Zealand | India | South Africa | China | Singapore

Viking is part of the Penguin Random House group of companies
whose addresses can be found at global.penguinrandomhouse.com

Published by Penguin Random House India Pvt. Ltd
4th Floor, Capital Tower 1, MG Road,
Gurugram 122 002, Haryana, India

First published in Viking by Penguin Books India 2004

10 9 8 7 6 5 4 3 2

ISBN 9780670058006

Typeset in Bembo by Mantra Virtual Services, New Delhi
Printed at Replika Press Pvt. Ltd, India

www.penguin.co.in

In loving memory of my parents
Jyotsnamay and Manashi Ray

Contents

~

PREFACE

The years of the national struggle threw up a rich array of strategic alternatives with which Indian leaders hoped to engage the British rulers and finally wrest freedom from them. During this period, Indian nationalist thought underwent deep introspection, grappling with the hypocrisy of a colonial rule that mouthed liberal values while denying them to a subject people. At the same time, the leaders had to confront their own ambivalence, which encouraged socio-economic egalitarianism while preventing any social upheaval that might jeopardize a united front against imperialism. The leadership of the Indian National Congress (INC) also had to respond to the 'modernizing' mission of the West by going through a process of self-scrutiny and reassessment of tradition, often valorizing it, often critiquing it. Through the unusually high level of debates, the ideal of freedom was broadened and constantly redefined. Perhaps the value of anti-colonial nationalism lay in this articulation just as much as in the freedom project itself, for it was to shape the making of the modern Indian mind. It is also important to note that intellectual history being evolutionary in character, the positions adopted by the national leadership on crucial issues of the day, and on other matters of social, economic and political importance, were constantly revised and fine-tuned. Nor were British and western attitudes an unchanging bloc, being equally complex and ambivalent and subject to constant evolution.

This is a study of three national leaders—Mohandas Karamchand Gandhi, Subhas Chandra Bose and Jawaharlal Nehru. It not only traces the history of their political interactions in devising strategies for India's freedom, but more importantly it also studies the plethora of intellectual and ideological ideals and aspirations which emerged in significant part as a result of these interactions. Democracy, federalism, secularism and the quest for social justice still remain very basic issues in today's India, more than fifty years after the country gained independence. This is also a study of the different mindsets of the three men, conditioned by diverse family backgrounds and education, and divergent temperaments and regional compulsions. The three protagonists often represented contrasting approaches to these issues, which mirrored the variety in India's multilayered identity. Gandhi and Subhas, despite ostensibly differing styles of political functioning which made them adopt non-violent and violent options respectively, were both rooted in Indian traditions and values. Gandhi and Subhas, both deeply spiritual, were open at the same time to western values, which had to be adapted to suit the realities of modern India.

Jawaharlal, in contrast, was an agnostic and steeped in the western traditions of scientific and enlightened liberalism, which alone, he felt, could free India from the burden of years of ignorance and superstition and take her along the path to progress and development. He, however, remained sensitive to the multiple layers of India's identity and admired Gandhi's instinctive feel for this underlying ethos. Destiny chose Jawaharlal to be India's first prime minister and hence the leader who steered the young democracy from a subject colony to an independent country charting its course of history. Subhas died shortly before the nationalist struggle ended, and Gandhi died soon after independence was won. It was left to Jawaharlal to devise strategies within the constraints of political consensus to advance his vision.

More than fifty years down the road, many of the sterling constitutional and parliamentary values that he espoused such as democracy have taken root, while many others such as secularism have faced contestation, requiring fresh responses to India's lived realities. It is an apt moment to revisit the thoughts of Gandhi and Subhas on these crucial issues, which continue to remain very relevant as a counterpoint to the Nehruvian vision. In many ways, it was the rich corpus of ideas that these three remarkable men articulated that helped shape the society and politics of independent India.

The special focus of this study is Subhas Bose, a choice governed by my own reading of his writings and the Indian National Army (INA) records, and the realization that the discovery of many relatively unknown details about his thoughts and accomplishments dramatically alter the stereotypical image of his being merely a challenger to Gandhi who met a tragic end.

In a style blending historical narrative with a rich variety of anecdotes, the rapidly unfolding drama of changing political and social realities has been captured by contrasting and juxtaposing the thoughts and responses of these men.

This work was made possible by the award of the Jawaharlal Nehru Fellowship in 2000. I am most grateful to Dr Sumit Sarkar for having read my manuscript and given invaluable comments; Dr Sabyasachi Bhattacharya for helping me to visualize the chapters; Dr Rajat Kanta Ray for being there to bounce off my ideas; Dr Gowher Rizvi for always encouraging me to believe that a book was there, waiting to be written; Mr Khushwant Singh for constantly reminding me of the rigours of writing; and Himachal, my husband, for creating the space in the midst of a demanding diplomatic schedule so that I could finish the book.

It is perhaps in the fitness of things that I should be in Rome, which is perched between the past and the present, to formulate my thoughts on the philosophical mindsets of the three leaders. As an interesting aside to the unending delights of this eternal city, I recall a certain afternoon sitting on a hotel terrace overlooking the Spanish Steps. While my eyes lingered on the imposing skyline, I remembered how Gandhi had savoured the sights of the city during his brief visit in 1931 with Mussolini, and I realized I had to steel myself to getting down to the business of writing. Over a cup of tea, my elegant Italian friend asked me politely on whom I was doing research at the moment. I replied that she would not know the relatively unknown Indian leader who had dramatically escaped the British with a forged Italian passport. 'Not Chandra Bose?' she asked, and while I looked at her incredulously, she explained that her husband had been a young boy in Kabul when his father, Alberto Quaroni, Minister in the Italian Legation, had helped Subhas secure the passport of one Orlando Mazzotta, and his mother had undertaken secret errands carrying messages to Bose. A small world, I sighed as I resolved to begin my writing the next day.

Reba Som
'Villa Vignarola'

October 2003   Rome

~

ONE

WHITHER INDIA?

Reminiscing about free India's journey over the course of nearly six decades after independence, Prime Minister Atal Bihari Vajpayee recently observed with pride that India had been successful in holding on to two of its most precious ideals, the unity of the country and the idea of democracy, not a mean achievement given the record of many newly independent countries, including some in India's neighbourhood.[1] The meaning of democracy had, however, evolved with every new experience, as Vajpayee's India of a billion plus people in the beginning of the twenty-first century has moved considerably from the democracy that Nehru had heralded in a country with a population of around 400 million in 1947. Some of the foundational values have remained, including the creed of democracy, which, like Nehru's description of India herself, was to remain both as a myth and an ideal, yet holding a vital relevance for a pluralistic nation.

In the years between independence in 1947 and his death in 1964, India in many ways was Nehru. Chosen by Gandhi to be his political successor, an idealistic Nehru, on assuming the prime ministerial mantle, departed from the Gandhian vision and sought to lead the country through a maze of traditions and superstitions on the path to a modern future. An international education and exposure to Fabian socialist thinking in his youth had instilled in Nehru the liberal values of equity, secularism and democracy. He was convinced that to lead a tradition-bound country like India from its colonized past on the road to development and progress, the state must extend to it a protective and firm helping hand. Japan's frenetic pace of development in the early twentieth century after hundreds of years of self-imposed isolation, which helped her to make the leap from a medieval to a modern state, had deeply impressed Nehru. Japan had never known the luxury of being sweet sixteen, Nehru had written. He was convinced that after centuries of colonial rule which had turned back the clock of its progress, India had to be steered in the direction of economic self-sufficiency by protecting it from competition from abroad. Key infrastructural areas in public sector development became government controlled as five-year plans were drawn up to chalk out the country's development. The government invested heavily in multi-purpose projects in key river networks, heralding them as the temples of the future. Nehru's prescriptive formula for development was grounded in liberal values, but in a country of multiple levels and realities such as India it could not offer any universal panacea. His deep commitment to democracy made him nurture with keen interest its institutions, from parliamentary functioning at the Centre to maintaining close relations with the chief ministers in the states. But he did little to cultivate alternative leaders who could follow him, so that the prospect of replacing Nehru seemed daunting. Although the transition after his death in 1964 proved smooth and successful, the nation had agonized over the question, 'After Nehru, who?'

Also, Nehru's natural distrust of the western capitalist world, perhaps an extension of the anti-imperialist focus of the national movement, and his admiration for the Soviet model of development made him place considerable faith in central planning and state control for young India's industrial and modernization programmes. With a British intellectual's typical disdain for the world of commerce and the free market, and guided by the conviction that the public sector needed to occupy the vantage points of the economy, Nehru's vision of socialist economics was to become the guiding policy of India over the next several decades. In hindsight it appears that Nehru's socialist world view had cocooned the country for too long from external competition, encouraging inefficient and unproductive state undertakings. Although the fledgling democracy had required careful nurturing, an extended period of protection turned state undertakings into complacent and non-competitive units while inadvertently creating a lingering malaise of corruption and bureaucratic red tape. Moreover, the deep contradictions between the state rhetoric, encouraging radical social and economic reform, and the vested interests of the ruling classes, which stood in the way of sincere implementation of such policies, soon became manifest.

Nehru's staunch secularism, which sought to keep religion and state in discrete categories, ensured that the communal and caste tensions that rumbled just below the surface did not erupt into the open. The reform of personal law in matters of marriage, divorce, inheritance and adoption among various religious groups, which the Constitution's directive principles of state policy had pledged to create through a uniform civil code, remained incomplete. As initiator of the reform measure, Nehru had to be content with merely the Hindu Civil Code, which, too, was passed over the course of several years in a truncated fashion. Nehru's intention had been to infuse the vast body of personal laws, which had been shaped over the years by tradition, with the spirit of practicality, progressiveness and justice, in keeping with the demands of changing times. It was never his intention to threaten the sense of identity and pride that each community doubtless felt and which was the essence of a pluralist society. Alive to this sensitivity, Subhas Bose had, in fact, spoken of the need to assure Muslims and other minority groups in independent India that they were fully 'entitled' to keep their 'personal law' without 'any change in this respect being imposed by the majority'.[2] Unfortunately, the ambiguity remained, blurring the progressive logic of bringing about greater gender justice and national integration through uniform personal legislation. Consequently, the original project, which had been buried for years, has been dug out periodically to fuel dubious bids to gain political mileage from its slogan.

The Nehruvian legacy of laying the foundations of a democratic structure has, however, stood the test of the aberration of the Emergency, imposed by his daughter for a short period (1976–77). Indira Gandhi confessed to not being committed to any political philosophy but adopting programmes which she considered opportune or pragmatic. While her populist slogans aimed at the nation's poor sounded practical and attractive, the authoritarian implementation of some of her programmes proved to be unpopular. It is to the credit of India's electorate, largely unlettered though politically astute, that it unceremoniously rejected Indira Gandhi in the general elections of 1977, but chose to vote her back into office in 1980, when the alternative Janata Party government fell victim to the divisive pressures of coalition politics. Although it was a chastened Indira Gandhi who became prime minister for the second time, she had to pay the ultimate price for her high-handed dealing of the Sikh separatist movement. Her assassination in October 1984 numbed a nation still loyal to the Nehruvian tradition, and the people chose to welcome her son Rajiv Gandhi as prime minister.

Rajiv brought with him a freshness of vision and an eagerness to release the country from the backwaters of stagnation and corruption in which it had become mired. However, the economic reforms he initiated with a youthful optimism proved more cosmetic than real. Besides, in his keenness to appear impartial and secular on issues concerning religious communities, he often took positions which helped the conservative rather than the progressive cause. In the 1989 general elections, Rajiv Gandhi was voted out of office, dogged by allegations of corruption in the Bofors gun purchase scandal. During the two-year minority government of the Janata Party's V.P. Singh that followed, two simmering issues of considerable social and religious tension surfaced which were to change, perhaps forever, the country's polity. One was sparked off by Prime Minister Singh's decision to extend affirmative action and implement the Mandal Commission recommendations made in 1980 concerning job reservations for other backward classes in addition to what already existed for scheduled castes and tribes. Protests took on a gruesome character when students from largely middle class and affluent families, feeling challenged by the new dynamics of social balance, immolated themselves on city thoroughfares. The other was the launch of a nationwide agitation by the Bharatiya Janata Party (BJP) to reclaim the supposed site of the birthplace of Ram in Ayodhya on which the Babri Masjid had subsequently been built in the sixteenth century.

In the general elections of 1991, the popular verdict was swayed by the sympathy wave in favour of the Congress Party in the wake of the tragic assassination of Rajiv Gandhi. The Congress government led by Narasimha Rao, which served its full tenure of five years (1991–96), will go down in history for two significant reasons. Of considerable importance was the initiative taken by the prime minister along with his finance minister, Manmohan Singh, to launch economic reforms which loosened the tedious system of government controls built over four decades, and opened up many areas of the economy to the private sector and foreign investment. The Indian economy, reeling under galloping inflation and dwindling national reserves, which had necessitated in mid 1991 the humiliating step of pawning the gold reserves of the country, now got a breather. As capital from abroad began to flow into productive investments as well as into the stock exchanges, the foreign exchange reserves rose dramatically and the budget deficit was reduced. Despite this, the rate of overall growth was relatively slow, with the rate of population increase still not arrested. However, the trend of economic growth having once been set and the logic of the reforms vindicated, there could be no real reversal of the pattern even though governments were to change.

The other significant event that occurred during Narasimha Rao's tenure was a national shame. While an apathetic government looked on, the Babri Masjid was destroyed in December 1992 by the frenetic supporters of the movement for the rebuilding of the Ram temple in Ayodhya that had commenced earlier. As communal passions were deliberately stoked, the country saw some of the worst communal riots and violence in its history. The lid was removed from the cauldron of communal and caste passions, and as its scalding contents poured out, something changed forever in India's politics and social identity. The constitutional credo of secularism and equality was no longer perceived as a satisfactory guarantee of safeguarding the multiple anxieties and concerns of a pluralist nation. Caste and religion emerged as defining factors in contemporary electoral politics as never before. The BJP, the dominant partner in the National Democratic Alliance, which came to power in 1999, redefined the thrust of the country's identity politics and development in a manner markedly different from that of the Congress Party, now in opposition. More than fifty years after independence and the midnight hour when Nehru had spoken about India's tryst with destiny, several themes emerged for debate. Significantly, however, democracy as a process continued, although it was redefined in the context of India's plurality, new realities and specific challenges.

The test of a mature democracy is to absorb new realities while maintaining the foundational and core values of the Constitution, irrespective of changes in the government. The experiences of the past decades have allowed various options of governance to be tried out in the true spirit of democracy. The monolith of the Congress Party has given way to the reality of coalition politics, while the thrust of economic liberalization initiated by the Congress government has been left undisturbed by the BJP government with the realism to detect its potential for further success. Consequently, in the international arena there has been a consistent projection of the country's concerns and priorities. The many voices clamouring for attention in a democracy should not be seen necessarily as the voices of discord but rather as representing different perceptions of matters of common concern. The Nehruvian formula of protection and control had served the needs of a fledgling democracy but eventually it outlived its usefulness. Similarly, the mere existence of directive principles of secularism and equality in the Constitution were perhaps not enough to satisfy India's myriad religious, caste and gender concerns.

The open contestation of these concerns, accompanied by recurring manifestations of ugly violence, makes it imperative to revisit the thoughts of the key figures of India's nationalist struggle. These leaders expressed not only differences concerning the strategies to be adopted in the anti-imperialist movement but also differences in envisioning India itself. Their ideas were not static; they underwent shifts with a steady evolution in their own thinking in response to the changing pattern of events, and they continue to be relevant even today and provide both the backdrop and intellectual parameters for the clash of ideologies between liberals and conservatives.

The two principal protagonists in this study, Mahatma Gandhi and Subhas Chandra Bose, represent two diametrically opposed positions in the anti-imperialist struggle. Gandhi's approach of non-violent non-cooperation was hotly contested by Subhas, who advocated a more forceful and confrontational approach including, if necessary, violent intervention with external help in the struggle against British imperialism. Subhas was the only leader in the Congress who dared challenge Gandhi's leadership by advocating an alternative programme. The differences between Gandhi and Subhas made them strike different postures and take up contrary positions. While the rhetoric of Subhas made him appear as an uncompromising detractor of the Gandhian line, Gandhi, too, exhibited a ruthless firmness in edging Subhas out of the Congress leadership. They were, as he explained to Subhas, 'sailing in different boats' in their quest for national freedom. However, in a situation almost reminiscent of a familial relationship between a stern father and a rebel son, Subhas was to retain till the end an abiding, albeit grudging, admiration for Gandhi's magnetic popular appeal, the strength of his moral convictions, and the ease with which he could identify with the essential soul of India. Gandhi, in turn, admired Subhas's burning patriotism, his irrepressible zeal and enthusiasm, his reckless courage and defiance of convention. When they parted company in 1940, Gandhi told Subhas that if his path proved to be the correct one, he (Gandhi) would be the first to admit it by sending him a congratulatory message. In his later years, when Gandhi sensed acutely that he was politically isolated, his thoughts dwelt increasingly on

Subhas, whose mission and arduous work in mobilizing the INA he came to acknowledge and appreciate. Perhaps the differences between Gandhi and Subhas had more to do with their different formulations of an anti-imperialist strategy than with the substance or their innate dislike of imperialism. Below their differing idioms of expression, they drew on the same wellsprings of Indian tradition and culture and shared similar values. In the context of India's multi-textured pluralist identity, both pleaded for informed tolerance and generous accommodation. Convinced that India's identity had to be fashioned from her uniqueness and the diversity of her experiences, both came to believe that home-grown solutions in response to ground realities would be more relevant than introducing concepts and ideals transferred from western liberal thought.

This conviction was in contrast to the beliefs held by the third protagonist in this study, Jawaharlal Nehru. Nehru's western education, international exposure and deep commitment to liberal thinking gave him notions of leadership which were markedly different from those of Gandhi. In age and educational background, he was closer to Subhas, with whom he formed a team of young Congress leaders which could provide a foil to the more conservative Gandhian direction. However, as they evolved over the years and formulated their individual ways of thinking, Jawaharlal and Subhas moved further apart, with Jawaharlal being favoured with the support and indulgence of 'Bapu', who chose him to be his political successor. Yet regarding general ideas about and instinctive approaches to India's concerns, Jawaharlal was far removed from the Gandhian position. Indeed, intellectually he was closer to the nation's poet, Rabindranath Tagore, who had stayed out of direct politics but lent his voice to most matters of national concern. Tagore's views, often powerfully articulated, were often in disagreement with those of Gandhi. Gandhi, in turn, gave spirited and explanatory rejoinders to his detractors, and in the process provided a rich corpus of intellectual material against the background of which younger leaders like Nehru and Subhas were to evolve their own arguments on important issues of the day.

Gandhi and Tagore, as well as Subhas and Jawaharlal, projected intensely patriotic voices representing distinct regional and generational realities of India, each being a valid depiction of India's pluralism. Nor were their equations with one another always confrontational despite differences in opinion. There was a mature acceptance of each other's point of view, which provided the key to the working of a consensual approach in the anti-imperialist struggle. It is perhaps both the richness of this experience and their tolerance of each other's opinions that helped create a democratic consensus, which has seen the country through several general elections and government coalitions in the more than five decades since independence. To address the dynamics, realities and challenges of contemporary India, it would be useful to recall the well-considered opinions expressed by the founding fathers on many important issues.

For the first seventeen years of independent India's existence, Nehru's leadership gave a firm socialist basis to the economic development of the young nation. In his impatience to draw a country from its long colonized past to a modern industrial reality, Nehru felt the need to strengthen the democratic processes through institution building and by keeping a check on the divisive differences of caste, gender and religion through the constitutionally accepted norms of liberty, equal rights and secularism. The limitations of this modernizing mission, however, became apparent when constitutional guarantees proved incapable of raising various groups to the same level of development. As India's pluralist identity cried out for attention, several areas of contestation appeared in the post-Nehru period. It would be worthwhile to highlight some of these areas and contrast the thinking of the main protagonists of this study on these issues if only to provide some pointers in resolving them.

Perhaps the most important subject of debate has been democracy itself. The Westminster pattern of democracy—of one person one vote, where the winner takes all—had never found favour with Gandhi. He believed that real democracy rested on a commitment to deep-seated values, which could not be negotiated for gaining short-term political mileage. The inherent potential for trading loyalties and buying electoral support in a democracy disgusted Gandhi, leading to his cynical outburst in *Hind Swaraj* comparing Parliament to a prostitute. To Gandhi, the nerve centre of India lay in the villages; and government structures, therefore, ideally had to be village-centric, with chains of command emanating outwards from this epicentre in concentric circles. There would be no hierarchy in this arrangement but interrelatedness. To the western-trained temperament of Nehru, the foundation of a new state based only on the principles of equality and goodwill, as Gandhi suggested, seemed too vague. He was convinced of the need to base the new India on a representational framework of democracy with an underlying corpus of liberal, egalitarian values. The importance of focusing on local self-government was, however, well recognized. It was only much later though that his grandson Rajiv Gandhi effectively carried forward the idea through the introduction of panchayati raj in 1989. An eminently successful initiative to empower villages with the tools of self-governing institutions, panchayati raj has been continued by succeeding governments and epitomizes how a democratic institutional structure can successfully realize the Gandhian vision of local self-governance.

In general, however, the functioning of the world's largest democracy remains a great challenge. Apart from the daunting task of managing the election process, democracy by definition means multiple options, choices and methods, which often make a pluralist country like India resemble a 'functioning anarchy'. The democratic practice of 'rule by the majority' renders voiceless those who are at the lowest tiers of social and economic development. The temptations of succumbing to power brokering and corruption that are inherent in the system have, from time to time, provoked serious debates about the merits of a presidential system, or even a more authoritarian government, as an alternative and presumably more effective system. Subhas Bose had moved from an initial commitment to democracy to a conviction that perhaps a presidential form of government at best, or an authoritarian government at most, for the initial years after independence, could steer the country towards order and accountability. As Congress president in 1938, Bose had closely observed the working of the Congress governments in the states and had been disturbed by the level of corruption that prevailed. While not unaware of the excesses of the Nazi and fascist governments of Germany and Italy in wartime Europe, Subhas chose to selectively appreciate the efficiency and order he found in these countries. It was with considerable conviction, therefore, that in 1944 he declared his support for an authoritarian government for India. India's brief experience with the Emergency imposed by Indira Gandhi has, however, convinced the nation that any straitjacket formula which stifles the voices of its myriad diversities would never be acceptable. India will have to work out its democracy not according to any western framework but in accordance with its own peculiar realities and evolving identity.

One of the key planks of democracy is secularism, which is vital for maintaining India's multi-religious identity. With his scientific and agnostic temperament, Nehru was a committed secularist and felt that the only way to take the nation forward on the road to progress and development would be to keep religious differences at bay by separating religion from politics. He believed that unequal levels of economic and social progress lay behind the existing communal divide. Therefore, it was only by creating conditions of modern, scientific and industrial growth that differences between communal groups could be gradually ironed out. Moreover, the traditional interdependence of the Hindu and Muslim communities, based on their distinctive and rich artisanal traditions, would prove to be culturally binding once economic progress levelled their disparate standards of living. Refusing to raise religion as an issue or give cognizance to deep-rooted differences in religious temperament, Nehru believed that the modernizing and inclusive principle of secularism would be a more mature way of handling religious divisiveness. However, in a country like India, with a pronounced religious identity, this policy did little to create respect for differences in belief or to nurture an understanding of the compelling commitment to faith that many had. Those belonging to the Hindu faith held on to the illusive comfort of being a majoritarian group, despite the vast linguistic and regional diversity of its adherents, while those belonging to Muslim, Christian and other religious faiths experienced an anxious and diffident self-consciousness often felt by minorities. As the studied silence of a secular state failed to soothe and reassure the heightened religious sensitivities of a populous country, the fringe elements of the key religions came to fanatically appropriate the dogma and privileged themselves as the exclusive spokespersons of their respective faiths. The nation's periodic lapses into communal insanity, the most recent being in Gujarat in 2002, when frenzied groups of both Muslims and Hindus let loose their unabated fury resulting in the most horrific violence, call for sombre introspection.

It is perhaps time to re-examine Gandhi's appeal for informed tolerance among the nation's diverse religious groups. Gandhi's secularism did not mean an abstinence from the use of religious metaphors. As the mass leader of India's millions, with a highly developed religious consciousness, Gandhi appealed to what he called the religion beyond religions—the body of moral and ethical values underlying all religions which created a generosity of spirit and an accommodation of difference. Although the occurrence of religious images in Gandhi's discourses and his references to the ideal of Ramrajya embarrassed the secular spirit of Nehru, Gandhi remained rooted in his traditional Hindu identity while reaching out with humanity, compassion and brotherhood to other religious strands that wove the composite fabric of India's identity. Moved by the values of catholic simplicity and Christ's message of sacrifice and suffering, Gandhi also recommended a reading of the Koran to dispel some of the ill-informed assumptions that had grown about Islam. Gandhi's interfaith prayer meetings, attended by people across religious, regional and gender divides, were intended to appeal to the underlying sameness of all faiths and inculcate values of humanity, compassion and generous accommodation. Without this basic human respect for each other, no political pact or understanding among the different communities could ever succeed. As Rabindranath Tagore recognized, as long as Hindus continued to regard Muslims as *mlechhas* or impure and Muslims continued to regard Hindus as kafirs or non-believers, there could be no cordiality between them. Only an informed respect for the other's beliefs could create cordiality between the different communities, while economic and financial interdependence could augur well for a nation's progress.

This philosophy was put to the test with considerable success by Subhas Chandra Bose in the INA, and drew the spontaneous admiration of Gandhi and Nehru, which Bose, however, did not live long enough to receive. Breaking long-ingrained prejudices of religion, caste, class and gender, Subhas was able to build a cohesive fighting force on the basis of the principles of equality and tolerance. The introduction of measures such as community living, inter-dining, participation in each other's religious festivals, promotion solely on the basis of merit, strict disciplinary action against all discriminatory social behaviour, helped overcome age-old superstitions, led to a new-found respect for the richness of India's diversity, and forged a bond and interdependence for the realization of a common goal. INA veterans have claimed repeatedly that this was nothing short of a social revolution.

In independent India, two issues which have come to acquire a new urgency are caste and women. It was Gandhi who not only focused on the plight of the marginalized but also devised programmes aimed at drawing them from the periphery of society onto the centre stage of action. For an entire period—the Extremist phase of the nationalist struggle—the problems of caste and gender oppression had been sidelined on the ground that addressing such 'social issues' should be postponed until after the achievement of political independence. Gandhi put both issues onto the national agenda.

During the Non-cooperation–Khilafat movement, Gandhi made the ending of untouchability a necessary precondition of bringing about swaraj within a year as he had promised. His ideas with respect to dalit groups, socially challenged by the caste hierarchy, did have many limitations, leading at times to sharp confrontations with Ambedkar. However, what ultimately emerged from these conflicts was the system of reservations for dalits and adivasis in legislative assemblies and government jobs, a necessary balancing of the principle of universal equal rights with the recognition of difference, through affirmative action on behalf of the underprivileged. With respect to caste, despite a continued valorization in part of an 'ideal' varna system, Gandhi was arguably more perceptive than most other sections of the national movement, which tended either to postpone the resolution of this issue until after freedom, or thought that it was resolvable through modernizing development and/or a simplistic reduction of caste to class. After independence, the policy of reservation for scheduled castes and tribes continued but infrastructural inadequacies slowed down the pace of their development and improvement. However, the realization of their own political potential as vote banks gave them a new-found confidence. Today, with the dalit voice being increasingly heard and dalit-led governments assuming power in many parts of the country, a new dimension has opened up in India's democratic politics. As dalits find themselves in the political limelight, they struggle to let go of the anger and bitterness caused by centuries of economic repression, political neglect and social rejection. To cope with the new socio-political reality, the upper castes in turn have to let go of their ingrained social and political prejudices and adopt a more accommodating and generous posture. This is where various constituents keep an anxious watch on the role of the state, which has to maintain a balance and reassure its citizens that it will protect the best interests of all. Any fear in this regard can spark off horrific violence as the protests against the Mandal Commission recommendations have demonstrated. Perhaps there is a need, never more than at present, to reassert the Gandhian philosophy of love and goodwill among communities.

Women, too, had been brought into the mainstream of the national movement principally by Gandhi, who was convinced that their non-violent nature and natural endurance would make them ideal participants in his non-cooperation movement. He called on women to actively participate in courting arrest, picket foreign cloth shops, and face brutal repression during the salt satyagraha. However, Gandhi kept their participation within well-defined parameters, as he never foresaw an active political career for women. A believer in gender equality of a kind, Gandhi felt that men and women had different but equally important roles to play; women as natural homemakers enjoyed a space distinct from that of men, who were providers. In Gandhi's colourful imagery, women who sought to ride the horse that men rode only succeeded in bringing down both.

Nehru instead saw women's participation in the freedom movement gradually leading to their seeking a larger social and economic freedom for themselves. Overcoming the marginalization and suppression that they had historically suffered, women would have the opportunity to empower themselves and rise in their own estimation. This could, however, never happen without women themselves taking the initiative and claiming equal opportunities and rights from a patriarchal society. The role of the state would be to provide the legal framework to support women's pleas for greater freedom. It was in this spirit that Nehru pressed hard for the incorporation of gender equality in the Fundamental Rights Resolution, passed by the Congress in 1931. He was convinced that if not spelt out, women's rights would remain unrecognized by default. He recalled the dignified reticence of the Indian women's delegation which had met Lord Montagu in 1917 to ask for voting rights but not reservation of seats. However, the mere enshrining of the principle of gender equality as part of Congress policy in 1931, or the detailed planning that Nehru initiated for women's development in 1938, did little to bring about any actual change in their situation since stereotypical prejudices remained deeply ingrained. Nehru stirred a hornet's nest of opposition in Parliament when, as prime minister, he initiated measures for the reform of personal laws; he realized ruefully that those who had voted in principle for gender equality in 1931 were not willing to back this through action. As a consequence, much of what Nehru initiated on behalf of gender equality, such as the enactment of the Hindu Civil Code, or the opening up of the civil services to women, or the appointment of women to key public posts, remained largely symbolical. So long as stereotypical assumptions remained and patriarchal mindsets continued, true gender equality would remain elusive. In this context, it is worthwhile to recall the vision of Subhas Bose regarding the role of women.

Like Gandhi, Subhas constantly spoke about the superior moral and spiritual strength of women, but, unlike Gandhi, he was unwilling to prescribe a separate path for them. Just as Indian men had to improve their physical stamina and counter the colonial stereotype of them in general, and of Bengali men in particular, as being weak and emasculated, women, too, had to counter the label of being *abala* or helpless. Perhaps for the first time in India's history, women were encouraged to march shoulder to shoulder with men and face the same challenges. While the sight of a marching women's contingent in the Bengal Volunteers in 1928 caused some mirth, it also shattered some stereotypes and helped improve the women's own image of themselves. Later, while forming the Rani of Jhansi Regiment in the INA in 1943, Subhas emphasized that the women's regiment was not a mere symbolic presence. The women, mostly recruited from plantation families, were largely illiterate and had led sheltered lives. They had to reinvent themselves, sporting cropped hair and army fatigues, rifle in hand, and march with the men on the battlefield while facing real danger, starvation and enemy fire. Only such equal participation, Subhas felt, could earn for the women equal treatment and shake the inbuilt social conditioning of centuries which had privileged men over women. Subhas's INA mission failed, and the Ranis of the Jhansi Regiment could never fulfil the larger mission that he had foreseen for them—namely to spread the message of women's equality, education and empowerment to India's remote corners after independence.

Today, more than half a century after India's freedom, the condition of women still remains unequal. Broad demographic data show an unfavourable sex ratio with regard to women, higher female infant mortality, a significant number of cases involving female foeticide, continuing incidence of child marriage, rising rates of reported dowry deaths and bride burnings, low levels of female literacy and work-force participation. However, today there is also a greater awareness of these areas of concern, and women's voices are being increasingly heard whether from decision-making positions at the panchayat level, or as assertive dalit voices in government legislatures, or as political lobbyists agitating for securing one-third representation for women in Parliament.

The international image of India had been a subject of serious reflection for both Nehru and Subhas. During the period of the national movement, both were appalled at the ignorance about India that existed in Europe and were convinced of the need for effective publicity to win support for India in her anti-colonial struggle. They, therefore, supported the formation of various Indian associations in many European cities consisting principally of Indian students and professionals, who were encouraged to become, in effect, ambassadors of India abroad and spread the word about India's rich cultural heritage and her current struggle against foreign rule. Subhas Bose, who was to spend several years in Europe as a political exile, took a particular interest in promoting the activities of these associations.

In the more than half century since independence, there has been a sea change in the way India has been perceived by the world. In the early years, the struggle to achieve economic development faced by the fledgling democracy evoked a condescending sympathy among more advanced nations. The lack of suitable infrastructure, and the resultant delay in the emergence of employment opportunities, discouraged a large number of qualified Indian professionals, who left India within decades of her independence. Non-professional Indian workers, too, found lucrative avenues of employment outside the country. The economic liberalization of the 1990s and the opening up of several sectors of the Indian economy to international investment, coupled with the proven excellence of Indians in the field of information technology and the substantial remittances sent home by Indians living abroad, have created the image of a resurgent India with a considerably bright future. The dream of Subhas Bose—that the twenty-first century would be India's—now does not seem merely a fond hope. The significant success that Indians have achieved in the professional work environment abroad has encouraged planners to dream of a similar success in India. As Prime Minister Vajpayee reflected, 'I often ask myself the question: if Indians can overcome all the odds and succeed spectacularly outside India, why can't we do so in India?'[3]

It is perhaps also worth pondering the significance of Subhas's success in having engendered in the INA the sterling values of tolerance and compassion among Indians irrespective of their many regional, religious, caste and gender differences. Any economic progress or development that modern India makes will be fragile unless it is grounded on popular goodwill. Unfortunately, this goodwill is being constantly vitiated by fanaticism, terrorism and the country's inability to accommodate the historically disadvantaged groups, women and minorities. There is no doubt that coexisting along with the 'shining face' of a burgeoning India is the dark face of continuing poverty, deprivation and unequal opportunities. It is a supreme irony that India today can be viewed in effect as two Indias: the smaller India, yet running into more than 300 million people as a fraction of her billion plus population, that is strident, aspiring and competitive, and the larger India, that is deprived and still awaiting the opportunity to share in the full fruits of democratic equity and development. Merely grounding the country on hallowed and exalted principles of social justice and egalitarian values as spelt out in the Constitution will not suffice. India's plurality and diversity need to be respected and accommodated through a spirit of generous understanding. What is needed to generate this spirit is an appeal to the intrinsic body of moral and ethical values, which Gandhi called dharma and Subhas described as 'love'. This was one of the cardinal principles that Subhas identified as being necessary to form the basis of India's collective life, the others being freedom, justice, equality and discipline.

Chapter Two, 'Sailing in Different Boats', focuses on the alternative strategies adopted in the struggle for freedom principally by two leaders, Gandhi and Subhas, keeping the story of Nehru's participation as an important counterpoint. But beyond the differences in political stance and rhetoric, there were also patterns in ideological thinking which were the result of a shared heritage and varied experiences in education and familial backgrounds. These patterns are explored in Chapter Three, 'Bapu, His Beloved Disciple and the Rebel Son'. Preoccupation with the anti-colonial struggle did not, however, prevent the leaders from thinking about India's future. While Gandhi and Nehru envisaged the shape of things to come and defined the priorities to be addressed by free India, it was Subhas who was afforded by circumstances the opportunity to not only dream of a future for India, but also to actually try out some of his cherished ideas in the alternative government in exile that he set up during the Azad Hind initiative. Chapter Four, 'Envisioning India', dwells at greater length on this hands-on initiative of Subhas after exploring the broad perceptions of the three leaders.

'Whither India?' Nehru had asked in 1933. He wrote:

> Never in the long range of history has the world been in such a state of flux as it is today. Never has there been so much anxious questioning, so much doubt and bewilderment, so much examining of old institutions, existing ills and suggested remedies. There is a continuous process of change and revolution going on all over the world, and everywhere anxious statesmen are almost at their wits' end and grope about in the dark. It is obvious that we are a part of this great world problem and must be affected by world events.[4]

Many of the observations Nehru made then continue to be relevant even today. Perhaps it is time today to take stock of where India is heading, consult the evidence of past thinking, and direct the nation's course on the path to an improved future.

~

SAILING IN DIFFERENT BOATS

Late at night on 16 January 1941, Sisir Bose, a young medical student, carefully drove his father's Wanderer automobile out of the gates of the Elgin Road residence of the Boses in Calcutta. The only passenger was his uncle Subhas Bose, who was escaping house arrest from under the very nose of the police guards stationed by the British authorities to keep watch on the house. A few weeks ago, he had been provisionally released from Presidency Jail on account of physical weakness brought on by a hunger strike, and was to be remanded once he recovered his strength. Had the guards peered at the rear seat they would have seen not Subhas but an unfamiliar bearded Muslim gentleman, in a long, brown, closed-collar coat, and a black fez cap on his head. The transformation from Subhas to the insurance agent, Mohammad Ziauddin, was so convincing that several hours later Asoke Bose could hardly recognize his uncle when he called on him at his residence in Bararee, near Dhanbad, more than 200 miles away from Calcutta.

Later, on the evening of 17 January, Subhas was escorted by his nephews to Gomoh station, where he boarded the Kalka Mail to Delhi, changing thereafter to the Frontier Mail for the onward journey to Peshawar. Met by contacts from the Kirti Kisan Party, linked to the CPI, whom he had assiduously cultivated earlier, Subhas planned his next move to Kabul. After a couple of days, Bhagat Singh Talwar, who took on the name of Rahmat Khan, accompanied his religiously inclined 'uncle', Ziauddin, on a pilgrimage to Adda Sharif in Kabul. Bhagat Singh was extra solicitous of this special uncle who appeared to be deaf and dumb, a careful precaution to avoid detection, helping Subhas through the rough wintry Afghan terrain on foot and on mule-back until they reached Kabul on 27 January.

Once in Kabul, Subhas spent more than six anxious weeks dodging attention while trying to figure out where he would be heading next. Efforts to establish contacts with officials of the Soviet government failed. The German Legation, however, was successfully contacted and kept in touch with him through their German representative of Siemens. Finally, he was put in touch with the Minister of the Italian Legation, Alberto Quaroni, who assisted him in getting a passport impersonating a clerk working in their office. Discarding his fez cap and long coat and donning western clothes, Ziauddin now became Orlando Mazzotta. An understanding between Germany, Italy and Russia allowed Subhas to travel across Russia on an Italian diplomatic passport. Accompanied by a German engineer, Subhas travelled by car on 18 March through the high passes of the Hindu Kush and crossed the Oxus to reach Samarkand, from where he took a train to Moscow. In early April 1941, he arrived in Berlin on a flight from Moscow. It had been more than two months since he had left Calcutta. Recalling his great escape later, Subhas commented that it had all the makings of a Sherlock Holmes thriller.[1]

Did Subhas really need to leave the shores of the country to realize his dream of liberating India? He confessed that had he any alternative he would have stayed on. The advice of President de Valera of Ireland, whom Subhas had met during his exile in Europe in 1934, that he should hasten back to India to be in the theatre of action, had always impressed him.[2] While in Germany, he bitterly regretted not being in India to participate in the Quit India movement in 1942. Then why was there such a sense of urgency in him to leave the country in quest of allies in his anti-imperialist mission? His great escape was not an impetuous move. He had studied his options well and taken a calculated risk. He tried sending feelers to Japan but his emissary was captured.[3] He had explored the option of getting help from Russia but to no avail.[4] For the contingency of a possible escape, he had cultivated German and Japanese officials in the Consulates of Bombay and Calcutta and made meticulous plans. Perhaps what had finally spurred him on was the realization that he could not work with Gandhi's strategy in the nationalist struggle.

Both leaders were strong willed and definite in their formulation of tactics, which were in direct opposition to one another. Like the stern father and the rebel son, there was a realization that they could not share a common space and had to pursue their different destinies. Gandhi was tired of trying to make Subhas toe his line. Pointing out that they were 'sailing in different boats',[5] Gandhi made it clear that he would be the first to congratulate him if his path proved to be the correct one. Subhas, too, came to realize that the pressure tactics that he had been consistently applying on the Gandhian position, to harness Gandhi's magnetic appeal among the masses and the bargaining position he had among the British, for a more confrontational position in the national movement would never succeed. Once outside the country, as the scope of a conflicting relationship between them was reduced, both men came to see in the other the same burning patriotism and unyielding conviction regarding their individual policies in the anti-British struggle. There was, furthermore, a realization that they shared common approaches in their perceptions of India beyond the immediate struggle, which found a resonance in their projected visions of the country's future. Anchored firmly in their sense

25

of Indianness and drawing from the same wellspring of traditional values and beliefs, both Subhas and Gandhi were actually much closer in their philosophical mindsets than is realized, as we shall analyse in the next chapter. However, for the larger part of their political lives they supported contrasting programmes, engaged in challenging rhetoric backing alternative leadership programmes and fought ruthlessly to the finish. It is this impression that has lingered in public memory. Although Jawaharlal Nehru, too, was a close associate of Bose in his bid to force the pace of the Gandhian movement, in personality and responses they remained distant. Nehru with his western upbringing and education did not share Gandhi's instinctive feel for certain realities of India's socio-religious identity, with which Bose empathized. However, as Gandhi's designated successor, Nehru's differences with the Mahatma were never publicly articulated, nor did he ever think of embarking on a parallel path.

This chapter describes the confrontation between the young Congress leadership, particularly Bose and Nehru, and Gandhi, which for Bose reached a point of no return. In trying to understand this story, it is important to see the regional compulsions and realities that moved Subhas. He inherited many of the perceptions and attitudes shared by the Bengal politicians, particularly his mentor, C.R. Das, towards Gandhi and the Gandhian style of politics, which invariably conditioned his approach and thinking. There were five major strands in this conditioning.

First, Gandhi's policy of non-cooperation had been received in Bengal with studied apprehension. For one, the strategy of boycotts, strikes and non-cooperation was not new to Bengal with its experience of swadeshi tactics, which had helped to undo in 1911 the British partition of Bengal in 1905. Gandhi's message could not, therefore, be credited with any novelty. It also evoked a wary response in a people who had recent memories of experiencing the discomfort of giving up their vocations and courting arrest. Moreover, the Montford Reforms of 1919, with their promises of greater devolution of power at the regional level, offered interesting possibilities to those who had ambitious of engaging in legislative politics. Boycott of the councils, a prominent plank in the Gandhian programme, did not, therefore, cause immediate enthusiasm. Besides, Gandhi's strategy of boycott, which called upon the Bengali bhadralok to stay away from educational institutions and law courts, very often their professional sites, while leaving undisturbed the economic activities of the indigenous mill owners, largely Marwari, created a feeling of unease. Gandhi was a relative newcomer to the nationalist scene and although the success of his South African experience gave him confidence, he trod the ground carefully as he tried to skilfully win over to his cause established national stalwarts such as Motilal Nehru and C.R. Das. The passing of the non-cooperation resolution, first at the AICC session in Calcutta and then decisively at the session in Nagpur in 1920, was not the result of Gandhi hypnotizing the Congress into capitulation as is often imagined,[6] but rather the outcome of hard bargaining between Gandhi and the stalwarts. While forcing Gandhi to agree to extend the scope and definition of the boycott to include an economic boycott as well, Das was also able to modify the call for staying away from legal and educational institutions to a 'gradual' rather than an immediate measure. Moreover, he seized upon Gandhi's promise of one year as the time sought for bringing around the British to agree to the nationalist demands, as the weapon to rein in the impatient and impetuous Bengal youth, many of them revolutionaries, and also to buy time before launching on another course if the present move proved unsuccessful. Besides, by using the

Congress platform in 1920 to announce the renunciation of the legal profession, which had earned him arguably one of the highest fees in the country, Das became overnight the Deshbandhu or friend of the nation. When Subhas, on resigning from the ICS, returned in 1921 to join the non-cooperation activities in Bengal, he responded to the regional dynamics by giving pride of place to Das, who was his hero and mentor, rather than Gandhi, who in any case had failed to impress him in a meeting held earlier in the year.[7]

Second, Subhas also inherited the sense of cultural incredulity that Bengal initially felt towards Gandhi and Gandhism. To Bengal, accustomed to a certain primacy of role in leading the national struggle, the leadership offered by a loincloth-clad Gandhi was received with cynicism. His call for compulsory spinning by charkha seemed to a people fed on the activist philosophy of Vivekananda a slightly absurd obsession with a non-intellectual manual exercise. Further, Gandhi's well-known attack on doctors and lawyers in his *Hind Swaraj* did not go down well in a society which prided itself on its traditional commitment to these two vocations. Besides, Gandhi's food fetishes and his commitment to vegetarianism caused some dismay among Bengalis who distinctly relished a non-vegetarian cuisine. The involuntary shudder of Gandhi as he walked past a goat sacrifice in the Kalighat temple, and his conviction that it should be banned,[8] was matched by the initial dismay of the inmates of Abhay Ashram to the Gandhian stricture of vegetarianism, which they finally altered to include fish, after convincing Gandhi that it was their only source of protein and historically an integral part of their diet.[9] Commenting on the condescending arrogance felt by the largely Shakta Bengali bhadralok to the Vaishnavas in general and to Gandhi in particular, Nirad Chaudhuri recounted the memorable occasion when Gandhi had stayed in the Bose

household as a guest in 1937.[10] To cater to Gandhi's strict
dietary needs and to live up to the family honour of traditional
hospitality, Subhas assiduously used his Calcutta Corporation
contacts to maintain a steady supply of fresh vegetables and
ensure that there was a daily line-up of she-goats from among
which Gandhi's secretary, Mahadev Desai, could inspect and
select the source of Gandhi's milk intake for the day.
Chaudhuri's caustic observation was that Mahadev Desai's
choice fell on the she-goat which could stare back at him
with a chaste and non-guilty expression.

Third, an aspect of Gandhi that was anathema to the Bengali
psyche was his unconditional condemnation of revolutionary
terrorism. Inspired by the activist cry in the novels of Bankim
Chandra Chattopadhyay and nurtured by Vivekananda's call
to shake off a customary lethargy and awaken to greater physical
prowess and determination, Bengal accorded considerable
respect and admiration to its rich revolutionary tradition. Most
of the political leaders found the bulk of their student and
youth support from among revolutionary groups such as
Anushilan and Jugantar, which, however, had to be harnessed
in the right direction. Although leaders and thinkers such as
C.R. Das and Rabindranath Tagore condemned the wanton
killing and bloodshed that terrorism unleashed and lamented
the misguided zeal of the youth, there was at the same time an
acknowledgement of their intrinsic commitment and
fearlessness. Gandhi's reservations about giving Congress
endorsement to a resolution saluting the martyrdom of
Gopinath Saha in 1924, his reluctance to acknowledge the
sacrifice of Jatin Das who fasted to death in 1929, a strategy to
which he himself often took recourse, or his inability later, in
1931, to persuade the British to alter the death penalty for
Bhagat Singh and his associates, troubled the conscience of
Bengali youth. Over the years, it remained a constant challenge

for Subhas to impress upon Gandhi the necessity of including in his periodic talks with the British authorities the issue of the release of Bengal's political prisoners, many of whom were revolutionaries.

Fourth, an issue on which both Bose and Gandhi shared the same conviction, and yet were constrained to adopt different positions because they operated at the regional and national levels respectively, was the communal question. Gandhi's desire to bring Muslim participation into the mainstream of the national movement, by appealing to the emotive Khilafat issue in 1917, found a parallel in the initiative taken by C.R. Das in 1923 to include the Muslims in a pact which would result in a generous seat sharing of all communities, with an edge for Muslims at both the corporation and the council levels. This was a remarkable measure especially so because the Muslims were in any case in a majority in Bengal. By bringing Muslims into the centre stage of political and municipal action, Das sought to give them greater confidence in a realm normally dominated by the Hindus. However, though the pact was adopted by the Serajgunj session of the Bengal Congress, Das was unable to get the national Congress to pass it at the general session. Subhas, too, was to inherit Das's passion for and commitment to communal harmony, but faced the same ambiguities when he tried to implement many of his well-articulated positions. While at a philosophical level he received Gandhi's support for his commitment to the policy of Hindu–Muslim harmony, at the regional level of working out the details of any arrangement, Gandhi, as continental leader, often found it difficult to support him. Also, he was often impeded by the contradictions of his own position.

Finally, the Gandhian pattern—of agitation, retreat and constructive activities—was not matched by the same rhythm in the strategy of other Congress leaders. Once the Bengal leadership joined Gandhi in the non-cooperation programme of 1920, expectations were raised about maintaining a certain tempo in the anti-imperialist campaign. That, however, never happened because Gandhi did not share the sense of urgency of Congress stalwarts Motilal Nehru and C.R. Das regarding contemporary events. For instance, Das felt strongly that the Congress should have responded in 1921 to the British offer of a round table meeting made soon after the hartal in Calcutta boycotting the visit of the Prince of Wales had proved successful. It would also be a face-saving arrangement for Das to placate Bengal's revolutionary youth who had been reined in by Gandhi's promise of gaining concessions from the British authorities within a year. However, Das was in jail and Subhas, his fellow inmate in jail, noted how distraught he was when Gandhi failed to resolve the situation. In vain did Das berate Gandhi in a statement declaring, 'You bungled it and mismanaged it. Now you turn round and ask people to spin and do the work of the Charka alone. The proudest Government did bend to you. If I had not been in jail, I would have forced the country to accept them.'[11] Similarly, in 1922, at the height of the non-cooperation movement, Gandhi's decision to call a halt after the violent attack on a police outpost in Chauri Chaura took the Congress stalwarts by total surprise. The frustration resulting from a repeated sense of missed opportunities spurred a decision among leaders such as Das and Motilal Nehru to branch off from the Gandhian direction and initiate an independent policy of constitutional politics. The Swarajist Party of Das and Motilal Nehru, formed in 1923 after bitter acrimony in the Congress between the pro-changers and the no-changers, spoke of contesting the council elections and once elected, sabotaging the work of the government by non-cooperation from within. Subhas, as the onlooker of these developments, observed first Das's deep frustration and disappointment with Gandhi and then his decision to steer an independent path. This impression was to shape many of Subhas's subsequent responses to Gandhi in the course of his own political career. He did not privilege Gandhi with any larger-than-life image and felt that he was as fallible as any other man. However, he was struck by the unique mass appeal of Gandhi and, after the death of Das in 1925, took upon himself the responsibility of keeping alive the thrust of the Gandhian challenge to the British while preventing any temporizing move that might break its momentum. He remembered well Das's analysis of Gandhi, 'The Mahatma opens a campaign in a brilliant fashion; he works it up with unerring skill; he moves from success to success till he reaches the zenith of his campaign—but after that he loses his nerve and begins to falter.'[12] Subhas felt it his mission to prevent the Mahatma from sliding and faltering. However, he failed to realize that while the newcomer Gandhi had been charitable to the independent line adopted by Das and Motilal, a mature Gandhi who proved himself to be the unquestioned leader of the masses would find Subhas's detracting moves very irksome and in the end would dispense with his challenge.

While C.R. Das was alive, the sheer strength of his personality was enough to keep together all the disparate political elements in Bengal, although the magic of the Bengal Pact was gradually wearing off. His sudden death in June 1925 created a leadership vacuum. With Subhas in jail, Gandhi stepped in to resolve the power tussle, entrusting J.M. Sengupta, a well-known barrister from Chittagong and a trusted lieutenant of Das, with a triple crown, namely of mayor of the Calcutta Corporation, president of the Bengal Congress, and leader of the Swaraj Party in the legislative council. After his release in 1927, there began a phase of intense political rivalry between Subhas and the Gandhi loyalist, Sengupta. Sengupta was supported by social workers such as Satish Chandra Dasgupta and Prafulla Chandra Ghosh, who ran ashrams inspired by Gandhian principles, and Marwari traders and business leaders such as G.D. Birla, whose economic interests were best served by Gandhian non-violence and the suspension of revolutionary activities. Subhas received support from a prominent Hindu bhadralok coterie consisting of Nirmal Chander Chunder, a wealthy Calcutta barrister, Nalini Ranjan Sarkar, a businessman from Mymensingh, Bidhan Chandra Roy, a distinguished physician, Tulsi Goswami, the Oxford-educated scion of the Serampore royal family, and Sarat Chandra Bose, an eminent lawyer who was the older brother of Subhas. This group, called the Big Five by a Calcutta journalist, actively participated in the dynamics of an evolving political leadership drama in Bengal. The fact that Sengupta and Bose hailed from two different parts of Bengal, one from the largely rural east and the other from the more urban Calcutta-centric west, lent a local colour to this competitive rivalry. Even the youth and student support that they garnered was according to this orientation. Thus, the pre-eminently revolutionary group Anushilan, based in Dacca, supported Sengupta while the Jugantar, based in Calcutta, supported Bose. Local newspapers captured the political conflicts, so that while the *Amrita Bazar Patrika* reflected the Gandhian position and the *Advance* represented Sengupta, the *Forward* and the *Liberty* were pro-Bose. This rivalry became so endemic and the rival factions so volatile and quarrelsome that the larger picture of the national movement threatened to get blurred amidst squabbles regarding election disputes in the BPCC or the AICC or the composition of the Bengal contingent to the Congress sessions, necessitating periodic interventions by an exasperated Gandhian high command.

In 1927, on his release from jail, Subhas made a committed

comeback to the Bengal political scene, winning a Swarajist seat in the council and replacing Sengupta as president of the Bengal Congress. Addressing students, workers and peasants in extensive political rallies and reaching out to Muslims in the spirit of the Pact that Das had created, Subhas sought to promote all-round mobilization for the national cause. At the all-India level, he sought to keep up a sustained pressure on Gandhi so that the goal of the Congress movement would be nothing less than complete independence. In this he found a close associate in Jawaharlal Nehru.

The deep-felt anguish experienced by Jawaharlal at the Jallianwala Bagh massacre of 1919 led him to opt out of his sedentary legal practice and join the Gandhian movement. Although disappointed and 'angry'[13] at Gandhi's sudden decision to withdraw the non-cooperation movement after the Chauri Chaura incident in 1922, Jawaharlal did not share his father's predilection for council politics. He felt that council entry would inevitably lead to the blind alley of constitutionalism and reformism.[14] During a two-year stint in Europe from 1926–27, when he participated as Congress representative at the International Congress against Colonial Oppression and Imperialism in Brussels, and attended Moscow's decennial celebrations of the 1917 Revolution, Jawaharlal came to be exposed to Marxist and radical ideas. He now realized that nationalism by itself was 'a narrow and insufficient creed. Political freedom, independence, were no doubt essential, but . . . without social freedom and a socialistic structure of society and the State, neither the country nor the individual could develop much'.[15] Jawaharlal returned to India with a wider outlook and a clearer perception of world affairs. Like Subhas, he saw the importance of increasing the pace of the national movement by holding out complete independence as the immediate political goal of the Congress. To Jawaharlal the social goal of ending socio-economic disparity was equally important but he realized that the Congress might not be willing to go that far. He, therefore, resolved to spread the socialist message outside the Congress among labour circles and the youth.

Jawaharlal returned to India just in time to attend the Madras session of the Indian National Congress in December 1927, presided over by Dr Ansari. For the past year, Jawaharlal had been deliberating on the necessity of forming a pressure group within the Congress to counter the activities of those who tried to hold the organization back. Complaining bitterly against the moderate mentality of the leadership, Nehru had written in January 1927 to the general secretary of the Congress, 'The mention of Independence frightens them and every effort is made to dissociate oneself from the idea or from its implications.'[16] At Madras, Jawaharlal was determined to change the goal of the Congress from dominion status to complete independence. He could not accept the usual argument that there was no real difference between the two because the former carried with it the right to secede. The assent to dominion status, Nehru felt, was an indication of India's mental degradation, for behind it was an unquestioning acceptance of the inevitability of a British presence in India. He complained to Gandhi, 'It passes my comprehension how a national organisation can have as its ideal and goal, dominion status. The very idea suffocates and strangles me.'[17] In his resolution in Madras, Jawaharlal defined independence to include full control over the defence forces of the country, financial and economic policy, and relations with foreign countries. Though not present in Madras, Subhas approved of the resolution as being 'a logical fulfilment of a process going on within the Congress for a long time'.[18] Moreover, the appointment of Nehru and Bose as general secretaries of the Congress Working

Committee for the coming year seemed to represent, Bose felt, 'a definite orientation towards the left'.[19]

Despite their exuberance, however, the conservative members of the Congress hardly took the young leaders seriously. Although Gandhi was absent from the Congress Working Committee meetings in Madras, he was very critical of Nehru's resolution and described it in *Young India* as 'hastily conceived and thoughtlessly passed'.[20] Privately, he warned Nehru, 'You are going too fast. Most of the resolutions you framed and got carried could have been delayed for one year.'[21] Smarting under Gandhi's chastisement of his performance in Madras as being of the level of a 'school boys' debating society', Nehru was sufficiently provoked to charge Gandhi's leadership as being hesitant and indecisive.[22] Gandhi challenged Nehru, saying that since their differences appeared so vast and radical, Nehru should unfurl his banner in a more 'dignified way' instead of carrying on 'open warfare'.[23] As a first step, he offered to publish their correspondence. Recoiling from publicity being given to his differences with Gandhi, Nehru pleaded that he was after all his 'child in politics, though perhaps a truant and errant child?'[24] Having secured his submission, Gandhi cabled Nehru reassuringly, 'Have no desire to publish anything from you.'[25]

Nehru's resolution in Madras, as he himself came to realize, was, in fact, not really taken seriously and was meant primarily to humour him. In Gandhi's absence, his followers were able to secure the removal of the parts of the resolution which clarified independence to mean full control of defence, finance, and economic and foreign policy. All that came to be passed was an innocuous statement of the Congress goal being full independence. The unreality of the independence resolution came out in that very session of the Congress, when another resolution condemning the all-white Simon Commission and appealing for its boycott was considered. As a corollary to this, it was proposed to convene an All Parties Conference which was to draw up a constitution for India. The Motilal Nehru Report, which emerged from the proceedings of this Conference, adopted dominion status as the Congress goal. In vain did Jawaharlal remonstrate that to make dominion status India's objective would be a 'wrong thing and a fatal thing'.[26] Nor were his threats to resign, along with Bose, from the posts of general secretary accepted. A disheartened Nehru was to write to Gandhi, 'I am always the square peg and the holes are all round. I feel very lonely.'[27] Professing his inability to support a constitution based on dominion status, Nehru registered, for the first and perhaps the only time, his act of defiance by forming an independent body, the Independence for India League.

Nehru defined the Independence for India League as being representative of the 'left wing element in the country and the Congress'.[28] Independence was defined as a composite ideal, which went beyond the mere political motto of complete independence and had a significant economic content. Accordingly, an impressive programme rich in socialist ideology was drawn up, which spoke of abolition of landlordism after payment of partial compensation, its replacement by small holdings of individual peasant proprietors with no right of alienation, writing off of agricultural debts, state acquisition of key industries, and so on. It also resolved to associate the Independence League with the League against Imperialism. Although provincial branches of the League were opened and much publicity given to its programmes, its achievements went little beyond rhetoric. As Subhas was to discover soon enough when the Bengal Tenancy Bill was tabled in 1928, regional compulsions forced him to take up a pro-landlord position in direct contradiction to his publicly articulated pro-tenant postures. Lack of coordination between the provincial leagues, and the intense rivalry between them and the central organization started in Lucknow, made the working of the League a farce. There was an absurd situation in Bengal, for instance, when the acute competitiveness between supporters of the youth leaders, Nehru and Bose, resulted in the emergence of two branches of the League, working at cross purposes.[29] The enthusiasm and zeal of the youth was better harnessed instead in a protest demonstration to boycott the arrival of the Simon Commission in 1928. However, the trail of violence that it left behind worried Gandhi, who pointed out that Jawaharlal's attempt at arousing the youth was merely encouraging 'mischief makers and hooligans'.[30] The moment seemed propitious for Gandhi to emerge out of his political isolation and take over the reins of the movement. The occasion was provided by the Calcutta Congress of December 1928.

The Calcutta Congress was presided over by Motilal Nehru, who faced the difficult task of trying to steer a sceptical Congress into acceptance of the Nehru Report. Both Gandhi and Motilal addressed the problem by pointing out that the debate between dominion status and complete independence was actually a non-issue, the focus being on a mere verbal duel and jugglery of words. Making light of the controversy by asking after all, 'what's in a name?'[31], Gandhi went on to explain more seriously, 'I suggest to you that it will be a grievous blunder to pit Independence against dominion status or compare the two and suggest that dominion status carries humiliation with it and that Independence is something that is triumphant.'[32] Summing up the conservative attitude, Rajendra Prasad explained, 'A dominion within the Commonwealth had complete freedom to manage its affairs and I felt therefore that dominion status would serve our purpose all right. Complete independence, no doubt, brings a certain prestige to a country but eventually every country has to seek some sort of relationship or affiliation with other countries. The British Commonwealth is a realisation of such an idea and I saw no harm in being a member of it.'[33]

The opposition of leaders like Nehru and Bose to the concept of dominion status was that it would be sliding back from the position taken at the Madras Congress, which would affect the international prestige and reputation of the Congress. Further, by accepting dominion status the immediacy of the Congress goal of independence would be compromised. Finally, Nehru argued that dominion status was meant essentially for people of the same race, those linked with Britain by social, religious and cultural ties. Acceptance of dominion status would be a morally degrading step for India, making the Congress 'beggars at the doors of the British Government'.[34]

Ultimately, Gandhi moved a compromise resolution declaring that Congress would adopt the Nehru constitution only if the British Parliament accepted it on or before 31 December 1930, a date he preponed after intense negotiation with Nehru, Bose and others to 31 December 1929. Explaining his consensus logic behind the compromise, Gandhi said, 'If we want unity, then adjustment and readjustment, a series of compromises honourable to both parties and to variety of opinions is to be effected.'[35] To Subhas and others, it was amply clear that the British would never respond to the Congress and that the issue of an imminent campaign had merely been postponed. But Subhas was not willing to give Gandhi the comfort of postponing the issue. On the crucial day of the passing of the resolution, he brought forward an alternative resolution to the effect that Congress should stick to the goal of independence. Taken aback, Gandhi put his reputation at stake, declaring that he would retire from Congress should the alternative resolution be passed. Bose's resolution was narrowly defeated, with 973 in favour and 1,350 against, with forty-eight abstaining. One of those who abstained was Nehru, who characteristically shrank from publicly opposing Gandhi although he was convinced that Gandhi's temporizing resolution would be a comedown from the ideal of independence. A troubled Nehru was to confess, 'It was surprising how easy it was to win me over . . . this happened on many occasions, and as neither party really liked the idea of a break we clung to every pretext to avoid it.'[36]

One of the developments that troubled Gandhi deeply and seemed to threaten his cherished non-violence was the feeling of unrest that he palpably sensed in the air. Even in Calcutta, at the Congress session of 1928, he saw with discomfort the military character of Subhas's volunteer corps in which was represented almost every terrorist party, ranging from Jatin Das, then engaged by the Hindu Socialist Republican Association to manufacture bombs, to members of the Shree Sangha and stalwarts of the Anushilan and Jugantar parties. Moreover, 1928–29 was a period of considerable labour unrest, and youth leaders like Subhas and Nehru were busy addressing striking workers and actively working for industrial settlements. It was also a period of peasant unrest, and with the successful termination of the no-tax satyagraha in Bardoli in 1928 under the leadership of Vallabhbhai Patel, Bose and others felt that Gandhi should give a call for a larger movement. While industrialists such as G.D. Birla and Purushottamdas Thakurdas saw the need to keep the revolutionary elements in the Congress in check by strengthening cooperation with those who advocated constitutional means to change the government, the government, too, saw the wisdom of making fresh overtures for peace. It was in this spirit that Irwin made a declaration on 31 October 1929 that through the realization of full responsible government, India would be enabled to obtain recognition as a self-governing dominion. Welcomed by liberal leaders and businessmen, conservative politicians responded to Irwin's offer with the Delhi Manifesto signed by Gandhi, Motilal Nehru and others. It offered to cooperate with the British in a Round Table Conference for framing a scheme of dominion status for India. Subhas saw red and immediately shot off a contrary manifesto along with a few others, opposing the acceptance of dominion status and also the idea of participating in the Round Table Conference. Nehru was as usual torn, his heart being with Subhas, but his conscience with Gandhi, who reminded him that in his capacity as president-elect to the Lahore Congress in 1929, he was duty-bound to sign the Manifesto, an act that he bitterly regretted.

Not that the senior Congress leaders believed for a moment in British sincerity in considering the Indian position. As Motilal comforted his son that the Delhi statement should be consigned to the dustbin, as the matter for immediate consideration was the mobilization of forces, Gandhi went on to observe, 'Slavery will not cease to be so by being referred to as independence and real independence will not become foreign domination by being called dominion status.'[37]

Jawaharlal Nehru was selected by Gandhi to be president of the Lahore Congress of 1929 in the hope that elevation to responsible office would make him rein in his own radical ideas while keeping the younger and revolutionary elements in the Congress in check. Jawaharlal was also in a more amenable mood, having confessed to Gandhi the 'hopeless failure' of his Independence for India League.[38] Although the declaration now of the Congress creed as complete independence was expected, the Gandhian proposal of legislative boycott caused serious reservations among many, including Bose and Sengupta, who thought boycott of the legislatures would be a blunder when the new constitution was being considered. Though Gandhi was able to secure the support of Motilal Nehru, the leading Swarajist of the day, and also win back the support of his protégé Sengupta, Bose went along a rebellious path. He now tabled counter resolutions declaring that for boycott to be indeed effective it should not only be legislative but also a fuller campaign involving total boycott of councils, courts, educational institutions along with a programme of general strikes with peasant, worker and youth participation, with a view to forming a parallel government. As he put it, rather dramatically, 'I am an extremist and my principle is—all or none.'[39] Gandhi responded with characteristic caution. He said, 'We ought not to bite more than we can chew.'[40] Ultimately, Gandhi's initial resolution was passed, although with a slim margin. However, the increasing spate of revolutionary activity, marked by political assassinations, bomb attacks and hunger strikes, worried him greatly. Although the hunger strike was a weapon that Gandhi learnt to use with perfection in his political bargaining with the British, he disapproved of its use by Jatin Das, Bhagat Singh and others for the amelioration of prison conditions. He rebuked Jawaharlal for approving of this fast, commenting that it was an 'irrelevant performance . . . like using [a] Nasmyth hammer to crush a fly'.[41] Gandhi's non-committal attitude towards Jatin Das's death from hunger strike seemed 'inexplicable' to the extreme nationalists such as Bose, who felt it strange that the martyrdom which had 'stirred the heart of the country did not make any impression on him'.[42]

Gandhi was convinced that for directing the civil disobedience movement that was imminent, the Congress Working Committee should include only those who shared his values of non-violence. Realizing that Jawaharlal was essentially non-violent and basically pliant, Gandhi let him remain. However, he excluded from it the names of Subhas and a few others, while including J.M. Sengupta, thus provoking a walkout from the AICC by Subhas and his associates; they then formed the Congress Democratic Party. There was very little difference in the objectives of the new party and the Gandhian Congress. Remaining within the Congress, it adopted as its goal complete independence by peaceful and legitimate means. His exclusion by Gandhi on the plea of establishing homogeneity in the composition of the Working Committee had taken Subhas completely by surprise. He felt his response was along the lines of the breakaway Swarajist Party initiative of C.R. Das. In a telegram to Mrs Das, he prayed for the guidance of the spirit of the departed Deshbandhu.[43] Nehru was again caught in a bind. Drawn to the Bose position, he agreed with Subhas that 'a time will come when a regular parallel government will have to be established in India'. However, he felt that 'vague and tall talk often defeats its very purpose'.[44] Moreover, as the Congress president he could hardly show his support for the dissidents. Bose, however, never forgave Nehru's sitting-on-the-fence attitude.

At the Lahore Congress of 1929, Gandhi felt compelled to accept the eventuality of a civil disobedience campaign against the British, although he was still uncertain about the exact programme he would follow. Worried by the language of militancy voiced by the radical elements in the Congress, he even considered it safer to offer civil disobedience alone. To Gandhi, this was not purely a political movement. The non-violent defiance of law under certain circumstances was a religious duty to him, intended to gradually bring moral pressure on the British. The philosophical content of his civil disobedience movement was anathema not only to the British authorities but also to the majority of the Congress who were taken by surprise, for instance by his formulation of 11 Points before the mass campaign was launched. Admitting the apparently 'childish' nature of the offer, Gandhi described his 11 Points as being 'very simple but vital needs of India', which would fill out the word independence and give it meaning to ordinary people.[45] The 11 Points combined such issues of general interest as 50 per cent cuts in army expenses and civil service salaries, total prohibition, and release of political prisoners, with specific bourgeois demands such as the lowering of the rupee–sterling exchange ratio, textile protection and reservation of coastal shipping for Indians, and basically agrarian themes including a 50 per cent cut in land revenue and abolition of the salt tax and government salt monopoly. Subhas felt Gandhi's formulation was intended to placate the big business groups which might have been alarmed by some of the Lahore Congress resolutions.[46] Indeed, Gandhi had assured Thakurdas that he would 'take no hasty step' in inaugurating the civil disobedience movement.[47] Nehru felt exasperated that Gandhi's list of obvious social and political reforms had taken the place of independence. 'Did Gandhiji mean the same thing when he used the term (independence) as we did or did we speak a different language?' he wondered.[48]

Gandhi's march to Dandi (12 March–6 April 1930) to manufacture salt inaugurated the civil disobedience movement. The decision to make salt in defiance of the prevailing salt laws was carefully planned. Non-controversial and without socially divisive possibilities, it linked the ideal of swaraj with a universal rural grievance. It was also a pre-emptive bid to prevent the growing party of violence from acting first.

For Subhas, the inauguration by Gandhi of the civil disobedience campaign was one of the 'most brilliant achievements of his leadership'.[49] And yet he failed to seize the opportunity to launch a spirited campaign in his provincial base. This was largely due to Bose's frustration at being excluded from the Congress Working Committee at Lahore, his rivalry with Sengupta, who steadily gained entry into the Gandhian camp, and his obsession with municipal politics.

Although at the Bengal provincial level, Bose was elected president of the Congress in 1929, Sengupta alleged rigging. As a result, the Bengal Congress split into two separate groups and there was the absurd situation when both undertook to conduct the civil disobedience movement in the state. The Sengupta-backed organization called the Bengal Council of Civil Disobedience (BCCD) had the involvement of revolutionaries of the Anushilan Party and also received the full participation of the Gandhians, particularly Satish Chandra Dasgupta, who marched Gandhi-style from Calcutta to Mahisbathan (24 Parganas) to make salt in violation of the law. The Civil Disobedience Committee of the Bengal Provincial Congress under Bose received the support of the Jugantar Party and the Bengal Volunteers. Its activities included picketing and propagating boycott in Calcutta and many of the district towns of Bengal. However, Subhas's attacks on the Gandhians remained unabated, and at meetings he announced that the loincloth and the bullock cart would not do as there could be no return to the ways of the village, as Gandhi wanted. Just as Nietzsche's ideal of the superman held the ground in Europe, Indians, too, had to shape their own ideals for the new man and the new society. He held out the ideal of the strong Indian, smartly turned out in uniform, the money spent on which, contrary to what many implied, was not a waste for it created an esprit de corps.[50] Gandhi hastened to pacify his disciple Satish Chandra Dasgupta saying, 'Subhas Babu will never pardon the loincloth. We must bear with him. He cannot help himself. He believes in himself and in his mission. He must work it out as we must ours.'[51] The in-fighting between the two major Congress factions undoubtedly weakened the overall Congress effort in Bengal, although the largest number of arrests during the years of the civil disobedience movement were in Bengal (15,000) as also the highest incidence of violence (136 excluding terrorist actions).

Gandhi had sought to maintain the focus of his civil disobedience movement so that his basic tenet of non-violence was not compromised. Apart from breaking the salt laws, he suggested the picketing of liquor and foreign cloth shops, resignation by lawyers and government officials from their posts, boycott of courts, and concentration on khadi work. So far as the programme of non-payment of taxes was concerned, he was still wary. While willing to allow non-payment of specific taxes like the *chaukidari* tax, for instance, he was hesitant to talk about an agrarian no-revenue campaign.

The agrarian issue could not, however, be postponed for long because the years of the civil disobedience movement coincided with the worldwide economic depression, which affected India through a very sharp fall in agricultural prices. Particularly hard hit were the smaller landlords and upper-caste rent receivers who were the most dependable Congress supporters at the district level. It was this group that sought to mount an agitation around issues such as reduction of revenue, irrigation charges, rent and debt burdens, and return of land confiscated at the outset of the campaign. The Congress leadership, on the other hand, tried its best not to let such campaigns escalate and become a class war threatening the social balance. Exhibiting a characteristic ambivalence, it displayed sympathy for agrarian problems and lent support to no-revenue campaigns as part of its anti-imperialist struggle but hesitated to sponsor a no-rent movement lest political consciousness be aroused on class lines. However, despite Gandhi's personal apprehension, the ground realities forced leaders with provincial bases such as Vallabhbhai Patel in Gujarat and Jawaharlal Nehru in UP to eventually sanction no-rent campaigns. In general, however, after the first flush of enthusiastic participation was over and police repression and reprisals began, the movement tended to grow out of Congress control. Tribal outbursts and the lead given by certain militant peasants threatened to radicalize the movement. Already concerned by the rising wave of terrorism, Gandhi now became wary of a populist campaign taking over and compromising his dearest doctrine of non-violence. His apprehensions were shared by leaders of the business community, who put considerable pressure on him to seek a way out by negotiating with the British. Although Gandhi had initially doubted the earnestness of the peace overtures of Prime Minister MacDonald, he was soon enough willing to read between the lines and seek an interview with the viceroy to discuss peace possibilities. The Gandhi–Irwin Pact of March 1931 was largely at Gandhi's initiative, supported by liberal leaders such as Sapru and Jayakar and business leaders like Thakurdas and Birla. Jawaharlal, who was recovering from the recent death of his father Motilal, was in no mood to quarrel and drew consolation from the fact that it was after all 'a truce and not peace'.[52] A less charitable Subhas charged Gandhi for being pressured into signing the truce by 'wealthy aristocrats and politicians who were dying for a settlement'.[53]

In the Gandhi–Irwin Pact, the token concession secured by Gandhi on salt was offset by his having to give up all demands for return of lands confiscated in the course of the agitation in various provinces. All that he obtained from Irwin was a promise that land not yet sold would be returned. Moreover, while civil disobedience prisoners were to be released, Bhagat Singh's death sentence was not commuted. Further, Gandhi's acceptance of Irwin's offer of federation with safeguards gave Nehru a 'tremendous shock'[54] while being equally unacceptable to Subhas. Faced with the tough task of getting Congress to approve of the Pact, Gandhi selected Vallabhbhai Patel, one of its strongest critics, to be president of the Congress session in Karachi (29–31 March 1931).

On 23 March, just days before the session was to open, Bhagat Singh and two of his fellow Lahore prisoners were swiftly executed. Many condemned the government for not showing more humanity and political sense. The youth movement, to which Bhagat Singh was a hero, blamed Gandhi for not having secured the commutation of his death sentence to life imprisonment. Gandhi and Patel were greeted on arrival at the Karachi station with a black-flag demonstration by supporters of Subhas. Gandhi insisted that he had pleaded unsuccessfully for a commutation in the sentence, but added that despite his bravery Bhagat Singh's actions had not benefited the country. Subhas was equally forthright in his address to the All-India Naujawan Bharat Sabha on 27 March and called Bhagat Singh the symbol of the unconquerable spirit of revolt in the country, which did not feel that the time for an honourable settlement had arrived yet.[55]

Although critical of the Pact, Subhas realized, however, that the Congress could not reject it and weaken the hands of Gandhi, whose popularity and mass appeal continued to amaze him. To the assembled young men in Karachi, Subhas's message, therefore, was to look beyond the Congress programme and work towards a socialist republic in India involving the youth and women, workers and peasants in programmes which would be guided by justice, equality, freedom, discipline and love. Unlike his role in the past two Congress sessions, Bose did not oppose Gandhi on any resolution. On the other hand, he drafted a statement on behalf of the left wing that although it did not approve of the Pact, it would refrain from dividing the House. This did not, however, earn him a place in the Working

Committee, which again went to his rival, Sengupta. Apart from approving the Gandhi–Irwin Pact, the Karachi Congress also passed a resolution on fundamental rights and economic policy, which has often been considered the price that Gandhi had to pay for the left's approval of his policy. Although Subhas regarded the resolution as an attempt to placate the socialist elements in the Congress, and Nehru considered it as a step in the socialist direction, the general democratic demands that it mentioned had no radical implications, and as Gandhi pointed out, zamindars and maharajas could rest assured that the Congress did not seek to destroy them.

Although Gandhi displayed considerable tact at Karachi in obtaining all-round support from varying elements within the Congress for the Gandhi–Irwin Pact, implementation was to prove much more difficult. For one, in the context of the continuing agrarian crisis, Gandhi's advice to the tenants to pay as much rent as was possible seemed unrealistic. The UP Provincial Congress was in a quandary. Leaders like Nehru suffered from an acute sense of guilt as they held themselves partly responsible for the plight of the tenants. To strike a balance, Nehru interpreted Gandhi's suggested scale of payment to be not the minimum but the maximum, which need not be paid if it entailed debt, or if the tenants suffered ill-treatment. He was at the same time very careful to avoid making the UP crisis a test case and embarrassing for Gandhi's peace efforts at the Round Table Conference.

In Gujarat, the demands for the return of confiscated lands, etc. were more specific and although Patel had steered the Congress into a clear acceptance of the Pact, he felt helpless in the face of peasant distress. 'I have never found myself in such a humiliating position all my life. If Bapu had been here, I would not have kept quiet,' he lamented.[56] Recognizing Patel's predicament, Gandhi secured from the British an agreement to hold a limited enquiry into the excesses committed by revenue officials in the Bardoli taluka. Armed with this dubious concession, Gandhi set sail for London. With his mind in despair, he wrote, 'The horizon is as black as it possibly could be.'[57] Although Patel used the face-saving promise of an enquiry to hold on to peace until Gandhi returned, Nehru found it impossible to prevent matters from escalating and he secured Gandhi's permission by cable to re-commence the no-rent campaign in several districts of UP, weeks before Gandhi returned in end December 1931 after an unsuccessful mission.

After the Karachi Congress, Subhas's resolve was to put an end to the petty squabbling in the Bengal Congress, which had caused considerable embarrassment to the leadership while providing vicarious amusement to detractors. On his way back to Calcutta, he issued a statement to this effect from Delhi. Second, although he saluted the revolutionary spirit of Bhagat Singh, and in Amritsar addressed an assembly calling for hundreds of Bhagat Singhs—causing the Home Department to wonder whether it was not a seditious speech[58]—Subhas increasingly came to believe that acts of terrorism simply would not work. Although this was Gandhi's conclusion, too, they started from different premises. Gandhi was absolutely opposed to terrorism because violence was evil and could not lead to any beneficial ends. Subhas concluded, like Aurobindo Ghose, that 'outburst of violent acts did much harm to the national cause. The followers of the cult of violence were no match for the authorities, in an armed conflict. But if scattered national forces were organised in a peaceful and non-violent way, they could achieve their objective much more expeditiously.'[59]

The Gandhian logic of mending fences, holding on to dissentient opinion and forging a consensus by making an emotional appeal to opponents, gradually appeared to Subhas to be the only way to bring political peace in Bengal. The

June 1931 elections for a new BPCC raised afresh charges of rigging and fraud by the Sengupta camp, necessitating the appointment of Aney as the sole Congress arbitrator to resolve the contentious issue. Subhas now decided to turn a new page in this long story of dissensions in the Bengal Congress which had started in the late 1920s. In a dramatic gesture reminiscent of the Gandhian style, he used the traumatic and tragic deaths of two prisoners at the Hijli detention camp in September 1931 to register his break from the past. He declared that the Hijli deaths appeared to him to be 'a Divine warning that we should close up our ranks and present a united front to our enemies'.[60] Resigning as BPCC president and as alderman of the Calcutta Corporation, he declared that no useful purpose could be served by retaining office if the cooperation of all sections of Congressmen was not secured. This gesture acted as a catalyst in resolving differences. In a new atmosphere of cordiality, all complaints were dropped and a new election decided for the next year. Aney congratulated the leading members for the splendid spirit of accommodation, reconciliation and self-effacement displayed by them in sinking their differences.

Although a spirit of accord was finally established, fate took Sengupta and Bose in different directions. Sengupta proceeded to England for health reasons in October 1931, returned in January 1932 to be imprisoned, and in July 1933 he died. Bose rushed to Bombay in December 1931 to receive Gandhi on his arrival from London and was arrested shortly after on his return journey by train. With his prolonged incarceration at various places, his health deteriorated and he became very ill with suspected tuberculosis and an infected gall bladder. During this period in jail, Subhas meditated on 'will power', reflected deeply on *swadharma*, and discussed matters of spiritual and religious concern with his friend, Dilip Kumar Roy, who shared his thoughts with Sri Aurobindo in his ashram in Pondicherry. Unwilling to take responsibility for his declining health, the government gave permission to Subhas to set sail from India to Europe, in February 1933, for health reasons. The letters that he continued to write to his friend Dilip on the sea journey show how deep was his religious sense and how Hinduism was an essential aspect of his Indianness. He wrote how his varying moods made him choose between Shiva, Kali and Krishna while his study of tantric philosophy convinced him of the extraordinary strength that was latent in *Mantra shakti*.[61] In the challenges of life that now faced him, he had much reason to delve periodically into this reservoir of strength and inspiration.

The second phase of the civil disobedience campaign (1932–34) was clearly not one of Gandhi's seeking and it never really got off the ground. Anticipating the Congress moves, the government retaliated by arresting all the prominent Congress leaders, imposing oppressive ordinances, and refusing this time to enter into any dialogue with Gandhi.

After he arrived in Europe, Subhas felt very encouraged on meeting Vithalbhai Patel, a Swarajist associate of C.R. Das and a strong critic of Gandhi, unlike his brother Vallabhbhai, the staunch Gandhian. Patel had been touring Europe and the United States extensively, advocating the cause of Indian nationalism through political networking. Convinced of the importance of this mission, Subhas decided to devote himself to the same cause in his years of political exile in Europe.

Gandhi's decision to call off the civil disobedience movement filled both Subhas and V.J. Patel with dismay. 'The Bose–Patel Manifesto', issued from Vienna in May 1933, was unusually strong in denouncing Gandhi. Possibly the handiwork of Patel,[62] it chimed in with Bose's thoughts. It concluded in no uncertain terms: 'As a political leader Mahatma Gandhi has failed.' It announced that the time was ripe for a radical reorganization of the Congress according to 'a new principle and with a new method', and with 'a change of leadership'. Very impressed with Subhas, V.J. Patel felt that he had finally found the ideal man who had 'all the merits of a great leader' and could 'carry on India's struggle without any kind of compromise'.[63] The terminally ill senior leader bequeathed to Subhas a substantial financial legacy, which could be used for continuing his mission of propaganda for the cause of India's liberation. Present at the bedside of V.J. Patel when he breathed his last in October 1933, Subhas lamented that he had again lost a mentor and staunch supporter, who had vindicated his point of view. Nor was he to enjoy the bequest, which was challenged in court by Patel's heirs and judged as being imprecise. However, Subhas took seriously the mission of propaganda he had inherited from Patel, and in three years (1933–36) he travelled extensively in most of Europe and west of the Soviet Union, meeting important leaders in many countries, helping Indian students, assisting in the growth of student organizations, encouraging binational cultural organizations with several European countries, and discussing economic relations with businessmen, industrialists and political leaders. As Mrs Vetter, a close associate and friend, commented, Subhas was almost myopic in the pursuit of his mission. With a passionate and consuming interest, he looked on to world politics only so far as it related to India.[64]

With the death of Patel, Subhas lost the confidant he had only just discovered. He now poured out his thoughts and analyses of Indian politics in a book called *The Indian Struggle 1920–1934*, with cathartic reflections on Gandhian leadership, which were, however, to make him intensely unpopular with the Congress leadership later. While acknowledging the unique control that Gandhi had over the masses, Subhas regretted that

Gandhi was surrounded by supporters who were blindly loyal without the ability of offering necessary and healthy criticism as Das and Motilal Nehru had done. His own efforts in this direction had been seen as representing a rebel mentality. Convinced that many of the 'blunders' of Gandhi as political leader could have been averted if he had good advisers, Subhas now turned to Nehru as being the only politician left who could pressure the Mahatma to tread a more confrontationist path in the anti-imperialist struggle. Lending Jawaharlal moral support by being by his side at the death of his wife, Kamala, in Switzerland in 1936, Subhas went on to encourage him about the decisive role that he was about to play as the next president of the Congress at Lucknow. In line with the thinking of Nehru, he spoke of the need for the Congress to take up the pressing issues concerning landlords and peasants, capital and labour, which could not be postponed indefinitely. To Nehru, he wrote, 'Your position is unique and I think that even Mahatma Gandhi will be more accommodating towards you than towards anybody else.'[65] Nehru also sensed Subhas's frustration and sympathized that he could not 'submit to indefinite exile'.[66] He held out the prospect of their working together by naming him a member of his Working Committee. Throwing caution to the wind, Subhas decided to return. However, as soon as his ship docked in Bombay in April 1936 he was arrested, to face another indefinite term of imprisonment.

Left to confront the Gandhian high command alone, Nehru now made the boldest assertion of his point of view in his career before being steered to total submission by Gandhi. Already in 1934, with the petering out of the second civil disobedience campaign and the absence of a gripping programme, Nehru had been slowly driven to the recognition that he had come to a parting of ways. Gandhi's sensational decision to fast unto death over the Communal Award decision by Prime Minister Ramsay MacDonald in 1932 on the untouchable separate electorate issue had amazed Nehru. Gandhi's religious justification for the fast, which sprang from his belief that separate electorates would 'simply vivisect and disrupt' Hinduism and had to be resisted, was anathema to Nehru.[67] While Gandhi fasted and a distraught India held its breath, Nehru felt 'annoyed' with Gandhi for choosing 'a side issue for his final sacrifice – just a question on electorate'.[68] In a note written soon after, Nehru confessed that there was hardly any common ground between himself and Gandhi and that he had been wrong in subordinating their differences to a larger loyalty for the cause of national freedom. 'No political organisation,' he now recognized, 'can represent conflicting interests without reducing itself to a flabby and unmeaning mass with no distinctive and distinguishing features.' He lamented, 'Our objectives are different, our ideas are different, our spiritual outlook is different and our methods are likely to be different.'[69] The inability of the Congress to spell out a concrete programme made Nehru restless. It 'surprised' and 'distressed' him that Congressmen, on meeting after two years of eventful campaign, did not re-emphasize the Congress political goal and stress the social and economic objectives. He accused the Congress leadership of being a 'pitiful hotchpotch, avoiding real issues' and pursuing a policy of drift.[70]

Gandhi's decision to devote himself completely to non-political programmes of individual protest or social uplift through a constructive movement had little general appeal. Questions like how to improve bullock carts or how to make molasses from toddy wine were considered rather tame and irrelevant in the context of an exciting and rapidly changing political situation. Gandhi's programmes for the upliftment of the harijans, including programmes of opening public wells for these socially challenged groups or his khadi programmes of compulsory spinning and weaving, were welcomed instead by the business community as a diversion from agitational politics.

Within the Congress, Gandhi's ideas of how to overhaul the organization were considered too radical even by his supporters. His proposals—which included the introduction of a khadi clause (which would exclude from Congress membership those who did not habitually wear hand-spun cloth), a spinning franchise (which required spinning of 500 yards of yarn per month for six months preceding the Congress delegate election), a six-month membership qualification to vote, and a drastic streamlining of AICC and PCC membership—were intended to weed out corruption and instil discipline. At the Bombay session of the Congress in 1934, the weight of Congress opinion watered down the most radical of Gandhi's proposals and softened the provisions of spinning and manual labour as enrolment qualifications. Gandhi's loyal lieutenants like Patel and Rajendra Prasad were quite relieved when he decided to retire from Congress in October 1934, leaving the mainstream Congress to put the house in order. They now used the amended Bombay constitution to considerably strengthen the Working Committee, whose members were to be nominated by the president, and gave it disciplinary powers so that it would be formally recognized as the controlling group in central Congress politics, which, in fact, it had become. This move was perceived by the Gandhian high command to be necessary not only for keeping in check the rising left consciousness in the country but also for making the Congress president accountable to the prevailing Gandhian opinion in the Congress. The full dividend of this strategy was realized soon enough, when both Nehru as Congress president (Lucknow, April 1936 and Faizpur, December 1936) and Subhas (Haripura, 1938 and Tripuri, 1939) were made to toe the official line. The outcome, however, was totally different, with Nehru being won over and Subhas edged out of the mainstream Congress fold.

Among the many strands in the rising left consciousness that troubled the conservative elements in the Congress at this time was the Kisan Sabha movement, which included many militant peasant leaders, who had taken over the direction of several agrarian campaigns once the Congress had applied the brakes with the stoppage of the civil disobedience movement. The Congress Socialist Party (CSP), officially inaugurated in 1934, while working within the Indian National Congress, supported many of the Kisan Sabha programmes such as the elimination of landlordism in zamindari and ryotwari areas, and liquidation of rural indebtedness. The use of Marxist terminology made the CSP pronouncements sound more radical than in fact they were. While Gandhi charged the socialists with having an intoxicating programme that frightened him, Jayaprakash Narayan asserted the need to go to the peasants not with a spinning wheel but with the militant force of an economic programme.[71] The years 1933 and 1934 also saw a significant labour revival following the post-Depression wage cuts and retrenchments. Militant communist leaders in the trade union movement advocated working within the CSP and the Congress to progressively align with the left nationalist elements.

This was also at the time when certain politicians showed a pronounced trend to return to constitutional politics. With the publication of the White Paper on constitutional proposals, followed by the Joint Parliamentary Report and the Government of India Act of 1935, this interest in constitutional politics came to be renewed with considerable commitment and involvement. The Gandhian Congress saw the wisdom of supporting a programme which had gripped the popular imagination in the absence of any better alternative, and hoped that it would divert attention from the radical pronouncements of the socialists. Sensing that left-wing radicalism could be a threat to Congress unity, the conservative Congress leadership sponsored the programme it had originally frowned upon, if only to keep the Congress united and keep it moving. The business groups, too, hoped to forge a common front between Gandhian constructive workers and advocates of council entry against the growing challenge from the left. Much of the funding for the election campaign was arranged through business support in Calcutta and Bombay.

When Nehru returned to India to assume what Gandhi called the 'crown of thorns', which the Congress presidentship at Lucknow in April 1936 was indeed to become for him, he had to take stock of both these developments: the rising left consciousness and the increasing interest in elections and office acceptance. Although intellectually Nehru supported the growing strength of left-inclined ideas and policies at this time, he was wary of the motley character of these elements. Of the CSP he wrote that it was a 'curious and mixed assemblage', adding, 'Even if I had been completely free I would not have suddenly joined it.'[72] About enjoying the fruits of office after electoral victory, Nehru's opposition was unequivocal. He was convinced that Congress participation in the Provincial Legislative Assembly elections could only be for wrecking the Constitution and under no circumstances could there be office acceptance. To observe the sea change in the Congress attitude, which now favoured office acceptance, was traumatic enough for Nehru, but as Congress president to steer the programme through was doubly harrowing. Nehru found it puzzling that Gandhi, who had shared with him until recently a strong opposition to the possibilities of election and office acceptance, was now encouraging those consumed with council politics to live out their obsession. With amused tolerance, Gandhi asked, 'Don't you think it is better for someone who is always dreaming of *jalebi* to eat it, and find out its actual taste?'[73]

Nehru sought to tackle the challenge by asserting an individualistic position, which only prolonged his agony. In his presidential address in Lucknow, he spoke extensively on socialism, which he declared was not merely an economic doctrine but a 'vital creed'. Unhesitatingly he denounced the Act as 'a charter of slavery' for which the Congress attitude could only be one of 'uncompromising hostility' and went on to declare that any idea of acceptance of office would be reformist and 'a vital error'.[74] He spoke of the need instead to address more real issues related to the economic balance in society and recommended in a resolution the abolition of zamindari, a 50 per cent cut in rents, and a moratorium on agricultural debts. Alarmed at his forthrightness, the conservative Congress manipulated the composition of the Working Committee in such a way that Nehru found himself in a minority without being able to protest, because the changes of 1934 had made the president responsible for its composition. Of the fourteen members of the Working Committee, no less than ten disapproved of socialism and disagreed with his ideas. Bose, in Nehru's original list, had been arrested, while the three socialists in it, namely Narendra Dev, Jayaprakash Narayan and Achyut Patwardhan, were of a milder persuasion. Nehru had himself to blame for the absence of a woman member on the committee, as he was to regret later. With such a composition, the Working Committee was able to water down most of Nehru's proposals. A frustrated Nehru lamented to Gandhi, 'A *hayadar* (self-respecting) President would probably have resigned but I being *behaya* (shameless) stuck on even though the majority of the Congress had decided against me on some vital issues.'[75] Gandhi remained unimpressed.

In the energetic election campaign that followed, Nehru now sought to gain lost ground and spread the socio-economic contents of his election manifesto to India's millions, while Gandhian loyalists were busy with the logistics of the election process. In a whirlwind tour of the country, Nehru made it clear that the 'Act has to be combated and rejected'.[76] In speeches in Bombay, he declared that class struggle was inherent in the social order and socialism was inevitable. He accused the mill-owners and members of 'big business' of allying with the government, asking for suppressive measures during the civil disobedience movement, and trying to drag India towards fascism.[77] Nehru's outbursts led twenty-one businessmen to issue a manifesto condemning his 'destructive and subversive programme',[78] while the conservative Congress leaders despaired of the adverse impact the speeches might have on the election prospects of the Congress. Gandhi now stepped in and, as he was to do with regard to Subhas's recalcitrance in 1939, he made the Working Committee members write a letter to Nehru threatening to resign. Gandhi knew that Nehru was pliable and would come around and also that the conservative leaders would respond to his direction. Reacting sentimentally to Prasad calling his activities 'harmful'[79] and Patel accusing him of an attitude of 'injured innocence',[80] Nehru wrote despondently to Gandhi, 'However tenderly the fact may be stated it amounts to this that I am an intolerable nuisance ... presumably the result of this will be that I shall retire and a more homogeneous committee will be formed.'[81] Gandhi pulled up Nehru for arrogance, intolerance and lack of a sense of humour. He asked Nehru to stop the 'tragic comedy' he was playing and not destroy himself by moving openly into opposition.[82] Gandhi also assuaged the hurt feelings of the conservative leaders and persuaded them to withdraw their resignations.

Nehru realized that his political career was at stake. Without

Gandhi there was no political future for him. Nor did he have any substantial following from among whom he could cull his own group of followers. There was a bitter truth in Gandhi's stern reminder that though he was in office, he was not in power yet. Gandhi had written, 'To put you in office was an attempt to find you in power quicker than you would otherwise have been.'[83] Nehru saw the wisdom of Gandhi's advice: 'Whatever happens, you must not be in opposition.'[84] By accepting the Working Committee members back, Nehru had also to accept his new role of protecting them against attacks from the Socialists, thereby compromising his original position vis-à-vis the left. From this time onwards, there was a noticeable toning down in Nehru's speeches and public pronouncements. Convinced that 'we cannot afford to split up and break up the Congress', he came to accept that 'we may even differ now, to agree later and work together'.[85] Nehru approached the crisis like a disciplined soldier, desisting from publicly challenging the Gandhian position anymore, although he was to privately agonize many a time. Birla observed with satisfaction, 'Jawaharlalji seems to be like a typical English democrat who takes defeat in a sporting spirit.'[86]

The next Congress session was to be held at Faizpur in December 1936, and since there were only eight months between the Lucknow and the Faizpur sessions, Gandhi was keen on Nehru continuing as president. Although Nehru's provocative public statement that his re-election would be a vindication of his programmes alarmed conservative politicians like Patel and Rajagopalachari, Gandhi was willing to take the gamble because he was confident he could restrain Nehru while keeping the Socialists happy with his choice. In the circumstances, the gamble paid off because in his presidential address at Faizpur, Nehru was studiously moderate and largely free from the sentimentalism and exaggeration of his election speeches. He spelt out the Congress goal as being full democracy and not socialism, which he hoped would ultimately come about by the logic of events. On the critical issue of office acceptance, the decision was deferred until after the elections were over. The agrarian programme also was an innocuous list of broad measures such as rent and revenue readjustment without mentioning extreme measures such as zamindari abolition.

In the elections, the Congress won 711 Provincial Legislative Assembly seats out of 1,585, with an absolute majority in five provinces out of eleven (Madras, Bihar, Orissa, CP and UP) and a near majority in Bombay. Ministry making, however, did not automatically follow. Nehru maintained his position that the importance of the electoral success, which had demonstrated Congress popularity, should not be lost over the spoils of office. However, realizing the tide of opinion in favour of office acceptance, Gandhi now stepped in. He offered conditional acceptance of Congress ministries in provinces where the party had won a majority, provided the governors did not use their special powers to impede their working. In the absence of a clear official acceptance of his formula, Gandhi seized an unofficial statement made by a liberal peer as a green signal. Ministry making in 1937 brought to an end a phase of acute tension and uncertainty within the Congress.

Nehru watched with amazement how Gandhi, who had initially opposed council politics, turned full circle to acknowledging the mounting craze for it. As Gandhi explained:

> But there has been no loss of principle here . . . My response is generally in conformity with the atmosphere . . . If it rains I use an umbrella, if it is cold I can wrap myself in woollens and in summer there is muslin . . . to cover me . . . There has been no change in my ideas. But

I express them in keeping with the prevailing wind . . .
Non-cooperation is not something I have accepted for
all time. When I find that India can advance through
cooperation, I will accept cooperation . . . Today we are
going into the Legislatures not to give but to take
cooperation.[87]

Further, Gandhi strongly disagreed with the old Swarajist logic
of entering the legislatures with the intention of sabotaging
their working in a spirit of non-cooperation. He elaborated:

To enter the Councils with a view to obstructing and
creating deadlocks after taking the oath of allegiance is
like entering the house as a tolerated guest and trying to
pull it to pieces . . . It is not working the Councils but
playing with them in a frivolous way. It may be politics,
it may be good tactics, it may be necessary and inevitable,
but it is not *dharma*.[88]

With office acceptance and serious preoccupations with
ministry making, the focus of attention turned away from the
socialist thrust. It was a humbled Nehru who now decided to
follow Gandhi's lead and logic. Gandhi happily wrote,
'Jawaharlal was more than good throughout. His innate nobility
asserted itself every time a difficulty cropped up. He is truly a
warrior, sans peur et sans reproche. The more I see him, the
more I love him.'[89] Prasad, too, wrote to Patel with satisfaction,
'I have a feeling that of late Jawaharlalji has been veering to
our view and differences which used to be so marked between
his viewpoint and ours on many points is less prominent
today . . .'[90] Patel was equally satisfied. He wrote to Gandhi:

We have been getting on beautifully this time . . . I
cannot speak too highly of Jawaharlal. He has done

wonderful work, and has been burning the candle at both ends. We found not the slightest difficulty in cooperating with him, adjusting ourselves to his views on certain points.[91]

A recently released Subhas, looking at the harmonious cooperation between Nehru and the Gandhian Congress, was not amused. However, his indifferent health, leading to prolonged periods of recuperation and recovery at Dalhousie and later Kurseong, kept him away from controversy. At the end of 1937, Gandhi, who visited Calcutta for the AICC session and stayed along with Jawaharlal at the Bose residence, decided that although Subhas was 'unsteady',[92] he was the only available choice for being the next Congress president at Haripura. In January 1938, Gandhi sent a cable to Subhas, who was then touring London, congratulating him as president-elect, adding, 'God give you strength to bear the weight of Jawaharlal's mantle.'[93]

Rushing back home, Subhas left for Haripura in February 1938, where he delivered, as president, the lengthiest and most significant speech of his career. He contextualized the Indian struggle as part of the anti-imperialist struggles of the world, exposed the mischievous divide-and-rule policies of the British, elaborated on his ideological preferences for socialism, and went beyond the struggle at hand to visualize the pattern of reconstruction and organization that was needed after the British departed. Elaborating on the concept of planning, he initiated, along with Nehru, the National Planning Commission, a pioneering process intended to launch India on the road to a modern industrial future.[94] The Haripura session was conducted harmoniously by Subhas. As Nehru judged candidly, Bose's role on the whole had been 'entirely passive' and he had 'functioned more as a speaker than as a directing President'.[95] Although the leaders of the CSP, CPI, supporters of M.N. Roy, as well as kisan and trade union spokesmen, held different positions on many substantive socio-economic issues, Subhas was careful to maintain a consensus position which would not alarm the Gandhian leaders. Not that he was hesitant about challenging the Gandhian line, but his supreme concern being the anti-British struggle at hand, he was willing to postpone dealing with other issues. He was convinced that it rested on him to steer the Congress to an all-out finish in the anti-imperialist struggle and prevent any Gandhian propensity for slackening the pace and making any compromise. He set great store by the position of Congress president and quite enjoyed its ceremonial aspects, from participating in the parade with fifty-one bullocks drawing his chariot, as at Haripura, or appearing on the cover of *Time* magazine, as in the 7 March 1938 issue.

Subhas's desire to seek re-election in 1939, however, drew no support or enthusiasm. Gandhi tried his best to persuade Azad and then Nehru to take on the responsibility, failing which he selected Pattabhi Sitaramayya as his candidate. Uneasy at the prospect of an election contest, the Congress Working Committee, in a statement on 24 January 1939, urged Subhas to reconsider his decision and allow Pattabhi's election to be unanimous. In vain did a disillusioned Nehru try to convince Subhas not to place much importance on the office. Speaking from experience, he observed, 'I have seen in the past the presidential elections do not make much difference to policy which is ultimately laid down by the Congress itself or the AICC.'[96] However, Subhas was not willing to step aside. Nor did he believe that between one president and another the question of policies and programmes was irrelevant. Indeed, he raised, rather grandly, the constitutional 'position of the Congress President to that of the Prime Minister or the

President of the United States of America who nominates his own Cabinet'.[97] Proceeding to outline the differences between his programme and that of the conservative leadership, he gave the election the complexion of a contest between two opposing Congress creeds.

The first issue that Subhas raised was that of federation. While the provincial autonomy provisions of the Government of India Act of 1935 had become operative, the federal parts, which called for the significant participation in it of the Indian states through their princes, had not. Although officially the Congress was totally against it, Subhas, on several occasions during the re-election campaign, spoke of the possibility that the right wing would compromise on the federation issue, which he, as an anti-federationist, had to resist.

Second, with war clouds looming ominously on the international horizon, Subhas thought it was an opportune moment to send an ultimatum to the British government demanding purna swaraj or complete independence and utilize any help that was offered by other nations, irrespective of what their internal policies or ideological persuasions might be, keeping foremost in mind India's own national interests.

Third, he sought to use the mandate of the position of Congress president to intervene in the provincial government in Bengal and stem the negative trend that he detected which portended ill for the future of communal peace in the region. Already the Communal Award of 1932, together with the conditions of the Poona Pact, which had induced Gandhi to break his fast unto death, had resulted in a fresh distribution of electoral seats in Bengal. In a house of 250, Muslims were to have 119 seats with a separate electorate and reserved seats, while the general non-Muslims were to have seventy-eight seats, of which some thirty were reserved for the scheduled castes. This arrangement was seen by caste Hindus as heralding the eclipse of their political power. In the elections following the Act of 1935, the Congress, while doing exceedingly well among caste Hindus, won only seven scheduled caste seats, most of which went to independents, and almost totally avoided contesting the Muslim seats. Muslim votes were split three ways, with the Krishak Praja Party (KPP) of Fazlul Huq winning 31.5 per cent, the Muslim League (ML) of Jinnah 27.1 per cent, and the independents receiving the rest. Unable to win a majority, the Congress declined to participate in the government and a coalition ministry was formed by the KPP with the ML. However, the KPP with its peasant programme and the ML with its patronage of landowning interests made strange political bedfellows. As the KPP elements in the government felt restive, the ML launched communal propaganda proclaiming 'Islam in danger' to keep the coalition intact. A large chunk of KPP members, however, parted company with Fazlul Huq, who played along with ML politics for a while to further his own political ambitions. Subhas firmly believed that the Congress should use the situation to its advantage by winning over the dissident KPP faction and aligning itself with them in a Congress–KPP–schedule caste ministry formation. He sincerely believed that only by returning from the political wilderness and entering the government could the Congress stem the growing communalization of Bengal politics.

Subhas's own power base in Bengal had been seriously eroded. The Big Five, which had provided him steady support after the death of C.R. Das, were no longer united. Nalini Sarkar had become a bitter Bose opponent and had entered Fazlul Huq's ministry as finance minister, while B.C. Roy as Gandhi's personal physician gradually became his trusted political representative in Bengal. The pure khadi types or Gandhi ideologues in Bengal, namely Prafulla Ghosh and Satish

Dasgupta, were loyal Gandhian allies and worked in tandem with industrialists like Birla, hesitant to change the existing political order in Bengal. With Sarat, his elder brother and political partner, Subhas continued to enjoy the support of the Bengal Volunteers, but in general he lacked a firm base and organized support structure.

On all the three counts raised by Subhas to justify his decision to stand for the Congress presidential re-election, the Gandhians opposed him. Subhas's raising of the federation issue, and his insinuation that many among the Congress leadership were secretly making deals with the British to be included in the envisioned cabinet,[98] raised many hackles because the various groups in the Congress had unanimously rejected the federation and Subhas's accusations were based largely on bazaar rumours. While Patel was pained,[99] and Gandhi was irked,[100] Nehru bluntly pointed out, 'No greater insult could be offered to a person than to suggest that he has secretly betrayed the cause he publicly stands for and even arranged a mutual distribution of ministries in the federation. It was a fantastic statement and it hurt to the quick.'[101] Even Sarat Bose, who had not been consulted, had been taken aback by his brother's hurried and impulsive outburst.[102]

On the issue of sending an ultimatum to the British taking advantage of the war situation, Subhas's stance was not greeted with any enthusiasm either. His foreign policy observations favouring the acceptance of help from any country inimical to the British, irrespective of their own persuasion, was viewed with cynicism and scepticism. A concerned Nehru declared, 'No enemy of the United Kingdom is necessarily our friend.'[103] Gandhi, too, had not been comfortable with Subhas's pace and the direction he sought to give the Congress. It was not unknown to him that Subhas had been in regular touch with the fascist officials at the German consulate office in Bombay and the Japanese consulate in Calcutta.[104] These clandestine meetings, which Subhas often attended in disguise, aided by Batlivala, an old theatre hand, made Gandhi uncomfortable.[105] This association militated against the non-violent core of Gandhi's thinking. Besides, Gandhi feared that Subhas might lead the country to a mass agitation for which the people were not yet prepared.

On the issue of intervening in Bengal politics and pushing the Congress into a coalition government, Gandhi was firmly of the opinion that the existing government should not be ousted. Taking the advice of Maulana Azad, Nalini Sarkar and Birla, whom he summoned to Wardha, Gandhi concluded that a reshuffle of the ministry would not serve the Congress well, and instead the existing government should be assisted to act more responsibly. Subhas was deeply hurt that Gandhi chose to ignore him and those actually running the Congress organization in Bengal while attaching more value and importance to the opinions of others. Gandhi's decision to remain 'wilfully blind', as he himself put it, proved costly and, according to Subhas's biographer, Leonard Gordon, was partly responsible for the eventual partition of India.[106]

The Tripuri re-election drama, which took place against this background, therefore, came to acquire elements of a Greek tragedy; here there was a certain ruthlessness and a complete absence of the generous accommodation which had been the hallmark of the Gandhian creed. Both Gandhi and Bose felt justified in sticking to their points of view, their temperaments being such that they thought it their dharma not to give up. It is also undeniable that the lifting of the ban on *The Indian Struggle* in 1938 gave wide circulation to its highly critical comments on Gandhi. The resultant bitterness and resentment became major stumbling blocks in the way of normalization of relations with Bose, even when he showed an eagerness for accommodation and reconciliation. The various stages of the Tripuri election battle were played out like a game of chess, where each move was met with a counter move, and eventually Gandhi, the superior player, checkmated Subhas, who was then made to quit.

The results of the Tripuri Congress presidential re-election, held on 29 January 1939, came as a total surprise. Subhas won by 1,580 votes to 1,375 over Sitaramayya, Gandhi's candidate. Gandhi's response was swift. Issuing a statement declaring that the defeat was more his than Sitaramayya's, he invited Subhas not to suffer a working committee with so-called rightists, but instead choose a homogeneous one without hindrance, adding tongue in cheek, 'After all, Subhas Babu is not an enemy of his country. He has suffered for it. In his opinion his is the most forward and boldest policy and programme.'[107] Encouraged by Bose's electoral success, which was the high watermark of leftist unity, M.N. Roy urged Subhas to create his own working committee under a new leadership. He reminded Subhas that Gandhi '*has been defeated*' and that 'there is absolutely no reason for you not to assert yourself'.[108] Subhas, however, was not convinced about the strength of his support. He increasingly realized the truth in Gandhi's assertion that the verdict had been more a censure of 'the old horses' or the conservative Gandhian leadership, particularly Patel, than an expression of support for Subhas.[109]

As Gandhi's statement had the immediate effect of making the contest assume the proportions of a straight confrontation between him and Subhas, support for Subhas began to crumble. Business leaders such as R.K. Dalmia, who had given Bose support on the basis of regional affiliation, were most confused. Dalmia confessed to Rajendra Prasad, 'If I had known that his (Bose's) policy is not in line with the orthodox Congress creed . . . I should have thought twice before associating with any of his activities.'[110] The Congress Socialists, too, who had chosen to carry forward their own programme of socialism while remaining in the Gandhian Congress, had no desire to go against Gandhi. Nor did Bose want a split in the Congress. He wanted to serve as president again, but he wanted to carry along with him all groups in the final confrontation with the British. Could he indeed have his *roshogolla* and eat it, too?[111]

On 22 February, twelve of the fourteen Working Committee members resigned. Jawaharlal Nehru and the Socialist, Narendra Dev, held out, Nehru's characteristic logic being that he would resign on his own without being part of the general statement which the Working Committee had issued. Although Nehru had been against Subhas's bid for re-election and had no faith in the left being able to shoulder the burden of carrying on the struggle alone, he was aghast at the old guard blatantly abandoning its policy of compromise, consensus and accommodation. Nehru sadly concluded that 'if that was to be their clear-cut policy, I had no place with them'.[112] Placed in this quandary, Nehru adopted, as he admitted to Subhas, 'a rather foolish attitude. I did not actually resign and yet I acted as if I had done so . . .'[113]

Between the elections at the end of January and the actual session at Tripuri in mid-March, neither the old guard nor Bose had decided on any particular course of action. Both had their own preoccupations: Gandhi was involved in the state people movement at Rajkot, where he had located himself, and Bose was battling a recurring and debilitating illness. The tide that had swept Bose to victory was already ebbing by the time of the Tripuri Congress. In a surge of feeling in favour of Gandhism, Congress veteran G.B. Pant now introduced at the AICC meeting a resolution declaring firm adherence to the fundamental policies of the Congress under the leadership of Gandhi, who alone could lead the Congress. It requested the president to nominate the new working committee in accordance with the wishes of Gandhi. The passage of this resolution by 218 votes to 135 robbed Subhas of the very raison d'être of his alternative leadership challenge to Gandhi. Pushed to the brink of choosing between Gandhi and Bose, the verdict was clearly in Gandhi's favour, with the crucial CSP block preferring to remain neutral and Nehru casting his vote with the old guard. Subhas never forgave Nehru. He lamented later, 'Nobody has done more harm to me personally and to our cause in this crisis than Pandit Nehru. If he had been with us we would have had a majority. Even his neutrality would have probably given us a majority.'[114]

Subhas reacted to the crisis with the mentality of a boxer.[115] He would not give up without a proper fight. After all, he was not willing to see his victory as a negative vote and liked to believe that it was an indication of the large amount of support for his cause. At the same time, he would not break with Gandhi totally, and when pushed against the wall he was willing to shake hands like a boxer and make up, as a rebel son with his stern father. To the Congress resolution that now was initiated by Pant, Subhas reacted strongly, calling it ultra vires and in violation of the Congress practice, hitherto followed, of having a composite working committee with different voices instead of a homogeneous body.[116] However, in response to this outburst, when Gandhi gave him an unfettered choice to appoint his own members, Subhas withdrew from precipitating a crisis. He became increasingly unsure of the quality of the support he had managed to build up. Even so, Subhas was not going to surrender completely. He was willing to make a compromise on his own terms. Accordingly, he now suggested a working committee with half the members of his choice and half of Patel's choice as an 'equitable choice'.[117] The Gandhian Congress, however, stood firm in rejecting any compromise with him. At the Calcutta AICC meeting, in May 1939, Subhas sent in his letter of resignation as Congress president. However, he made a final plea to Gandhi that he would accept as binding whatever committee Gandhi appointed since it was his 'determination to implement Pantji's resolution'.[118] Gandhi remained unmoved and even disowned the Pant resolution due to an ambiguity in its wording.

Nehru was distraught. He exclaimed, 'To try to push him (Bose) out seems to be an exceedingly wrong step.'[119] Despite Subhas's harsh indictment of him, Nehru had genuinely tried to broker peace between two stubborn men. In vain did he beseech Gandhi to tend to more crucial matters within the Congress rather than remove himself from the scene and camp in Rajkot. And in vain did he plead with Subhas to leave the formation of the working committee entirely to Gandhi and promise his loyal support to whatever was decided, a recommendation that Nehru had followed in a similar situation a couple of years ago. Nehru was, however, basically pliable and had an instinctive reverence for Gandhi, with whom he could differ but whom he did not dare defy.

Subhas launched his ultimate act of defiance by rallying all the elements opposed to the Congress leadership and forming a kind of national 'left-wing' organization. He founded both the Forward Bloc (a pressure group within the Congress) and the Left Coordination Committee (formed of four Forward Bloc, three CSP, three CPI and two Royist members) to consolidate all the left forces in the country in the impending fight against British imperialism. However, with no united programme to bring them together except an anti-Gandhian stand, the Forward Bloc was reduced to 'a negative grouping, an anti-block', as Nehru put it.[120] It appeared to have a certain nuisance value though, as it galvanized opinion against AICC resolutions enforcing stricter control in the organization. Bose called an all-India protest day against these resolutions on 9 July, which, however, turned out to be a fiasco since both the Congress Socialists and M.N. Roy dissociated themselves from it. Gandhi, however, would not let off Subhas so lightly from what he considered was a gross abuse of party discipline. He first asked Subhas to resign from the Congress, and on his refusal, he personally drafted the resolution to ban him from holding any executive office in the organization for three years. In vain did the nation's poet, Rabindranath Tagore, protest against the ban and request Gandhi to take it back in the 'supreme interest of national unity'.[121]

Gandhi's response was telling. He knew he was being ruthless but felt it was the only way to make Subhas 'open his eyes'.[122] Explaining that he had accepted Subhas as a son, he was proceeding to do what he had done with his recalcitrant eldest son, Harilal, whose wayward behaviour had prompted Gandhi to cut off relations with him. Gandhi wrote in the *Harijan* in early 1940, 'The love of my conception, if it is as soft as rose petal, can also be harder than flint.'[123] He admitted experiencing 'the pain of wholly associating himself with the ban' on Subhas. However, he asked Andrews to assure Tagore that he still regarded Subhas as a son even though he was behaving 'like a spoilt child of the family'.[124]

The weakness of Bose's position at the central level undermined his position at the provincial level. His opponents in the Bengal Congress gloated over his defeat, and in the new working committee formed by the new Congress president, Rajendra Prasad, two of them found a place, P.C. Ghosh and B.C. Roy. The Fazlul Huq ministry, making full use of the infighting within the Bengal Congress, ended by legislative action in 1939 the Congress domination in the Calcutta Corporation. Thus, the Congress, unable to join a coalition ministry in Bengal, also lost control over the Calcutta municipal politics which it had been enjoying for decades. The Working Committee now called the BPCC to elect a new president, and when the Bose-dominated body unanimously elected Bose as president, it was dismissed and a small ad hoc committee headed by Maulana Azad was appointed in its place. With the coexistence of both these bodies from late 1939, factionalism in Bengal reached an all-time high, with the Congress central executive even appointing an auditor to go into the so-called financial irregularities of the Bose-led BPCC.[125]

Subhas now released his pent-up energy through the Forward Bloc, making whirlwind tours around the country and feeling encouraged by the large audiences that he attracted. However, his speeches largely dwelt on his rebellious challenge to Gandhi, 'an act of dare-devilry'[126] which he proudly contrasted with the constitutional mentality of the Gandhians. The programmes he offered were not very convincing and neither was his support base very reliable. Nehru lost patience with 'the arrant nonsense' about a rival Congress that Subhas kept speaking about. Jawaharlal confided to a friend, 'Subhas Bose does not seem to have an idea in his head and except for going on talking about leftists and rightists he says little that is intelligible.'[127]

With the German attack on Poland in September 1939 marking the start of World War II, the focus now changed. Congress ministries were asked to resign. In the discussions on the war situation which Viceroy Linlithgow had with the Congress, Subhas Bose was also invited to participate. Subhas did not sympathize with the fate of Britain, reiterating instead his earlier views about utilizing the war situation to India's advantage. Without anyone to share his views, Subhas now turned back to Bengal where he stole some of the limelight by beginning an agitation for the removal of the Holwell monument in the summer of 1940. The monument, which had been built in mid-eighteenth-century Calcutta as a memorial to the victims of the so-called Black Hole tragedy, was an eyesore for both communities of Indians, Hindus and Muslims. Arrested along with others, Subhas was, however, not released even after the government decided to do away with the monument and his co-prisoners were set free. Sensing that the British government was planning to keep him in detention for the period of the war and realizing that his political options within the country were limited, Subhas now hatched his sensational plan of escape, first from the British prison and then from the country. Commencing a fast unto death in protest against his unjust imprisonment, he frightened the jail authorities into letting him out in a few days as his indifferent health posed hazards. From under house arrest he wrote to Gandhi about the need for a mass movement. Gandhi replied that their paths had to be different for they were sailing in different boats.[128] On 16 January 1941, Subhas escaped house arrest and subsequently left India, taking the British authorities and his countrymen by total surprise. He was never to return.

Once out of the country, and free from the constraints of pursuing different policies within the same political space, the rebel son reached out to the stern father. Gandhi could not but be impressed by the sheer 'irrepressible' nature of Subhas, which resulted in 'the fireworks' that he had predicted.[129] Operating in the larger arena, both men could go beyond their differences and follow the burning sense of mission that each had and acknowledge the commonality of vision they shared for the India of their dreams. Once Bose was dead and India almost free, when news trickled in about the phenomenal communal and gender unity that Subhas had created in his Azad Hind initiative, Nehru joined Gandhi in acknowledging the worth of the dream that Subhas had dared to dream.

~

THREE

BAPU, HIS BELOVED DISCIPLE AND THE REBEL SON

The intellectual history of India in the nineteenth and twentieth centuries reflected an evolving national consciousness which assessed, critiqued, challenged and came to terms with the colonial experience. Under colonial rule, Indian beliefs and practices were scrutinized through the western lens of reason and utilitarianism. A contrasting paradigm of modernity and tradition was drawn up where modernity was equated with westernization and progress, and conversely tradition was associated with Indianness and backwardness. Challenged by the onslaught of British racial arrogance and cultural superiority, the nationalist response was complex and ambivalent.

Indian nationalist thought was confronted with the insincerity of colonial rule, which advocated parliamentary constitutional values while keeping them from the subject people. At the same time, the Indian National Congress, too, in its struggle against colonialism was ambivalent about major socio-economic issues as it attempted to maintain a consensus among disparate groups while seeking to take the movement forward. The national leaders of the Congress oscillated between encouraging mass movements and putting the brakes on when these threatened to get out of hand and jeopardize the interests of other constituents of the party with landed or business interests. Gandhi's classic juggling of positions between agitation, retreat and constructive activities in the anti-imperialist movement was a response to this necessity. However, the different and strongly opposed stances in his position baffled his critics and followers alike, for they showed him in different lights as a radical reformer, a moderate compromiser, a visionary and an idealist. In reality, however, this change in stance was a natural outcome of the interaction between the shifting forces of imperialist action and reaction and the various constituent groups of the Congress national movement.

The Congress leadership displayed a similar ambivalence in its response to the 'modernizing' mission of the West. In a process of understanding itself, it redefined tradition, often lauding it, often faulting it. The considerable debate, dialogue and discussion that this provoked helped the ideals of freedom to be seen on a larger canvas.

By and large, the nationalist leaders were deeply disturbed by the state of Indian society and looked for means to regenerate it. Barring a small group of traditionalists, who glorified the Indian past and chauvinistically dismissed all western influence as undesirable, the majority body of opinion believed in a syncretic approach arising from an interaction between the western and the traditional systems. Sociologists have seen in this pattern of interaction a distinct difference between those who approached cultural synthesis rooted in a traditional position, called the critical traditionalists, and those who favoured a synthesis rooted in an essentially modern stance, called the critical modernists.[1] Thus, critical modernists are seen as those who believed in a successful combination of the best aspects of western and Indian systems, while the critical traditionalists are seen as those who sought instead to weed out the evils in the legacy of Indian tradition. While they appreciated some of the Enlightenment values of socio-political liberty and equality, they disagreed about the role of modern technology and industrialization. They felt that India had to evolve its own institutions keeping in mind its peculiar ethos and native genius. In this categorization, Gandhi has been seen as a critical traditionalist, while Nehru is regarded as a critical modernist. Attractive though these categorizations may appear, it is important to realize that intellectual history is evolutionary in character. Thus, many of the statements of the national leaders were not necessarily absolute, and they covered considerable ground over the years in revising or buttressing their initial positions. A typical case was that of Subhas Chandra Bose, whose beliefs combined aspects of both these points of view, thus belying any simplistic attempt at categorization. However, the postures and stances adopted by the national leaders tended to create a public impression which cast them into certain moulds far more rigid than was really the case. In his assessment of Bose, his biographer Leonard Gordon observed that Subhas shared a few points in common with Nehru but much fewer with Gandhi.[2] However, Gandhi and Bose were actually much closer to each other in their perceptions and attitudes than is usually recognized. Also, Bose and Nehru, despite commonalities in their education and upbringing, had fundamentally different mindsets, which led to their drifting away from each other although they had begun their political careers as part of the same team.

The loincloth-clad Gandhi, who appeared to Romain Rolland as 'the little Indian St. Francis' and who defended the philosophy of non-violence, stood in stark contrast to the military general Subhas, who asked for his countrymen's blood in lieu of freedom.[3] In the public eye, Subhas and Gandhi appeared to stand side by side in the nationalist movement, like the tiger and the elephant in the jungle until their respective territories were challenged.[4] Subhas's unique open challenge to Gandhi's leadership, the only individual within the Congress leadership to have actually done so, and his formulation of an alternative strategy in the anti-imperialist struggle, placed him squarely in an opposing camp.

The contrasting images of these two leaders were heightened by their different regional backgrounds. Gandhi hailed from Gujarat, was predominantly vegetarian, and the product of the Swami Narayan tradition espousing faith in the Vaishnava concepts of tolerance, love and compassion. He entered the political arena at a time when Bengal was at the centre stage of the nationalist agitation. Indeed, after the successful swadeshi agitation in Bengal—with its programmes of boycott, picketing and protest, which led to the undoing of the Bengal partition of 1905—Gandhi's call of non-cooperation in 1921 did not generate immediate enthusiasm in the province. There was even indignation that the Gandhian programme was not original, having been tried out already in Bengal. Moreover, Gandhi's insistence on spinning seemed tame and slightly absurd in a state which had been inspired by the activist mantra of its philosopher, Vivekananda, and the rallying cries of its celebrated novelist, Bankim Chandra Chattopadhyay. The Nobel laureate, Rabindranath Tagore, complained to Gandhi, 'Poems I can spin, Gandhiji, songs and plays I can spin, but of your precious cotton what a mess I would make!'[5] Subhas was to inherit some of these misgivings.

Making his debut on the stage of Indian politics as the lieutenant of the Bengal leader Chittaranjan Das, who was Gandhi's rival, Subhas was to gain first-hand experience of how his leader could successfully fashion an alternative programme of council entry after Gandhi's non-cooperation movement had been called off in 1922. To Subhas, therefore, Gandhi was not an icon who could overawe him into submission. There was in his approach to Gandhi the questioning and critiquing attitude of the younger generation towards the older. On the one hand, he recognized Gandhi's unique contribution to the national movement, that of making it for the first time a mass movement. He acknowledged that Gandhi, as 'India's man of destiny', had converted the Congress from 'a talking body' into a 'living and fighting organisation' by 'his single-hearted devotion, his relentless will and his indefatigable labour'. While lauding his policy of unification that reached out to 'Hindu and Moslem, the high caste and the low caste, the capitalist and the labourer, the landlord and the peasant' alike, nevertheless, Subhas's overall verdict on Gandhi's performance was severe. 'He has failed,' Subhas concluded.[6] Among the many reasons that he identified as being responsible for this failure was Gandhi's 'old age'.[7] He was convinced that the reason for Gandhi's temporizing moves, as for instance when he signed the pact with Irwin in 1931 and attended the First Round Table Conference, was because he could not sustain the civil disobedience movement as he lacked the vigour and enthusiasm of the younger generation of politicians whom Subhas claimed to represent. Subhas went on to say that Gandhi's use of religious idiom and his obsessive emphasis on non-violence in any other country would have 'led him to the cross or the mental hospital'.[8] His dismissive and impatient outbursts against Gandhi drowned out the basic admiration he had for the Mahatma's extraordinary mass appeal. He stood out as an upstart in his behaviour towards Bapu, which earned for him considerable disapproval among the close-knit group of Gandhi's followers. When his book *The Indian Struggle*, initially banned in India after its publication in 1935, was allowed into the country a few years later, it put up the backs of the Gandhi loyalists in the Congress, particularly in view of its unfortunate timing as Subhas had by then decided to take on Gandhi's candidate in the Congress presidential re-election.[9]

Subhas described the political differences between himself and Gandhi in terms of a left–right clash. To Subhas, 'right' meant an old-fashioned and inflexible approach which could not spontaneously engage in action. Also, the Gandhian hesitation in addressing socio-economic issues simultaneously while engaged in political agitation seemed to the young Subhas an indication of a conservative mindset.[10] To him, 'left' meant an uncompromising and sustained approach to active politics without succumbing to the temptation of calling for a truce or making a deal. He was willing to call Gandhi a 'leftist' in 1921[11] when he launched the non-cooperation movement, but felt that he had adopted a conservative point of view subsequently. However, Subhas's narrow definition of left versus right was not acceptable to either Gandhi or Nehru. Nehru protested that the loose application of terms such as 'left' and 'right' caused confusion, as 'a person may be very "left" or advanced in a political and nationalist sense and yet "right" in a social sense'.[12] An exasperated Gandhi told Subhas, 'I wish you would choose better and indigenous terms to designate the parties of your imagination.'[13] Eventually, Subhas himself moved away from this simplistic definition when he realized in his home state, Bengal, the difficulties of opposing the landed interests while pushing the political agenda along. However, he continued to use the labels to emphasize how 'static and hidebound' Gandhi had become,[14] and to present, in contrast, his own alternative strategy of direct action against imperialist rule.

The strong rhetoric of the late 1920s and 1930s used principally by Subhas and politicians of leftist inclinations to critique the Gandhian line, and present an alternative strategy, created the impression that the two men were poles apart ideologically. This impression was reinforced by their regional and generational differences, their well-articulated differences on the issue of violence versus non-violence, and above all by the labels of left and right, which were commonly bandied about in the contemporary political usage and reportage of the day. However, in the 1940s, the altered international and national circumstances, as well as the experiences of the preceding decades, made Subhas look upon the project of national independence through a slightly larger lens. He now looked beyond the goal of independence towards the need to restructure India's socio-economic system and polity. His experience with the Planning Commission when he was Congress president at Haripura in 1938 shows how all-round his vision had become. He could now interact meaningfully with the industrialist classes, and at the same time accommodate Gandhi's favoured project of handloom and cottage industries. His Azad Hind experience in south-east Asia beginning in 1943 provided him an opportunity to work on a programme encompassing all, across the barriers of class, caste, religion and gender; this was the blueprint for his vision of what post-independence India should be. During this period, he saw himself not vying with Gandhi, but instead working in tandem with him in a complementary fashion. Gandhi, too, in the years following Subhas's escape from India, mellowed considerably in his attitude towards him. Indeed, his Quit India call in 1942, given in spite of opposition from many Congress loyalists, seemed not only to loosen his dictates on non-violence but was also a reassuring statement of his commitment to press on in the nationalist agitation without compromise, which younger colleagues like Subhas had over the years unsuccessfully implored him to do. This change in attitude might appear to be a dramatic volte-face, but may not necessarily be so if one looks at the basic compulsions which motivated them both. Gandhi and Subhas, stern father and rebel son, for all their political and ideological differences, drew on the same wellsprings of inspiration, and were actually much closer to each other in basic temperament than is realized.

In the face of the British challenge, both Gandhi and Subhas acted from the conviction that there was a need for national self-strengthening. Non-violence, to Gandhi, was not a passive movement, but rather one that called for consummate inner strength so that the non-cooperator could withstand the penalty of breaking the law without recourse to counter violence. Gandhi felt that the rishis, who had discovered the law of non-violence in the midst of violence, were greater geniuses than Newton.[15] He explained, 'Strength does not come from physical capacity. It comes from an indomitable will.'[16] Subhas, too, was motivated by a steely determination and an unbending will. He drew upon the revolutionary tradition of Bengal, sharing the revolutionary's passion, dedication, discipline and unswerving focus but without supporting the policy of sporadic killings. His espousal of the armed option as part of a consistent military venture was to come later. Gandhi, too, saw his role in leading the Congress movement as a disciplined soldier, and the examples of Mazzini and Garibaldi in fashioning the unification movement in Italy inspired both Gandhi and Subhas. Underlying this resolve was a deep-rooted spiritual commitment to selfless sacrifice, and both Gandhi and Subhas were deeply moved by the exhortation in the Gita preaching 'nishkama dharma' or commitment to duty without any expectation of reward. There was also in Gandhi's overall thinking an all-pervading feeling of compassion, love and tolerance, as well as a deep concern for the socially disadvantaged. Thus, Gandhi and Subhas shared certain abiding values and strands in thinking which made them essentially more similar to each other in mindset than is apparent at first glance. In contrast, Nehru and Subhas, although closer in age and intellectually similar in training and education, had less in common. Although Subhas had begun his political career on the same side as Nehru, as young hot-headed leaders determined to force the pace of the Gandhian movement, their opposing mindsets made them eventually drift apart.

★

Subhas Chandra Bose was born in 1897, the ninth child in a family of fourteen children. His parents, Janakinath and Probhabati Bose, belonged to two prominent Kayastha families, the Boses of Mahimnagar and the Dattas of Hatkhola. During Subhas's early years, his family resided in Cuttack, where his father was a prominent lawyer. Subhas was a diligent and successful student with an excellent academic record throughout. During these formative years of student life, his impressionable mind was subjected to several abiding influences.

Religion fascinated Subhas and he delved into the scriptures and the tantras and tried unsuccessfully, in the first year of college, to look for a spiritual guru in the Himalayas.[17] This quest left him disgusted with the hypocrisy of the priestly classes and the sacrileges they committed in holy places. Throughout his life, he kept alive this faith and drew strength from his beliefs. Brought up amidst the ritual observances of religion in the family, Subhas always cherished memories of such occasions. The fifteen-year-old Subhas wrote to his mother how much he missed the typical atmosphere of Durga Puja. He recalled with nostalgia the melodious chanting of sacred hymns, the sound of the conch shell and the gong, the sacred aroma of flowers, sandalwood and incense, and the ritual partaking of prasad/bhog or holy food offered to the goddess.[18] Incarcerated in Mandalay Jail in Burma in 1925, Subhas pleaded with the jail authorities and organized the observance of Durga Puja.[19] His deep interest in the tantra shastra continued, and as an ailing Congress president at Tripuri in 1939 he wore the innumerable amulets sent by well-wishers to ward off the alleged evil effects of the tantra spell (*Maran kriya*), which supposedly had been set on him.[20]

After standing second in the matriculation examination from Calcutta University in 1913, Subhas entered Presidency College to study philosophy. He was to complete his graduation, however, from Scottish Church College in 1919 with first class honours. Subhas's short stint at Presidency College was significant, particularly because of his involvement in the much-publicized Oaten affair, which became a defining moment in his life. Professor Oaten, who allegedly had made derogatory references to India, had been manhandled by some students in 1916, of whom Subhas was one; this led to his expulsion from Presidency College. This incident had a crucial significance in the mental development of Subhas. He hardly felt like a hero when the incident occurred. If anything, he was more concerned that his record as a good student would be affected by his expulsion. He even hoped that his innocence might be proved and that he would be let off.[21] Only later, when the event had made a hero out of him, did he realize its full importance. He expressed his regret to his brother, Sarat, in a letter written from Cambridge for not having summoned enough courage to openly admit that he had beaten the professor.[22] Looking back on the incident, Subhas wrote, 'Little did I then realize the inner significance of the tragic events of 1916. My Principal had expelled me but he had made my future career. I had established a precedent for myself from which I could not easily depart in future.'[23] It would have heartened Subhas to know that Oaten not only forgave his errant student's action, but also recognized in him 'the genial patriot fire that brightly glowed in India's mighty heart' which was stilled when, 'Icarus-like', Subhas plummeted to his death in the seas.[24]

The racial arrogance of the British rulers had irked Subhas considerably. In his student years he noticed with distaste, for instance, how on tramcars the British would often be 'purposely rude and offensive to Indians' by putting up their feet on the front seats occupied by Indian passengers.[25] He tried to counter this insult in two ways. First, he made a conscious effort to shake off the colonial image of Indians in general, and Bengalis in particular, as being frail and emasculated. He tried to infuse the Indian consciousness with a greater vigour and manly discipline. Second, he tried to improve Indian efficiency and excellence by perfecting the acceptable social graces of the British and challenging them both academically and professionally.

In advocating greater physical fitness, well-being and discipline for Indians, Subhas was reflecting the mood of his generation. The well-known invective against Bengali men by Macaulay, Law Member for India in the 1830s, as physically feeble to the extent of effeminacy and mentally weak to the point of helplessness, had been repeated in many official discourses.[26] The nationalist reaction to this characterization had been a grudging recognition of physical effeminacy, which was ascribed to a lack of adequate exercise and faulty diet. There was a conscious effort at refashioning the nationalist identity by making a transition from the frail hero to the virile and manly Indian. Physical fitness was promoted in community fairs such as the Hindu melas patronized by the Tagore family, and indigenous skills in lathi or bamboo stick play and wrestling were encouraged in gymnastic schools. The exhortations of the philosopher Vivekananda (1863–1902) to Indians to wake up as a nation, to remove the mental cobwebs of superstition, and to acquire spiritual and physical fitness and strength, provided the inspiration for this call of regeneration.

On a lighter side, there was also a movement in indigenous literature and popular culture towards self-ridicule and introspection. The Kalighat *patachitras* captured in cartoons the ironic image of the feeble man being castigated by his physically imposing wife. The myth of the strong wife was reinforced by recasting the woman in revised roles, from the neglected and the weak to the spiritually strong and supportive, and raising her to the elevated pedestal of a goddess. To the English-educated bhadralok class, it was necessary to invent an image of Bharat Mata combining the attributes of Kali and Durga, so that the woman could not only emanate strength but also keep at bay the threat of man's sexual overtures. In the nationalist discourse, woman's participation as co-worker in the national movement could be assured only by placing her beyond lust, in the form of a mother goddess immortalized by the celebrated novelist, Bankim Chandra Chattopadhyay (1838–94). Also, putting the woman on a pedestal and lauding her role as being born to sacrifice and suffer took away her voice or capacity to protest.

There was also a challenge to the nationalist male to desist from sexual thoughts, to equate all women with mothers and sisters, and to focus on the struggle at hand. Vivekananda's formula of celibacy and asceticism for reclaiming lost manhood found favour among many. In the bhadralok recasting of the woman's role, there was also the additional dimension of qualifying her to be compatible with her English-educated husband, so that he would not stray into the arms of prostitutes. The recommended behaviour for the *bhadramahila* included mastering the skills of music and dance and acquiring greater education, so that she could share in her educated husband's delight in English literature and later provide the foundations of learning for their children. There was, however, a studied consciousness that a woman's emancipation should be limited, so that she could be 'recast' according to a prescription whereby her character and personality were refined and reorganized according to carefully delineated parameters.[27]

Subhas came to inherit most of these trends of thought, but over the years he critiqued many of the assumptions and evolved in his own way of thinking. He was convinced of the need for India as a nation to build up physical stamina and acquire fitness and strength. Vivekananda's observation that 'salvation will come through football and not through the Gita' made sense to Subhas, who regretted his own neglect of sports in his early years.[28] Reflecting on his childhood, he observed that lack of sports facilities and the preference of Bengali middle class parents for studies over sports had turned him into a 'goody goody', obedient son 'busy devouring ethical verses in Sanskrit'.[29] It was exactly this 'goody goody' nature of the Bengali character that he proceeded to attack later in an effort to arouse the Bengali bhadralok from a sense of complacency and cultural superiority into which they had been lulled by their acquisition of English education. 'Good boy will not achieve anything. That he who is "good" at studies eventually attains prosperity—is an utterly wrong ideal,' he wrote. He recommended that students should inculcate a spirit of adventure and wanderlust, and indeed should learn to become 'wayward'.[30] He lamented that students were becoming bhadralok and 'gradually giving up such manly practices—as swimming across the river, climbing fruit-bearing trees, snatching fruits and eating them, going out on picnics, walking long distances—20 to 40 miles in groups, playing *lathi*, wrestling etc'.[31] English education had mongrelized the true Indian character and created the 'Firengi Bengali', who was English educated but lacked contact with the life of Bengali society.[32]

Subhas tried to compensate for his own rather tame childhood by dabbling in adulthood in physical training, drills and musketry with the university unit of the Indian Territorial Army. He discovered a certain 'pleasure in soldiering, and a feeling of strength and self-confidence' in the experience.[33] Defeating his instructors at Fort William in a shooting competition, or participating in a guard of honour parade for the governor at the university convocation, reinforced his faith in being able to excel in areas where the British had a known mastery.

Subhas's postgraduate studies were interrupted when he proceeded to Cambridge, at the behest of his father, to prepare for the Indian Civil Service (ICS) examinations. His exposure to British society made a deep impression on him. Being very sensitive, he could easily detect the 'feelings of superiority' the British had 'beneath a veneer of bonhomie'.[34] On the one hand, deeply affected as he was by the indiscriminate killing by British troops of unarmed people in Amritsar in 1919, an enraged Subhas commented, 'Nothing makes me happier than to be served by the whites and to watch them clean my shoes.'[35] On the other hand, he acknowledged, 'They have many faults but in many matters you have to respect them for their virtues.'[36] It was this realization that made Subhas eager to confront the British on their own terms. In his zeal to prove Indian efficiency and excellence, he sought to perfect the acceptable social graces of the British, much to the annoyance of his friend Dilip Roy, who wondered whether Subhas was not indeed betraying a certain 'inferiority complex not easily visible except to a small group of lynx eyed observers'. Dilip recounted how at Cambridge Subhas would feel outraged by his friend's customary posture of sitting in a dhoti in an asana pose or by his habit of gesticulating. He would protest, 'You must learn to talk in a stifled voice and don't, for mercy's sake, fling your hands about like lassos. You mustn't Dilip, no, not even behind closed shutters, for beware, murder will out.' His favourite motto being 'In Rome do as Romans do', Subhas advised, 'Leave behind an impression of flawless spruce-ness.'[37]

It was in the same spirit that Subhas approached the Civil Service examinations. He felt that he had to excel in an examination dominated by the British elite, and then express his nationalist ardour by resigning from it. Finishing fourth in the ICS examinations, Subhas decided to resign and take up 'national service'. In his resolve to resign from the ICS, he was inspired by the example of Deshbandhu C.R. Das. Explaining his decision, Subhas wrote, 'If C.R. Das at his age can give up everything and face the uncertainties of life—I am sure a young man like myself, who has no worldly cares to trouble him, is much more capable of doing so.'[38] Bose wanted to set an example for members of other services since he realized that before him 'in the whole history of British India, not one Indian has voluntarily given up the Civil Service with a patriotic move'.[39] From Cambridge, Bose wrote to C.R. Das, declaring his intention of joining the national movement. On his way back to India in 1921, he decided to stop en route in Bombay to meet Mahatma Gandhi. Recording his first impressions of this meeting, Subhas expressed dissatisfaction at Gandhi's inability to spell out in detail the programme he was about to commence. The characteristic Gandhian tendency to avoid cut-and-dried formulas and instead leave all options open failed to impress the young Subhas impatient for action. C.R. Das, on the other hand, under whom Subhas began his political apprenticeship, fitted his bill as an ideological mentor.

Subhas began his political career in the thick of the non-cooperation movement and engaged himself in a variety of activities under the leadership of Das in Bengal. Involving himself in national education, he remained for a while the conscientious principal of Bengal National College, despite the empty benches in the classrooms.[40] After organizing boycott movements and working closely with newspapers such as *Banglar Katha, Forward* and *Atma Shakti,* Subhas became involved in the drama of Swarajist politics, championed by Das and Motilal Nehru. The Swarajists recommended council entry as an alternative to the Gandhian programme of non-cooperation, which had been suddenly called off in 1922. These were also instructive years for Subhas in corporation politics, where, as chief executive officer, he worked closely with Das, who was the mayor. Social work, too, claimed his time and his distinguished participation in flood relief operations in north Bengal recalled the voluntary work he had assiduously engaged in during his student years in taking care of cholera and small pox victims. Subhas's close interaction with Das was abruptly terminated by his sudden imprisonment in 1924. Death claimed Das in June 1925, and Subhas was not destined to see his mentor again. However, this brief period of political apprenticeship proved to be crucial in shaping his mindset, not merely because of the variety of activities in which he became involved but, more importantly, because of the philosophical impact that his guru came to have on him.

Subhas acknowledged that his close relationship with Das during the brief spell of eight months (1921–22), when they were co-prisoners, had had a profound impact on his formative thinking. For one, it was Das who made him aware of the richness of Bengal's culture and tradition. He confessed to the celebrated novelist, Sarat Chandra Chattopadhyay, that but for Das he would never have realized the depth of his love for golden Bengal.[41] He reflected deeply on the cultural strains influencing the Bengali psyche and identified three dominant ones. The pursuit of *nyaya* and *smriti* made the Bengali naturally argumentative, eloquent and articulate. The influence of Vaishnavism and Vedanta gave a spiritual foundation to Bengali beliefs and made Bengalis naturally emotional and sentimental, a quality, Das said, that had to be cherished with pride and not be embarrassed about.[42] Vaishnavism, integral to Das's religious beliefs, made him reach out to people of diverse political and religious backgrounds in a spirit of love and compassion. He placed great faith on working out 'pacts' or compromises so that differences, whether within families, among friends, in communities or in political life, could be resolved in a mutually acceptable manner.[43] It was in this spirit that Das reached out to Muslims in a historic accord made with them in 1923. Similarly, he sought to draw the underprivileged sections of society in his all-inclusive slogan of swaraj for the masses and not only the classes, thereby giving a political platform to Vivekananda's social message. The influence of Das's thinking could be found in Subhas's programmes later when he sought to reach out to a large cross section of society across economic, social, religious and gender divides. The deep spiritualism of Das and his mission of sacrifice for the country's cause also left an indelible imprint on Subhas's mind. The image of Subhas as a military leader tends to overshadow his underlying commitment to *seva* and *tyag* or self-denying sacrifice, which he had made his ultimate goal.

One quality of Das that Subhas valued considerably was his tolerance of dissenting opinion. He recalled how openly and fearlessly views were expressed at meetings with Das and 'wordy battles' fought. However, there was never any 'pettiness' in the way that Das dealt with such expressions of difference.[44] Allowing differences to be aired, he would encourage the formulation of a strategy of action and focus on it with single-minded devotion. This passionate and unswerving commitment to the realization of the declared political goal was strongly shared by Subhas. Recalling this, he observed:

Whatever he (Das) desired, he desired with all his life, mind and utterance. He would go mad over it. The utmost impediments were unable to frighten him or force him to withdraw. Like Napoleon Bonaparte who, seeing the Alps standing before him, had said, 'There shall be no Alps', the Deshbandhu also wholly ignored difficulties and obstructions.[45]

Bose learnt his lesson well from Das. He took his inspiration from the activism of Vivekananda, dismissing Gandhi's slackening of the pace of the national movement from time to time as a sign of weakness, and being impatient with Nehru's indecisiveness.

Intellectually, therefore, Subhas saw dissent as a healthy expression of an alternative point of view, which strengthened the movement and took it forward by helping it to evolve. Philosophically, he explained it in terms of Hegelian dialectics as a necessary and natural evolution in the direction of the movement. He believed that when the mainstream of a movement began to stagnate, it became necessary for a left wing to stimulate progress, resolve the conflict through an agreement or adjustment, and carry the movement forward. In course of time, this left wing became the mainstream of the movement. The dialectical progress—with the 'thesis' throwing up its 'antithesis' and resolving the conflict through a 'synthesis', which then became, in the next stage of evolution, the 'thesis'— profoundly influenced the thinking of Subhas. He situated his dissent from Gandhi within the framework of this discourse. As he explained, 'Progress is neither unilinear, nor is it always peaceful in character. Progress often takes place through conflict.'[46]

One of the powerful influences on the mindset of Subhas was the concept of mother, which he equated with the motherland and through which he sought a resolution of his own evolving thoughts on women and the question of gender equality. In his prescription of physical fitness for Indians to overcome the colonial label of effeteness, Subhas had included women on the same terms as men. He visualized a determined body of 'freedom intoxicated' men and women who would take upon themselves the task of delivering India no matter what the suffering and sacrifice may be.[47] In this vision of Indian women, Subhas sought to give the lie to the age-old description of women as the weak and frail sex. He wrote, 'So long, the woman was weak—now we must make women strong and brave . . . To achieve independence is not merely man's job. It is also woman's job. One half of society are women, therefore if India's women do not wake up, India will not wake up.'[48] In organizing a separate women's contingent in his Bengal Volunteers, which made its presence known during the Calcutta Congress in 1928, and later by organizing the Rani of Jhansi regiment in his Azad Hind Fauj in 1943, Subhas displayed an awareness of democratic gender relations. At the same time, this depiction of women permitted Subhas to maintain a comfortable distance from the emotional demands of gender relationships which he could not handle.

From his adolescent years, Subhas had struggled hard to come to terms with the concept of sexuality.[49] At an age when mixed-sex socialization was not very common and matters of sexuality seldom discussed, Subhas tried very hard to 'suppress or transcend' the growth of sex consciousness, which he considered 'unnatural and immoral'.[50] Relying on Vivekananda, he tried to overcome his weakness by focusing instead on higher spiritual goals like patriotism or nationalism. He was inspired by Vivekananda's ideal of making the motherland the queen of his adoration. In according women the place of mother, sister or colleague marching alongside men, Subhas felt he could escape from having to deal with them on a human, personal and emotional plane where he was vulnerable. He tried to follow Ramakrishna's dictum of sublimating the sex instinct and regarding every woman as a mother.

Subhas's respect for his mother was absolute, and as he wrote to Probhabati, 'We are reared on mother's milk—therefore, nothing can be more educative and elevating than what instruction and guidance we get from the mother.'[51] Subhas also enjoyed a closeness with Basantidebi, the wife of C.R. Das, to whom he would turn for emotional support after the sudden death of Das left him without direction. Exhorting her to take on the mantle of political leadership, he appealed to her as the 'mother', whose cult was integral to the spiritual quest of Bengal.[52] Subscribing to the Bengali nationalists' equation of the motherland with Durga or Kali, Subhas associated the mother and the motherland with being all nurturing, all sacrificing, all embracing, like Ahalya Bai, Meera Bai, Durga Bai—all role models he often cited. The obsessive attachment of Subhas to the figure of the 'mother', along with an inherent shyness which prevented him from socializing with women, generated a myth about him as being a confirmed celibate and a spiritually committed person. Dilip Kumar Roy recalled that the reputation of Subhas as a student was that of 'a pure character—no girl dare darken with her shadow even the shadow of his shadow'.[53] Roy suggested that this attitude was the result of 'a Victorian Puritanism dressed up in the neo *Brahmo* garb of standoffishness'.[54] During his student years in England, Subhas apparently never talked to women, far less mixed with them. Indeed, he was a 'puritan', disliking those who drank or cracked bawdy jokes. He warned against the 'formidable temptations of European culture—wine and women'.[55]

In view of this reputation, it is not surprising, therefore, that when Subhas met Emilie Schenkl in Austria in 1934 and wed her in secret in 1937,[56] the marriage remained undisclosed until he divulged it to his brother, Sarat, only on the eve of his submarine journey to Japan in 1943, two years before his death. Many were disillusioned by the news and felt that Subhas had surrendered himself only too predictably. Nirad Chaudhuri thought Subhas's involvement with an ordinary woman like Emilie was nothing short of disaster.[57] Indeed, Nirad Chaudhuri's dismissal of Emilie as ordinary echoes the class contempt with which many from among the German aristocracy in the German Foreign Office had viewed her.[58] Class considerations had certainly not bothered Subhas, who had seen in Emilie an efficient, affectionate and caring person who had welcomed him into her immediate family and provided the emotional support and care that were so crucial in his fleeting and stressful career. In his relationship with her, Subhas had evolved in his own thinking on women. He acknowledged as much when he wrote to her, 'I thank you for loving me and for teaching me to love you ... I have loved the woman in you—the soul in you.'[59] In 1937, writing his autobiography, *An Indian Pilgrim*, Subhas confessed that it had been 'midsummer madness' to have wasted his energy in his youth trying to suppress the only too natural sex instinct.[60] During this period, Subhas spent much time reading Freud and Jung and gave much thought to interpretations of dreams and psychoanalysis.[61] It was a mature Subhas who advised his nephew, Asoke Nath, in 1939 to marry of his own choice following 'a period of friendship and intimacy' and after studying 'at least one good book on sex and its problems'.[62]

Although Subhas had been able to shed his inhibitions about women, sexuality and marriage, he could not rise above the expectations of the bhadralok husband of his wife. In Emilie, he found a person he could guide, mould and scold, much as a proverbial Indian husband, without her expressing any rancour. So solicitous was he about her well-being that he would perhaps never have suspected that he was being dominating or possessive of her. As his close associate, S.A. Aiyar, was to write about Subhas, 'He was a democrat at heart and a dictator in effect . . . he was conscientious and fastidious in his democratic ways, and yet I know in my heart of hearts that he had his own way every time.'[63] While encouraging Emilie to have a career in freelance journalism, he was insistent about correcting and ultimately rewriting every draft she wrote for the *Hindu*. He did not fail to reprimand her with comments such as, 'Very Bad! Very Disappointing! English also is bad!', or point out factual errors in her article 'which an Austrian should be ashamed of'.[64] Protective about her, he discouraged her from giving lessons to Indians since they tended to be flirtatious.[65] The stereotypical bhadralok image of the ideal wife finds resonance in Subhas's repeated counsels to Emilie on how she should live her life. His prescriptions included regular physical exercise, lessons in domestic hygiene and economy which would make her 'useful in later life', knowledge of bookkeeping, skill in playing a musical instrument for entertaining herself and her family at times, learning needlework, knitting, embroidery, and a little bit of philosophy.[66]

The Subhas who sailed out in a submarine in February 1943 for the south-east Asian sector of the war in the last phase of his life and career was a much evolved individual. Completely free of the restraining Gandhian influences within the Congress, mature in his dealings with women, and liberated from social inhibitions, for instance with regard to alcohol,[67] Subhas was free to enthuse the Indian National Army, which he organized with his unique and characteristic 'genius of enthusiasm—of inspiration'.[68] The all-women Rani of Jhansi regiment within the INA was conceived as a fighting unit and not as a mere symbolical showpiece. By persuading the families of Indian plantation workers to allow their wives and daughters to march in uniform, with cropped hair and in military formation, in the Rani of Jhansi regiment, Subhas had achieved a minor social revolution, the significance of which was lost in the context of the overall failure of his venture.[69]

★

Mohandas Karamchand Gandhi, the fourth and last child of his father's fourth and last marriage, was born in Porbander, Gujarat, on 2 October 1869. Bania by caste, the Gandhis were grocers hailing from Kutiyana in Junagadh state. Enterprise and good fortune steered Gandhi's grandfather to the post of a diwan or chief minister of the princely state of Porbander, a position that his son also held with uprightness for twenty-eight years before giving it up for the same office in Rajkot, another tiny Kathiawar principality. Although Gandhi's father had no formal education himself, he gave his children the comforts of an established home life and the opportunities of education. At home, Mohandas had access to books on religion and mythology and was subjected to the strong influences of his mother, Putlibai, whom he remembered for her 'saintliness' and 'deeply religious' nature.[70] However, the young Mohandas never became a strict adherent of any religious observances and practices.

Marriage at age thirteen to the same-aged Kasturba saw Mohandas graduating prematurely from adolescence to manhood without the intervening period of youth and awakening. This brought with it the attendant problems of rebelliousness, leading to subsequent journeys of self-discovery. Looking back, Gandhi recounted how tormented he had been by 'the shackles of lust'.[71] His obsession with his early marriage threw out of proportion the larger goals of life. As he battled to regain this focus, he came to attach a concept of sin to sex, which continued into his later years. He never forgave himself, for instance, for the intimate moments he had spent with a heavily pregnant Kasturba while his father breathed his last and he held himself responsible for the fate of his child, who died a few days after birth.[72] He also lived with a sense of guilt for not having educated Kasturba, whose resistance to studies in these early years only matched his preference for lovemaking. Taking the blame on himself, Gandhi felt that if his affection 'had been absolutely untainted with lust she would be a learned lady today'.[73] Kasturba never learned to read or write anything but elementary Gujarati, her native language.

Gandhi took his role of husbanding seriously at all levels. He was to confess how jealously he had tried to guard and control Kasturba's movements, which she resented deeply. Later in life, Gandhi forced Kasturba to accept his stipulations of austere living with its requirements of celibacy, cleaning of latrines and denial of advantageous opportunities in educational and career improvement for their children. Gandhi acknowledged that he had been a 'cruelly kind husband',[74] while Kasturba, over time, came to see beyond the idiosyncrasies of her husband the self-denying honesty of a man who acted from his convictions alone. However, in her silent strength, courage and capacity for suffering Gandhi found a live prototype for the Sita who he idealized as a symbol of Indian womanhood. Gandhi's dislike of gymnastics and sports in these early years and his uncomfortable awareness of a lack of courage, which made him sleep with a light on in his room, led him to a journey of self-discovery. He followed the recommendation of his friend, Sheik Mahtab, that meat eating would result in bravery and prowess as it had with the English rulers. The result was disastrous because although he summoned the courage to break the familial taboo and eat the meat, he could not literally sleep over it, as he seemed to hear a live goat bleating inside his stomach.[75] The rebellious phase in Gandhi's life continued for a while not only with meat eating and the attendant awkwardness of having to tell lies but also included a visit to a brothel where sheer panic resulted in a quick exit.[76]

After graduating from high school, Gandhi proceeded to England to take a law degree, financed by his brother and promise-bound to his mother that he would not touch wine, women or meat. After some initial discomfort, Gandhi found to his relief a vegetarian eating house and was also heartened to see publications and clubs expressing interest in vegetarianism. Without compromising at this stage on his food preferences, Gandhi felt the need to adapt himself to the sartorial and social preferences of the British society in which he found himself. Anxious to face the British on their own terms, he invested his energy and money on a trendy wardrobe complete with a tailor-made suit from Bond Street, a gold double watch chain, leather gloves, silver-mounted stick, bright burnished silk top hat, stiff starched collars and flashy ties. He also sought to acquire social skills by playing bridge, which he enjoyed, taking dancing lessons, which revealed his ineptness at moving to rhythmic music, and violin lessons, which, too, he had to abandon for lack of talent.

The studied sartorial elegance did not, however, dislodge Gandhi's inherant shyness, which left him at a loss for words on several public occasions. His quest for self-discovery led him, then a third-year student, to study the Gita, in English translation, for the first time. To many of his questions and doubts he found answers, which were philosophically and spiritually satisfying. With its allegorical significance, the Gita, Gandhi felt, viewed the soul as the site of a battlefield, where Arjuna, as the representative of higher impulses, fought the evil, and Krishna, as the inner voice and conscience of the individual, gently reminded him of his choices and took him through the acid test of renunciation. Gandhi also studied the New Testament and was deeply inspired by the Sermon on the Mount, which he found shared similarities with the Gita. Gandhi's first religious readings set him on an introspective course, strengthened over the years, to deal with life's varied experiences and gain more understanding.

On completing his studies in 1891, Gandhi returned to India, which seemed to him infinitely poorer as death had claimed Putlibai in his absence. Moreover, his tongue-tied shyness proved disastrous in his first attempts at establishing a legal career. After a couple of unsuccessful years in India, Gandhi went to South Africa to fulfil a legal assignment, the success of which gave his life a new direction. With his new-found confidence he felt he could take up the cause of racial discrimination that he and fellow Indians, derisively called 'coolies', constantly faced.

Several years later, when asked by Dr John Mott, a Christian missionary, to cite the most creative and defining moment in his life, Gandhi referred to an agonizing night he had spent on a railway station at Pietermaritzberg in 1893.[77] Travelling by train from Durban to Pretoria in pursuit of the legal case that had brought him to South Africa, the newly arrived Gandhi had faced the ignominy of being physically thrown out of a first-class carriage at the insistence of a white passenger. Huddled through the night in the cold waiting room, Gandhi had reflected on his experience. He was to write later that his active non-violence began from that date. On the successful completion of his assignment, as he was preparing to leave for India, local Indians urged Gandhi to assist them to oppose a proposed Bill which threatened to deny their right of franchise. Gandhi was destined to stay on, setting up his legal practice and making South Africa his home for the next twenty years.

Gandhi's experience in South Africa proved momentous in

preparing him for the leadership role in India's freedom movement that he was to play. First, he acknowledged that for every act of racial discrimination in South Africa there were also acts of kindness from the white population. His approach was, therefore, discerning and humane. He believed that while moral pressure had to be brought to bear on the white leadership to recognize the legitimate needs of the coloured population, it was also imperative for Indians to acquire certain social graces and a basic English education so that their claims to better treatment could be legitimately grounded. He forced a complaining Kasturba and their children to wear socks and stockings and use cutlery at mealtimes to which they were naturally unaccustomed. Gandhi's sense of fair play made him extend his support to the British during the Boer War although his personal sympathies were for the Boers. By organizing Indians to form an Ambulance Corps, which was engaged in the crucial task of caring for the war-wounded, Gandhi strengthened the case for the Indians to demand a fairer treatment in return.

In course of time, Gandhi realized that his misplaced trust in British goodwill would not lead to the amelioration of the living conditions of Indians. Various issues of discrimination troubling the Indian population—ranging from prevention of free travel without compulsory registration, denial of rights to own fixed property, compulsion of living only in demarcated areas, invalidation of all non-Christian marriages—became rallying cries around which Gandhi was able to galvanize participation of the local Indians. His method of protest was novel. It involved a non-cooperative civil resistance which, he explained, could not be adequately conveyed by the rather negative expression 'passive resistance'. Gandhi's preferred description was satyagraha or a crusade invoking the force of truth, love and non-violence. It embraced the path of suffering for a righteous cause. And his soldiers of satyagraha had much to suffer, from physical beatings to incarceration, from forfeiture of property to penury. Taking a fair share of this suffering, Gandhi kept the movement alive with his inspiring dedication and commitment. Discarding western clothes for a knee-length white smock, an elongated loincloth and sandals on his feet, Gandhi inspired respect as the uncrowned leader of the discriminated community. After a series of half measures and disappointments, there was finally a settlement in June 1914 between General Smuts, representing the South African government, and Gandhi, representing the Indians. According to the Indian Relief Bill, which subsequently became law, several of the contentious issues were resolved although several more continued to remain. To Gandhi, however, it was a Magna Carta whereby the abstract principle of racial equality was vindicated and the racial taint removed. Moreover, it was a vindication of civil resistance and demonstrated to Gandhi the immense possibilities that the unleashing of this moral force offered.

To Gandhi, perhaps the greatest victory was in having converted the foe, General Smuts, into a friend. He presented him with a pair of sandals he had made in prison, which Smuts wore every summer at his farm near Pretoria before returning them to Gandhi on his seventieth birthday in 1939 as a gesture of friendship. Smuts was to write:

> It was my fate to be the antagonist of a man for whom even then I had the highest respect . . . he never forgot the human background of the situation, never lost his temper or succumbed to hate, and preserved his gentle humour even in the most trying situations.[78]

While pressing on with his efforts to mobilize Indians in the struggle for greater political rights, Gandhi spent the large part of these years in South Africa in an important exercise of community living. In Phoenix Farm near Durban and later in Tolstoy Farm near Johannesburg, Gandhi could put to practical use many of his preferred ideas of frugal, self-sufficient, egalitarian, healthy and tolerant social living. It also gave him an opportunity to provide shelter to the families of incarcerated satyagrahis or civil resisters. The experience of community living in South Africa was to serve as a blueprint for the ashram life that was to follow in India. It was the right blend of social commitment and awareness, practical economic sense and spiritual discipline, which brought about greater tolerance, compassion and service.

Gandhi's values were not based on an academic commitment to any set ideology. He evolved in his ideas after reading randomly and experiencing the lessons of life. Consequently, his solutions to socio-economic problems or his formulas to resolve contentious political issues were unconventional, unique and home-grown, based on his instinctive feel for human nature and a trust in his inner compulsions. Gandhi was profoundly inspired by those aspects of what he read which echoed his own thinking as they gave the necessary approbation and legitimacy to his beliefs. He once wrote, 'It was a habit with me to forget what I did not like and to carry out in practice whatever I liked.'[79] Gandhi did not leave at a theoretical level the lessons which profoundly influenced him from his readings. He proceeded to apply them to his lived experiences.

One of the most profound influences on the thinking of Gandhi was the Gita, the study of which he continued in South Africa. It became his daily discipline to learn verses from the Gita, which he had pasted on the wall, as he brushed his teeth every morning.[80] The key teaching from this 'spiritual reference book', Gandhi felt, was not the literal exhortation to violence on the battlefield, but the development of strength to stay committed and focused on one's goals after forsaking all expectations of results and remaining detached from worldly comforts and allurements. Explaining his mission to be a *karma yogi*, or one committed to the path of action, Gandhi wrote, '*Karma yoga* is the *yoga* (means) which will deliver the self (soul) from the bondage of the body, and in it there is no room for self indulgence.'[81] A testing board for Gandhi's thoughts in these early years was his jeweller friend, Raychandbhai, in Bombay. Gandhi saw in him a true *karma yogi* who combined his devotion to his calling with honesty, dedication and spiritual wisdom.

Another major influence on Gandhi's thinking was the British essayist, John Ruskin (1819–1900), whose book, *Unto This Last*, Gandhi came across quite fortuitously. Given the book by a friend to read on the long train journey from Johannesburg to Durban in 1903, Gandhi was deeply moved by its message. It preached the dignity of manual labour, urged the living of a simple life, and stressed the incapacitating complexities of the modern economic system. Acknowledging that the book had marked 'a turning point in my life',[82] Gandhi shortly after embarked on his experiment of community living on the Phoenix Farm, near Durban.

In the thick of his protest movement against the South African government's attempts at forced registration of Indians, when Gandhi was in jail, he borrowed a book from the prison library which again moved him intensely. Henry David Thoreau (1817–62), the American poet and essayist, was repulsed by the ignominy of Negro slavery and had chosen for himself a life of inner strengthening and peace in an isolated cottage outside Concord, Massachusetts, where he dwelt, doing all his own work, growing his food and enjoying full contact with nature. Refusing to pay taxes to a government for which he had lost respect, he chose instead to go to jail. In his provocative political essay, 'Civil Disobedience', Thoreau's message was that it would be more honourable to be faithful to one's own convictions than to be law-abiding. He was convinced that even if a few committed people could exhibit courage to resist a government's tyranny, there would result a peaceful revolution. Gandhi, who was well into his satyagraha and in jail, found these words close to his heart. He discovered in them a resonance of the teachings of the Bhagwat Gita, with which Thoreau, too, was familiar. Acknowledging that the 'masterly treatise' had left a 'deep impression' on him,[83] Gandhi was to carry these lessons into his civil disobedience years in India.

Another book which Gandhi found time to read in the quiet of the jail was Tolstoy's *The Kingdom of God is Within You*. In it he found the anti-establishment Russian author launching a tirade against the Church for missing out on the intrinsic teachings of Christ as well as attacking governments for failing to provide peace for their subject peoples. In the course of his life, Count Leo Tolstoy (1828–1910) had come to renounce his family and his considerable wealth and fortune, had adopted working clothes and dedicated himself to humanitarian programmes of village education, famine relief, manual labour and philanthropy. His blunt observations—that one is not free because one does not free oneself, and that the wherewithal of change lies in the choices one makes, since the Kingdom of God lies within—greatly appealed to Gandhi. In a letter, Gandhi apprised Tolstoy of the farm near Johannesburg that he had named after him, which was dedicated to achieving economic and spiritual self-sufficiency. Tolstoy acknowledged the receipt of this letter as also a copy of Gandhi's book, *Hind Swaraj or Indian Home Rule*, written in 1909. Having read the book with great interest, Tolstoy wrote to Gandhi that its underlying philosophy of passive resistance, which was of the greatest importance not only for India but for the whole of humanity, was 'nothing else than the teaching of love uncorrupted by false interpretations'.[84] Gandhi was to receive the letter several days after Tolstoy had breathed his last.

Hind Swaraj remained a comprehensive statement of Gandhi's understanding of 'tradition' and 'modernity', with his doctrine of swaraj prescribing India's political future and diagnosing its civilizational malaise. He was to comment years later that the ideas expressed in it had evolved but his essential thinking had remained unchanged. With characteristic bluntness, Gandhi wrote in *Hind Swaraj*, 'The English have not taken India, we have given it to them. They are not in India because of their strength but because we keep them.'[85] Lambasting modern western civilization for its perceived lack of morality, Gandhi sought also to expose the weaknesses in Indian society which had made it an easy prey for foreign occupation.

Gandhi's trenchant criticism of the modern western philosophy of life, called western because its principal site was the West, was directed at many of the dominant themes of post-Enlightenment thought—namely Reason, Science and History. He felt it impertinent to claim that any of these concepts could offer a privileged access to Truth. As he wrote, 'Mere intellect makes one insane or unmanly. The reasoning faculty will raise a thousand issues. Only one thing will save us from these and that is faith.'[86] It is because of this lack of faith that western civilization, which only sought to increase bodily comforts, appeared to Gandhi to be 'irreligion'.[87] Civilization to Gandhi was 'like a mouse gnawing while it is soothing us'.[88] Machinery as the chief symbol of modern civilization was thus 'a great sin'.[89] Carrying forward the same argument, Gandhi attacked British institutions introduced for exploitative purposes. Thus, he felt that the railways had disturbed the country's indigenous balance, creating artificial famines and carrying diseases which otherwise would have been localized. His attack on lawyers and doctors was based on his moral analysis that these professions were profit making rather than humanitarian. Instead of resolving legal or health issues with any degree of finality, they were prolonging and perpetuating them for money-making purposes. Gandhi also criticized that great bastion of democratic idealism, the Parliament, for being constantly manipulated by its current master, the government in power, leading to a 'prostitution' of its principles and policies.[90] Many of these startling and extreme comments of Gandhi have to be considered in the context of his broader frame of argument. He himself moved away later to a pragmatic acceptance of certain modern developments, which he felt could have an important role in India's future. Thus, he came to accept the idea of shipbuilding, iron works, communally owned powerhouses, and heavy machinery for public work.

Gandhi felt that a bankruptcy of moral values was responsible for the malaise plaguing both Indian and western civilizations and emphasized that by invoking the foundational values of civilization, both the East and the West could come together, giving the lie to Kipling's famous comment that the twain could never meet. Gandhi's highly idealistic prescription called for the regeneration of moral strength and 'soul force', which would raise both western and Indian civilizations to a higher plane where they could communicate from the position of truth and conscience. As Gandhi put it, 'The force of love is the same as the force of the soul or truth.'[91] Satyagraha would involve refusing to do anything repugnant to one's conscience, suffering the consequences of sticking to an indomitable will, and overcoming hurdles through self-discipline and self-transformation. To Gandhi, *swadharma*, or performance of one's duty as highlighted in the Gita, was essential, for as he said, 'If I do my duty, that is, serve myself, I shall be able to serve others.'[92]

By seeking to apply traditional values in pursuit of activist and this-worldly concerns, Gandhi comes across as a modernizer of tradition. On the one hand, he believed in the need to inculcate a religious sense and invoke ethical values, and at the same time he pleaded for religious and cultural tolerance. He, however, continued to use Hindu imagery in his discourses to bolster his arguments and held out the ideal of Ramrajya as his model, which he defined simply as 'the Kingdom of God on Earth'. Similarly, while defending the caste system as being an accepted worldwide structural division accommodating multiple professions caring for the diverse social and economic needs of society, Gandhi lamented that the underlying philosophy of equality among the castes had been lost in India. Attacking hierarchy and discrimination for having 'mongrelized' the varna system, Gandhi went on to chide British imperialist arrogance as much as the brahmin's sense of superiority over the shudra. As he explained, 'I have fought this doctrine of superiority in South Africa inch by inch, and it is because of that inherent belief that I delight in calling myself a scavenger, a spinner, a weaver, a farmer and a labourer.'[93] This consciousness fuelled his sustained war against untouchability that was to follow in India.

When Gandhi returned to India in 1915, he carried with him the confidence of having successfully conducted a series of non-violent confrontations with the white racist authorities of South Africa. The nationalist scene in India was confused. The Moderate and the Extremist planks of the Congress movement had been played out, and the Swadeshi agitation which had galvanized Bengal after its partition in 1905 had lost its momentum after the division of the province was rescinded in 1911. The weapons of boycott, strikes and non-cooperation used successfully during the Swadeshi period, along with positive programmes of village reconstruction and the building of indigenous industries, were not sustained. Revolutionary terrorism continued in a sporadic way. Gandhi's long absence from India and lack of a specific regional base not only gave him an objective perspective on the prevailing situation, but also freed him from the limiting regional pressures. As a 'continental leader',[94] he moved with care and tact. His successful campaigns among the Champaran farmers (1917) and the Ahmedabad millworkers (1918) had already earned for him a reputation as a leader. In the aftermath of the Jallianwala Bagh massacre (1919) and the Rowlatt Act, when he initiated his programme of non-violent non-cooperation in 1921, he was afforded an opportunity to try out his own peculiar style of politics.

Gandhian politics invoked the moral conscience not only of the participants in its movement but also of the authorities that were challenged. Unorthodox in design and pattern, Gandhi's programmes used topical issues of imperialist discrimination as rallying cries so that large numbers could be galvanized across the divides of caste, class, religion and gender to offer protest along strictly non-violent lines. Conscious of the limitations of sustaining such intense moments of agitation, Gandhi provided for avenues of retreat when the civil resisters could dedicate themselves to constructive activities of village development, concentrate on matters of social concern like untouchability, and build bridges of communal harmony to soothe frayed nerves. To provide a discipline that could keep agitated minds constructively occupied, Gandhi prescribed compulsory spinning, which to him made economic and spiritual sense. Community living in his ashrams also fostered a spirit of tolerance, compassion, self-sufficiency and practicality.

While developing the Congress as a mass organization to spearhead the anti-imperialist movement and wrest political concessions from the British authorities, Gandhi cared little about the trappings of office, and for the most part of his political career, he chose to remain on the fringes of the party while being its guiding spirit. In conducting the struggle for independence against the British, he had also no prescriptive formula for the future development of the state to come. He was more concerned that the freedom that was to be won should be seen not in the narrow sense of ending foreign rule but rather in the larger sense of achieving a moral freedom from the injustices of social and economic disharmony and religious intolerance.

One of the most significant concerns of Gandhi was to bring women into the mainstream of the national movement as equal participants. As he put it, 'I would have no use for that swaraj to which women have not made their full contribution.'[95] He believed women, with their innate moral strength and capacity for suffering and inborn compassion, would be the natural advocates of non-violence and satyagraha. While a believer in full gender equality, Gandhi, however, felt that separate roles had been apportioned to men as breadwinners and women as homemakers, and he was unwilling to see women going beyond their prescribed role. Therefore, he made sure to keep women's participation restricted within the parameters of non-violent pickets and marches. It is perhaps this care that ensured the participation in large numbers of women in the national movement with the full consent of the men in their families. In many ways, it was a revolution that Gandhi initiated by lifting the veil of segregation and bringing women out of their households, sometimes for the first time ever, to participate as equals in the common movement of liberation.

★

Jawaharlal Nehru was born in Allahabad on 14 November 1889, the only son of the prosperous lawyer, Motilal Nehru, whose handsome earnings were matched by a fondness for the good life. In the westernized and affluent surroundings of his home, Jawaharlal felt quite spoilt. His mother, Swaruprani, created in him an interest in Indian folklore by reading to him stories from Hindu mythology and the epics—the Ramayana and the Mahabharata. However, he did not share her religious beliefs and was led to believe by his father and other male members of the family that religion with its various rituals was 'a woman's affair' in which the women members of the family had to be humoured.[96] Although shortly after, under the influence of his resident tutor, Ferdinand Brooks, he came to be exposed to theosophical thoughts and philosophical concepts from the Upanishads and the Gita, these naturally went over the head of a thirteen-year-old boy.

He was sent to Harrow, the exclusive British public school, at the impressionable age of sixteen, and passed his student years at Harrow, Trinity College, Cambridge and the London School of Economics, without any commendable distinction. His performance was well below the level of his talent, which disappointed his father. Looking back on his student years, Jawaharlal described his primary mood as having been a vague kind of Cyrenaicism or hedonism.[97] He favoured the various diversions of London society—music, concerts, golf, tennis, waltzes, club life, cricket—and found himself constantly out of pocket, having to ask an alarmed Motilal for supplementary grants. Apart from dabbling in London society life and pursuing his law studies which 'did not take up much time', Jawaharlal read extensively and was attracted by the Sinn Fein movement in Ireland.[98] On passing the Bar finals, Jawaharlal returned to

India in 1912, a young man of twenty-three. He described himself in a self-deprecatory style as 'a bit of a prig with little to commend me'.[99] Nehru's long stay abroad had helped to form an international outlook and he was always to view the problems in India in a holistic way as part of a larger world scenario. As he put it later, 'I came to think that these separate problems, political or economic, in China, Abyssinia, Spain, Central Europe, India or elsewhere, were facets of one and the same world problem.'[100]

Jawaharlal returned to the life of lavish entertainments for which Motilal was known, and obediently joined his father's chambers. In 1916, he was married with much pomp to Kamala Kaul, a young Kashmiri Brahmin girl Motilal had selected for him in 1912, and subsequently groomed and trained in deportment to match his son. To Jawaharlal, the legal practice was not too inspiring, and as he was to confess 'The average lot of the lawyer, especially a junior one, is to deal with petty and rather dull cases.'[101] Politics did not actively involve him either, and apart from a passive interest in the Home Rule League agitations, Jawaharlal did not become seriously involved in the politics of the day.

It was with the advent of Gandhi on the Indian political scene that there came about a sea change in Nehru's political thinking and indeed his way of life. It was an inspired Jawaharlal who led an unsure and hesitant Motilal to the change in lifestyle that Gandhian politics heralded. Looking back, Jawaharlal was to acknowledge that acceptance of Gandhian leadership, as also the civil disobedience and jail-going that followed, made a man of him.[102]

Jawaharlal's first meeting with Gandhi was during the Lucknow Congress in December 1916. At that time, Gandhi appeared to be 'very distant and different and un-political to many of us young men'.[103] However, with Gandhi's success at

Champaran and Kheda and the firm lead he took during the Rowlatt satyagraha, Jawaharlal was inspired into accepting Gandhi's leadership. It was an important breakthrough for him—'Here at last was a way out of the tangle, a method of action which was straight and open and possibly effective.'[104] Although to Motilal the concept of jail-going and lawbreaking seemed strange and the idea of his dear son doing this was preposterous, he slowly saw the logic in Gandhian thinking after the 1919 Amritsar happenings and the legal enquiry into them. However, the acceptance of boycott and non-cooperation meant Motilal giving up a lucrative legal practice and making a complete break from his past life of ease and comfort. Jawaharlal recognized that this was not an easy decision for a man on the eve of his fifty-ninth birthday. For the young Jawaharlal, the transition was much simpler, and though he was completely dependent financially on his father, he readily simplified his way of life and standard of living. Up to this point, Jawaharlal's politics had been those of his class, the bourgeoisie: 'In 1920, I was totally ignorant of labour conditions in factories or fields and my political outlook was entirely bourgeois.'[105] It was his experience during the non-cooperation movement, the prison sentences he served, and his interest in the UP agrarian situation that gave him the much-needed insight. Although Gandhi's stoppage of the non-cooperation movement in 1922, after the Chauri Chaura incident, made young Jawaharlal 'angry' and filled him with 'amazement and consternation',[106] he never opted for the alternative programme of Council entry that his father Motilal, along with C.R. Das, advocated at that time. Jawaharlal was careful not to get drawn into the no-changer/ pro-changer debate since neither group attracted him. The Council party, he felt, was veering towards reformism and constitutionalism and being led down a blind alley, and the no-changers, ardent followers of Gandhi, seemed to Jawaharlal to lack dynamism since they followed the letter rather than the spirit of the teachings of the Mahatma.[107]

Instead, municipal politics kept Jawaharlal occupied. Between 1923 and 1925, as chairman of the Allahabad Municipal Board, he gained first-hand experience of official administration. Despite the constraints under which he operated, he approached his job with refreshing new ideas and a quiet efficiency which the authorities grudgingly had to recognize. A two-year stint in Europe from 1926 to 1927 exposed Jawaharlal to European political workers and movements, lending a new depth to his thinking and activities. His participation as the representative of the Indian National Congress at the International Congress against Colonial Oppression and Imperialism, held in Brussels in February 1927, brought him into close contact with leading intellectuals and exposed him to Marxist and radical ideas. His visit to Moscow in December 1927 with his father, in response to an invitation to attend the decennial celebrations of the 1917 revolution, provided a first-hand glimpse of communist life which impressed him deeply.

In 1927, Jawaharlal returned to India in time for the Madras Congress. Nehru's biographer, S. Gopal, observed, 'He who had sailed from India as a dedicated disciple of Gandhi returned a self-conscious revolutionary radical. Although always to be deeply influenced by Gandhi, he was never again to be wholly a prisoner in the Gandhian mould.'[108] It can be argued, however, that although Nehru viewed Gandhian programmes critically, he agonized alone when he found he could not agree. He would never make a break with Gandhi—as often urged by Subhas—and remained a prisoner to his sense of loyalty and emotional dependence on Bapu. He sensed that a break with Gandhi would mark a split in the national movement and weaken it considerably. It would also lead to an eclipse of his own political prospects since without a regional base and support structure of his own, it was Bapu's support and grooming that were vital for his political future. However, Nehru's liberal education and belief in western Enlightenment values made him view life and its problems from a completely different point of view from that of Gandhi, underscoring the fundamental difference in their philosophical mindsets. Without publicly articulating his differences with Gandhi, Nehru preferred to speak about them at length in his *Autobiography*.

Perhaps the biggest difference that Nehru had with Gandhi hinged around the latter's sense of religiosity, which informed his politics. From a non-religious start in his childhood, Nehru had gone to England where his studies and scientific temperament had made him an agnostic. While a believer in the importance of spiritual values and certain social standards of behaviour, he was not attracted by the metaphysical aspects of Hindu religious texts. He was troubled, therefore, by Gandhi's references to Ramrajya as the ideal halcyon age of the past or his attempt to explain the great Bihar earthquake of 1934 as divine wrath for the sin of untouchability.[109] Also, Gandhi's constant recourse to fasting as self-purification to atone for society's sins was to Nehru 'incomprehensible'.[110] He was intrigued by Gandhi's ability to use the emotive power of religion to pull the strings that move people's hearts, almost like a magician.[111]

Nehru questioned Gandhi's basic logic in extolling the virtues of the inner change to the detriment of external progress. Indeed, he wondered whether it was not a sense of inferiority that led to Gandhi's assertion of eastern spiritual superiority, underplaying the advances made by the West in external development.[112] Gandhi's disparagement of railways, telegraphs, hospitals, lawyers and doctors in *Hind Swaraj* seemed to Nehru to be 'an utterly wrong and harmful doctrine and impossible of achievement'. Gandhi's logic of self-discipline, self-sufficiency and sacrifice, which lay behind this doctrine, was lost on a rational Nehru, who argued against Gandhi singing in praise of poverty and suffering and recommending the ascetic life as a social ideal.[113]

Similarly, Nehru could not fathom Gandhi's concept of democracy. After criticizing the institution of the Parliament and discrediting the importance of numbers or majority representation, Gandhi proclaimed himself to be 'a born democrat'. His metaphysical definition of democracy, as based on service and sacrifice using moral pressure, was again inexplicable to Nehru. With the Westminster pattern of democracy being Nehru's ideal, he looked at the legal solution to society's ills as the ideal way out. To Gandhi, however, the solution to society's woes lay not necessarily in statutes but rather in a change of heart and a willingness to address the wrongs of society. His readiness to rely on the exploitative classes of India such as feudal princes, landowners and capitalists to hold their wealth as a common trust for the general weal of the people sounded totally utopian to Nehru. Calling Gandhi's description of himself as a socialist to be some kind of 'muddled humanitarianism',[114] Nehru was puzzled that Gandhi was guided by 'certain vague, unmeasureable spiritual values' which allowed him to coexist with evils such as the ruthless struggles and exploitation of groups and classes, while he found bad habits such as smoking and drinking and sexual indulgences totally unacceptable. To Nehru, these were bad in themselves but not to the extent of the former. As Nehru put it, Gandhi 'attaches vast importance to the self-regarding sins or failings and very little to social sins'.[115]

Similarly, to Nehru, at times Gandhi's total belief in the doctrine of non-violence seemed a little obsessive. As he put it, 'Violence itself, though bad, cannot be considered intrinsically immoral. There are shades and grades of it and often it may be preferable to something that is worse.'[116] To Romain Rolland Nehru confided that Gandhi, by committing everyone to his creed of non-violence, with its implied sufferings, was actually practising a form of violence. The liberal in Nehru was troubled by Gandhi's disregard of the basic principle of the right of choice.[117]

Gandhi's attitude to sexuality, his argument that sex was permissible only for procreation, his refusal to recognize that there could be any natural attraction between man and woman other than those in a family with blood ties, seemed 'unnatural and shocking' to Nehru.[118] Nehru clearly attached no idea of sin to sex and never concealed the fact that he took delight in the company of women with whom he could share an aesthetic and emotional closeness. His relationship with Kamala, dogged as it was with illness, incarceration and her premature death, had a certain element of magic which never wore off.[119] Analysing his own thoughts on man's love for woman, Nehru wrote, 'Love, as I conceived it, and as it came to me, was something different, something electric, something often painful. It was not the conception of duty owed or an obligation to be discharged. I would hate to have someone feel that it was his or her duty to love. I want no such purchase.'[120] He reasoned, 'Evidently Gandhiji thinks ... that if the sexual affinity between man and woman is admitted, every man will run after every woman and vice versa. Neither inference is justified. For him it is a "soot or whitewash" question, there are no intermediate shades.'[121] He confessed, 'I presume I am a normal individual and sex has played its part in my life but it has not obsessed me or diverted me from my other activities. It has been a subordinate part.'[122] Nehru made no secret of the fact that his friendship with women friends like Padmaja Naidu or Edwina Mountbatten gave him the vital intellectual and emotional strength that kept him going through periods of grave stress. Physical intimacy, if there had been any, would be a mere detail in the totality of this truth. There was no patronizing arrogance in Jawaharlal's relationship with his women friends. Underlying his deep respect and understanding for their growth and development as independent personalities there was an emotional bond of sharing. If Sita was Gandhi's model woman to be emulated, it was Chitrangada, the Manipuri princess immortalized in Rabindranath Tagore's celebrated lyrical drama, whom Jawaharlal admired.[123] The image of Sita, as handed down by the past and recast by Gandhi, was associated with self-sacrifice, an infinite capacity for suffering, chastity and a moral power to inspire men with higher notions. In the legend of Chitrangada, the princess made it clear to her prospective husband, Arjuna, that her condition of marriage was that she should be treated equally, neither raised on a pedestal and deified nor treated with disdain and neglected. Nehru wrote that ultimately Kamala seemed to come to him as Chitrangada herself saying, 'I am Chitra. No Goddess to be worshipped, nor yet the object of common pity.' [124]

What impressed Nehru most about women's participation in the civil disobedience movement was its equalizing impact. Not only did it bind women from diverse socio-economic backgrounds to a common cause but also made women feel that they were co-sharers with men nationalists in India's destiny. To Nehru, the natural corollary to women's participation in the national struggle was the beginning of a greater struggle for finding a proper identity in the Indian social milieu and enjoying equal rights with men. He was perhaps one of the few leaders who sensed this inevitable turn in the women's movement and actually heralded it. He loudly proclaimed, 'I have the greatest admiration for the women of today. I have faith in them. I am not afraid to allow them freedom to grow because I am convinced that no amount of legal constraint can prevent society from going in a certain direction. And if you put much legal constraint the structure breaks.'[125] It became Nehru's mission as prime minister to try and push through legislation in the teeth of opposition from partisan and conservative opinion to ensure greater equality for women in personal law. Although his gains were limited to the Hindu community, he was to remember the personal law bills as the highlight of his tenure.[126] In his liberal mindset, there could be no higher forum than Parliament for securing the individual rights of citizens. To Gandhi, who was no less committed to gender equality, the definitive factor for enabling greater rights for women was to achieve a change of heart in the men of the household so that they could be generous in admitting women as co-workers in the national struggle.

Seeing Gandhi as an impossible paradox at times, Nehru concluded, 'Perhaps in every other country he would be out of place today.'[127] This echoed Subhas's conclusion that 'born in another country he (Gandhi) might have been a complete misfit'.[128] Nehru, however, refrained from the harsher words that Subhas also used.[129] Instead, Nehru tried to gauge what caused Gandhi to maintain such a miraculous hold over the imagination of the nation. He felt that the prophetic-religious personality of Gandhi and his peasant appearance drew, like a magnet, fierce loyalties and attachments. In the ultimate analysis, 'He is the quintessence of the conscious and subconscious will of those millions.'[130] Similarly, despite his own reservations about the khadi movement with its hand-spinning and hand-weaving programmes, which seemed 'a throw-back to the pre-industrial age', Nehru came to appreciate its profound symbolical value. 'Khadi became the uniform of national freedom.'[131] He further realized that it could be only with Gandhi that he could fill the vital gaps in his own 'mongrel' education[132] and discover the real India, where lay his political dreams.

★

Of the three, Subhas and Gandhi were born leaders; they sensed it was their mission in life to lead. 'The locomotor restlessness and energy' that Erikson described as being outstanding to Gandhi was very much a quality of Subhas as well.[133] Dilip Roy, the college friend of Subhas, has reminisced how the infectious enthusiasm of Bose had pressured fellow students to initiate discussions in debating groups about national issues and take up social causes.[134] With his arresting personality, striking looks, record for being a good student, and reputation for daring the British, as evident in the Oaten incident, Subhas became, quite easily, the darling of the youth in Bengal. Under the tutelage of his political mentor, C.R. Das, Subhas received many opportunities for furthering his leadership potential. His experience as the youngest mayor of Calcutta, the leadership of the Bengal Congress, his immense popularity in his urban constituency, his acknowledged prominence in youth politics, his considerable success in the initiative of flood relief in rural Bengal, earned him extensive admiration and prepared him for the arduous role that lay ahead. In the vacuum created by the untimely death of Das, many looked to Bose for the lead. Roy wrote to the incarcerated Subhas in Burma, 'We all look up to you as our future beloved political leader. Yes we of the present generation pin our faith on you as the one man who can lead us and that at no distant date either.'[135] Indeed, on his release from prison in 1927, and in the absence of Das, he felt it his responsibility to keep the torch of Bengal alight and prevent it from suffering a political eclipse. Subhas was not willing to accept Gandhi in the same role of mentor and tried unsuccessfully to persuade Basantidebi, Das's widow, to don the mantle of the deceased leader. Subhas carried with him regional misgivings which saw with Gandhi's rise a decline in Bengal's own political importance and a reduced role for the Congress to represent Muslim interests in a state with a Muslim majority, which could have ominous implications in the future. Exhorting his fellow Bengalis to take the lead in the movement to expel the British,[136] Subhas came to be convinced that destiny had chosen him to quicken the pace of the movement which had slackened under Gandhi. He saw it as a natural stage in the evolution of the movement explainable by the Hegelian logic in which he believed. He feared that opportunities do not get repeated in history and when they come, they had to be seized. Thus, the outbreak of World War II was a signal to him to intensify the national movement against the British, a logic that the Gandhian Congress hesitated to accept and adopted only later, in 1942, when Subhas was well out of the country.

Gandhi, too, sensed that his mission was to lead. After shaking off his initial diffidence and shyness, he had been able to keep up a sustained agitation in South Africa where he successfully led Indians in a unique campaign of non-violence. He returned to India with a formula which had proven successful against the racist discriminatory regime of South Africa. He felt instinctively that he was being shown the path by his inner light, and his lead had to be followed. From his followers he expected discipline and loyalty and complete trust in his judgement. Indeed, he called himself the 'generalissimo of the *satyagraha*'.[137] He took pains to point out that his movement instead of being a passive force was 'an intensely active force when properly understood and used. It is much more active than violent resistance. It is direct, ceaseless but three fourths invisible and one fourth visible.'[138]

Nehru, like Subhas, was also the darling of the masses. Belonging to a prominent family and blessed with good looks and charisma, he was easily acceptable to the people at large. However, he was diffident about his leadership skills and often embarrassed by the spotlight in which he found himself. His nomination as Congress president in 1929 by Gandhi, who declined his own recommendation by the provincial committees, caused him much surprise and a consequent reluctance which he expressed charmingly in his *Autobiography*. 'But I did not come to it by the main entrance or even a side entrance; I appeared suddenly by a trap-door and bewildered the audience into acceptance. They put a brave face on it, and, like a necessary pill, swallowed me.'[139] In course of time, he became acutely aware of the restraining influence of the office where Gandhi had cleverly put him to take the wind out of his sails. Although ideologically he was attracted to the thinking of the younger left-inclined politicians, who would not settle for the Congress goal as being anything less than complete independence, he could not rebel against the Congress leadership as Subhas did periodically.[140] Thus, as Congress president at the Lahore session of 1929, Nehru opposed Subhas storming out to form a short-lived alternative party in protest against the Gandhian programme of non-cooperation, which he protested was not broad based enough. The tug of war in Nehru's mind continued, and as Subhas put it, 'His (Jawaharlal's) head pulls one way and his heart in another direction. His heart is with Gandhi.'[141]

The office of the Congress president which came unexpectedly to Nehru in 1929, and was repeated twice in 1936, was, however, steadily avoided by Gandhi, who shied away from holding party office and even chose to give up the party membership in 1934 while preferring to remain the spirit behind the Congress. Subhas, who saw his Congress presidentship in 1938 as an endorsement of his leadership, was determined to continue the next year, too, to ensure that his lead was sustained. However, history decided otherwise, and despite his re-election he was made to resign by a hostile Gandhian Congress. Both Gandhi and Subhas, whether in office or not, were very sure of their leadership roles and pressed on with their respective programmes and priorities according to their basic convictions. Nehru, on the other hand, despite his definite ideological preferences, never had an independent programme to unfurl, and while constantly honoured by office, was to remain in it as an overawed and often amused outsider. Having to constantly don the mask of a public personality in spite of being essentially a very private individual, Jawaharlal was provoked to write a piece for *Modern Review* of Calcutta in November 1937, entitled 'The Rashtrapati', under the pseudonym Chanakya after the Machiavellian Maurya minister of the fourth century BC, famous for his views on statecraft. Realizing that he was merely playing a part, Nehru wrote:

> Jawaharlal has learnt well to act without the paint and powder of the actor . . . He goes to the peasant and the worker, to the zamindar and the capitalist, to the merchant and the peddlar, to the Brahmin and the untouchable, to the Muslim, the Sikh, the Christian and the Jew, to all who make up the great variety of Indian life. To all these he speaks in a slightly different language, ever seeking to win them over to his side.[142]

Subhas, who did not mince his words, was piqued by this aspect of Jawaharlal's personality, which he described as an 'amorphousness' in letting himself be moulded by Gandhi and others to any shape and pattern they may choose. Listing Jawaharlal's 'inexplicable popularity' with the 'good graces of

Madame Luck', Subhas wrote:

> The peasant hails him as his spokesman, labour as their
> protagonist, the communist patronises him, the capitalist
> dotes on him, the artist hails him as a pathfinder in belles
> lettres, the mill-owner gushes over him, ignoring the
> disconcerting fact that he is actually spinning away
> without conviction to prove a worthy heir to Gandhiji
> and a friend to the *daridranarayan*, a world he abhors.[143]

Subhas would probably have had little patience with Jawaharlal's
lamenting his predicament as Congress president, which he
said made him feel that he was riding a tiger, unable to neither
rest nor dismount.[144]

What gave Subhas and Gandhi this phenomenal strength
of conviction and belief in their own sense of mission? For
one, it was their personal experience of imperialist arrogance
which made them suffer the pain of humiliation and, in turn,
steeled them with a determination to overcome. While the
defining moment of Gandhi's life was his experience at the
Pietermaritzberg railway station in South Africa, for Subhas
it was the agonizing Oaten affair. They both went on a journey
of self-exploration, gradually giving up western stances and
enhancing their own self-esteem and confidence by adopting
a truly Indian way of life. Second, for both Gandhi and Subhas,
the personal threshold of pain was very high, as they had an
inborn austerity which made the renunciation of creature
comforts easy. Subhas had once explained in a letter to a
friend that in moments of physical ailment he had the
maximum clarity in thought. 'You feel more and more that
man is after all a disembodied soul and the body is only a
passing raiment. One's vision of the future becomes clearer
and one's convictions grow stronger.'[145] Tagore applauded

this when he wrote to Subhas as the 'Leader of the Nation', 'Your strength has sorely been taxed by imprisonment, banishment and disease, but rather than impairing, these have helped to broaden your sympathies—enlarging your vision so as to embrace the vast perspectives of history beyond any narrow limits of territory . . . '[146]

To Gandhi, 'The dignity of man requires obedience to a higher law—the strength of the spirit.'[147] For Gandhi to give up his western attire, comfortable lifestyle and steady income and adopt the loincloth came naturally from his deepest convictions. For Subhas, the decision to give up the ICS and the comfortable lifestyle it promised and enter the uncertain arena of politics also came from a deep fervour and commitment. In many ways, both men were lonely crusaders who unhesitatingly went forward in pursuit of their own missions even when they could not carry others with them. Tagore's famous song, 'If no one responds to your call, travel alone', was one of Gandhi's favourites and was also Subhas's inspiration.[148]

Underlying this strength of resolve in both Subhas and Gandhi was a deep-rooted sense of spiritual motivation. Although sceptical of the fanatic fringe in religion, which the sadhus often represented as Subhas discovered in his search for a guru,[149] he was certain that there was a national need 'to revive faith in religion'.[150] He lamented, 'We have lost our religion . . . and are now a weak, servile, irreligious and cursed nation.'[151] Gandhi, too, while remaining wary of the hypocrisy and selfishness of certain religious teachers, whether brahmins, mullas or dasturs, was unequivocal in asserting that ethical education was very important since 'India will never be godless and rank atheism cannot flourish in this land'.[152] While both Gandhi and Bose were rooted in the traditional Hindu values that they were born with, their exploration of religion made them receptive to many influences. Drawn to the philosophy of the Gita, with its mission of nishkama karma or duty without any expectation, Gandhi was equally influenced by the catholicity and compassion of Christ's teachings, in particular his Sermon on the Mount. On a visit to the Vatican, Gandhi was moved to tears by a painting showing Christ's agony on the cross.[153] Evolving an ecumenical position, Gandhi meant by religion 'not formal religion or customary religion but that religion which underlies (or transcends) all religions'.[154] Speaking of the need to inculcate moral and ethical values of justice, equality, tolerance, sacrifice and service, he sought to embrace all, across the divides of caste, class, gender and religion, through this all-encompassing formula of love. Accepting the occupation-oriented logic of the caste system, Gandhi sought, however, to break down its hierarchical value system and underscore the equal importance of all castes. While his rhetoric contained Hindu imagery, throughout his life Gandhi sought to draw the Muslim community into an embrace of equal participation in the national movement.

Subhas was raised in a traditional Hindu family where observances of ceremonies and rituals were frequent. Inheriting the Bengali tradition of exalting the image of the mother to stand for both the goddess Durga and the motherland, Subhas remained an enthusiast of Durga Puja and in his jail cell there was always a corner for his prayers. Later in life he was to invoke the name of Kali as an auspicious start for the beginning of his fast unto death at Presidency Jail, Calcutta in December 1940.[155] Since the fast was part of his larger design to ultimately escape the British, he sent word secretly to his nephew to offer special prayers at the Kali temple.[156] Subhas confided to his friend, Dilip Roy, that his varying moods made him constantly oscillate between the three divine forms—Kali, Krishna and Shiva. While Shiva as the ideal yogi held a fascination for him, Kali as the mother also had a powerful appeal, while Krishna the compassionate god inspired his Vaishnava beliefs.[157]

In spite of this outward observance of religious practices, Subhas, like Gandhi, looked towards the essence of all religions for his basic inspiration. A student of philosophy, he delved into several philosophical texts and believed that there was a divinity within man that shaped his direction. He felt that there was a purpose and design in nature, and that man was an instrument in the hands of the Divine.[158] Subhas often referred to the mighty stream of divine energy, reminiscent of what Bergson called the *élan vital*, into which man had to ultimately surrender himself.[159] This consciousness made him philosophical in accepting life's hard knocks and yet going forward with undiminished enthusiasm and undeterred resolve. In a speech in Berlin, just prior to his escape to south-east Asia, he said, 'There is not only joy, but there is also sorrow. There is not only a rise, but there is also a fall. If we do not lose faith in ourselves and our divinity—we shall move on through darkness, sorrow and degradation towards renewed sunshine, joy and progress.'[160]

Influenced by C.R. Das's Vaishnava ideal of an all-encompassing compassion, Subhas, like Gandhi, spoke of love as an ideal, which along with justice and equality, would bind all groups across the barriers of class, caste, religion and gender.[161] Although deeply religious personally, Subhas realized the need in a multi-religious country like India to invoke a spirit of communal harmony. In a speech at Poona early in his political career in 1928, Subhas spoke of the need to rein in fanaticism, which was one of the greatest obstacles in the path of progress, and facilitate cultural rapprochement between communities through a 'dose of secular and scientific training'.[162] Economic consciousness would bring together classes threatened by vested interests from across the religious divide, thereby spelling the death of fanaticism and communalism. Nehru, too, believed strongly in secularism, which he made a key plank in his post-independence planning. However, Nehruvian secularism meant a surgical division between religion and state, which in a country like India with an essentially religious ethos was problematic, as subsequent events in independent India have repeatedly shown.

In his philosophical beliefs, Subhas claimed to have evolved from an initial faith in maya, the world of illusion, to the pragmatic world of a dynamic reality, where there was space for 'the widest toleration'.[163] He saw the solution to India's communal troubles lying in an informed coexistence rather than cultural exclusiveness.[164] He declared, 'It is necessary for the different religious groups to be acquainted with the traditions, ideals and history of one another because cultural intimacy will pave the way towards communal peace and harmony.'[165] In his conviction that society was required to be based on moral values drawing on all religions, Bose was very close to Gandhi's thoughts. Gandhi did not wish to explain away religious differences in an overarching unifying formula. At his oft-held prayer meetings, Gandhi pleaded for religious and cultural tolerance. He declared in a significant statement, 'I very much like the doctrine of the many-ness of reality. It is this doctrine that has taught me to judge a Mussalman from his own standpoint and a Christian from his.'[166] Subhas recommended that a policy of 'live and let live in matters religious' would help bring confidence among religious minorities in a post-independence India.[167] He believed that the communal problem was a creation of the British divide-and-rule policy as the Ulster problem in Ireland and the Jewish problem in Palestine had been. During the Cripps Mission to India, Subhas lashed out in a radio broadcast from Germany against the British for using the Muslim League as a religious tool, against Indian unity, for dividing a people.[168] Subhas had been hopeful that communalism would cease with the end of British rule. In his vision for the future, there was to be no 'state religion',[169] so that complete religious and cultural freedom for individuals and groups could be guaranteed. Judged from this point of view, Gandhi's Khilafat agitation in 1916, which drew Hindus and Muslims together in a common cause, was close in spirit to Subhas's INA initiative.

With this ingrained spiritual sense, both Subhas and Gandhi spoke of the strength that came from sacrifice (*tyag*) and service (*seva*). It was this deep commitment and burning conviction that made them both easily sacrifice family interests for the cause of the country. Subhas explained to an aspiring political worker, 'One's duty to one's relatives is superior to one's duty to oneself. And one's duty to one's country is superior to one's duty to one's family.'[170] The ultimate lesson that both Subhas and Gandhi drew from their spiritual journeys was a process of inner strengthening with an unswerving focus on the goal they had set themselves. While the example of Mustafa Kemal Ataturk, creator of modern Turkey, was the inspiration for Subhas, Gandhi was much impressed by the example of Mazzini during the Italian unification. An indomitable will is what both adopted as their weapons. Gandhi's non-violence was in essence an expression of an unbending strength in the face of provocation. It sought to bear moral pressure on the adversary and eventually achieve in them a change of heart. Although Subhas's strategy of a military initiative with the help of the Axis powers seemed far removed from the Gandhian line of non-violence, at another level he was counting on a change of heart that came closest to Gandhi's confidence in being able to touch the core of human loyalty and emotions. Subhas hoped to be able to subvert the morale of the Indian Army by sustained propaganda, first among the prisoners of war to form the nucleus of the Indian Legion in Europe and then the INA in Singapore. Then he hoped to influence the Indian component in the British Army in India to rally round an invading nationalist army. Moreover, he sought to enthuse the army not by material encouragement but by invoking 'soul force', 'superior morale' and sheer tenacity.[171]

To Nehru, Gandhi's stress on the ideal of an ascetic life, replete with suffering and denial, seemed esoteric, backward looking and unattractive. He was astounded that Gandhi avoided real issues of socio-economic inequity and instead spoke of bringing about a change in people's hearts. This, to Nehru, was 'the pure religious attitude to life and its problems. It has nothing to do with politics or economics or sociology.'[172] Nehru's practical view of life, his scientific temperament, and his disinterestedness in the metaphysics of religion, made him a marked contrast to Gandhi, who constantly delved in other-worldly discourses. Neither did Nehru share the religious view of life that Subhas had. In an attempt to understand why two men with so many common factors in their upbringing and education should have had an 'instinctive disaccord', Dilip Roy concluded that the essential difference between Nehru and Bose hinged on their conflicting approaches to religion. As he put it, 'The mystic in Subhas could never be assuaged when the great Kashmiri repeated the communist mantra about religion being the opium of the soul.'[173]

The spiritual inclinations of both Subhas and Gandhi did not lead them to the reclusive life. Instead, they plunged into active politics as *karmayogis*. As Gandhi put it, 'In this age, only political *sannyasis* can fulfil and adorn the ideal of *sannyasa*. No Indian who aspires to follow the way of true religion can afford to remain aloof from politics.' He recommended, therefore, 'the politicisation of spiritualism', that is seeking liberation through political action, as well as the 'spiritualism of politics', or the conduct of politics solely according to ethical principles.[174] This was a view that found a ready echo in Subhas's thoughts. Indeed, the retirement of Aurobindo Ghosh, the erstwhile revolutionary firebrand, to the ashram in Pondicherry as a yogi committed solely to a life of meditation, seemed a disappointment for Subhas. He wrote to Dilip Roy, a devotee of Aurobindo, about his fears that perfect seclusion might result in 'the active side of man to get atrophied if he remained cut off too long from the tides of life and society'.[175] He was 'heartened' by the 'inspiring' words of Romain Rolland:

> But we men of thought must each of us fight against the temptation that befalls us in moments of fatigue and unsettledness, of repairing to a world beyond the battle called either God or Art or Freedom of the spirit or those distant regions of the mystic soul. For fight we must, as our duty lies on this side of the ocean—on the battleground of men.[176]

Along with a sense of conviction in their life's missions, both Gandhi and Bose were temperamentally very strong willed and adamant about their judgement of priorities. The unbending streak in Gandhi's character, which prompted Romain Rolland to call him the 'sacred mule',[177] caused perpetual dismay among his followers, who tried in vain to dissuade him from his periodic fasts to attain political ends. Subhas, too, was unshakeable in his resolve, and as Gandhi himself remarked, 'You are irrepressible whether ill or well.'[178] Subhas took his inspiration from Tennyson's *Ulysses*, 'To strive, to seek, to find and not to yield.'[179] Gandhi's obdurate tenacity found a match in Subhas's daring audacity. Subhas often quoted a poem from his childhood about the hero William Tell, emphasizing that his knee would bend to God and God alone.[180] Gandhi, too, spoke of the greatest bravery lying in the resolute refusal to bend the knee to an earthly power, no matter how great.[181] In vain did Nehru try to mediate between the two headstrong men, as during the serious Tripuri crisis over the re-election of Subhas as Congress president.[182] The election drama brought into the open the differences in approaches, priorities, methods and mindsets of the three leaders. As Jawaharlal put it, behind the political issues there were psychological issues and these were much more difficult to resolve.[183]

In this crisis, both Gandhi and Subhas had acted from their convictions and were driven by their inner compulsions although they were at cross purposes. Subhas had been asked by Gandhi to 'cheerfully submit' to party discipline, and when he declined, he was edged out.[184] However, his determination to chart out an alternative course to the Gandhian line led him to form his own party, the Forward Bloc, which despite its loud rhetoric, could never provide a viable alternative to Gandhi.

The reaction of Jawaharlal to this crisis demonstrated a totally different philosophical mindset and a contrasting response. From the beginning, although Nehru had supported Subhas in his youthful challenge of the conservative Gandhian Congress, he would never encourage any divisive move that could break its unity. He, therefore, pleaded with Subhas not to contest the elections and tried to demystify the position of Congress president, having held it several times himself. At the same time, his democratic temperament was unhappy with the Congress resolution, with its insistence on a homogeneous working committee and asking the current members to resign. He pointed out that it had been a Congress tradition to allow several points of view to be represented in the apex body, and that although some homogeneity was needed, it should not be narrowly interpreted. Therefore, he did not resign with the others but acted as if he had. This was Nehru's quandary: intellectually, he resented the pressure tactics of Gandhi to make Subhas buckle under and yet he could not go along with Subhas in his defiant and rebellious path. Instead, he tried to play the role of the mediator. He prevailed upon Subhas to meet Gandhi and mend fences while he persuaded Gandhi to be more charitable towards Subhas. He succeeded with neither. While Gandhi ignored his mediation, Subhas lashed out, saying that nobody had harmed his cause in the Tripuri crisis more than Jawaharlal.

The Tripuri drama proved a catalyst in bringing into the open the simmering hostility between Subhas and Jawaharlal, which was ventilated in a series of long letters exchanged between the two.[185] Years later, when Hiren Mukherjee was to ask Jawaharlal the background of his bitter relationship with Subhas, he referred to this correspondence as being self-explanatory.[186] While Subhas's tone in this correspondence was aggressive and accusatory, Jawaharlal's response as a British public school product was reticent. Jawaharlal pleaded guilty, in good grace, to Subhas's allegations against him of being indecisive and vacillating, but they both traded charges of faulty ways of functioning. While Subhas criticized Jawaharlal for his long-winded and verbose formulations of Congress resolutions, Jawaharlal, in turn, charged Subhas with having been a non-directing president. He pointed to the psychological differences with Subhas, while the latter confessed that he had no patience for the sentimental politics of Nehru, and his Hamlet-like indecisiveness. Jawaharlal emerged from this crisis confused, anguished and agonized. He almost winced at Subhas's open outbursts and remained astounded by Gandhi's unforgiving stance.

In their styles of functioning, both Gandhi and Bose employed an element of drama. Gandhi's innovative use of an emotive issue such as the salt tax, which made him undertake his famous Dandi march, successfully galvanized the masses across the divides of caste, class, religion and gender, in the civil disobedience movement in 1930. Subhas's call in 1940 for an all-out agitation to demolish the Holwell monument, a symbol of imperialist assault against the Nawab of Bengal, touched a chord in every patriotic heart in Bengal across religions. Much later, while in Rangoon heading the Azad Hind Army, Subhas visited the tomb of Bahadur Shah Zafar to make it the rallying point for an impassioned participation by Hindus and Muslims alike for the cause of India's freedom.[187] Gandhi adopted periodic fasting as a weapon of political bargaining to wrest concessions from the British Raj. Subhas, too, resorted to this tactic from time to time for highlighting pressing concerns such as pathetic prison conditions or the demand for the release of political prisoners. However, Gandhi never approved of anyone else adopting fasting as a bargaining tool. His disapproval of Jatin Das's fast and his silence after his premature death left the younger generation of political leader hurt and confused. In the typical scenario of a generation clash, Subhas questioned how Gandhi could disapprove of others adopting a strategy that he himself had perfected.[188]

Another trait that Gandhi and Bose shared was their unique and phenomenal ability of persuasiveness, which won them the most unlikely of followings. Almost single-handedly, Gandhi turned the Congress into a mass movement, and Subhas, in a foreign country, faced with adverse international circumstances, forged an unprecedented alliance with the Axis powers, on the one hand, and the local population, on the other. Describing Gandhi in his evocative narrative prose, Nehru wrote:

This little man of poor physique had something of steel in him . . . in spite of his unimpressive features, his loin-cloth and bare body, there was a royalty and a kingliness in him which compelled a willing obeisance from others . . . His calm and deep eyes would hold one and gently probe into the depths; his voice, clear and limpid, would purr its way into the heart and evoke an emotional response . . . This process of 'spell-binding' was not brought about by oratory or the hypnotism of silken phrases . . . It was the utter sincerity of the man and his personality that gripped . . . [189]

In his pen sketch of Gandhi, Romain Rolland spoke of the little man with bare, skinny and stilt-like legs like a heron, a bespectacled countenance with large ears and toothy smile, whose embrace reminded him of a big friendly dog rubbing his wet nose on your shoulder. And yet there was in his embrace 'the Kiss of St. Dominic and St. Francis'. Gandhi's brief stay in Europe in 1931 brought on reactions that ranged from the sublime to the ridiculous. While Italian women were seen imploring him to predict the ten lucky numbers for their weekly lottery, at public meetings in Lausanne and Geneva, where Gandhi spoke frankly about capitalism and labour, the bourgeoisie of the League of Nations felt peeved, while the sympathetic dairymen of Vevey hoped to serve the King of India. [190]

Subhas Bose, too, could move hearts. As his long-time associate in Europe, Girija Mookerjee, analysed, Subhas was not a particularly great orator, his delivery being slow and his choice of words being far from dynamic. However, the honesty and conviction with which he spoke, the enthusiasm that he generated, and 'the homeliness with which he touched unsophisticated hearts' had an electrifying impact and won him many converts.[191] Subhas was to reap the benefits of this phenomenal gift of mass appeal as he went along his stormy career. Sivaram observed, 'In political showmanship and the tactics of mass appeal, Subhas Chandra Bose was a real genius and an accomplished expert.'[192] Recalling the impact of the first speech of Bose in Singapore, delivered in simple yet forceful Hindustani on 4 July 1943, Lakshmi Sahgal wrote how he had totally convinced all with his 'utter sincerity and iron determination'.[193] Thus, both Subhas and Gandhi had an immediate and emotive impact on the masses. Nehru, too, addressed the masses constantly, and while the image of the handsome idealistic Congress president in Lahore on a white steed lingered in public memory, in idiom and stance he remained far removed from their lived reality. Nehru's Faizpur presidential address provoked the *Times of India* to comment, 'There is no doubt that his review of the globe, China to Peru went clean over the heads of the thousands that sat shivering in a corner of India, who would have appreciated much better, a discussion of problems nearer home affecting their hearts and home.'[194]

To both Gandhi and Bose, who were charting out novel paths in the Indian national movement, it was very important to carry public opinion with them. Gandhi used his prayer meetings to address large gatherings and enthuse them about his programmes. He also carried on a regular programme of educating the public on various pertinent issues and raising their moral and political awareness through regular columns in his publications, *Harijan* and *Young India*. With his phenomenal grip over people's emotions, Gandhi proved to be an expert in soliciting monetary contributions for his various projects, from khadi to Harijan relief. Targeting not only the rich, he declared that he was proud that he could make the poor empty their pockets for those poorer than themselves.

From auctioning off garlands which he said were a waste of money, to selling his autographs for a donation, and coaxing young women to part with their jewellery, his begging bowl was constantly replenished by his ingenuity.[195]

Subhas, too, in the course of time, came to fine-tune the business of addressing the masses and raising their awareness level regarding the pressing issues of the day. He tried to make the most of his years of forced exile in Europe, from 1932 to 1936, as an ambassador of India in bondage, devoting himself to comprehensive networking and establishing contacts in government and non-government circles in the different European cities. He travelled widely, meeting important political leaders and intellectuals ranging from Dr Eduard Benes in Czechoslovakia, Mussolini in Italy, de Valera in Ireland, Romain Rolland, André Malraux and André Gide in France, and at the same time reached out to the Indian population, particularly the youth and students. Disappointed by the colossal ignorance about India, Subhas felt strongly that at every international Congress there should be Indian representation. Consequently, he visited, supported and helped set up Indian centres and associations in a wide number of places.

The considerable network of contacts that Subhas had successfully built up in these years stood him in great stead when destiny made him flee from house arrest in India and reappear in Berlin in the war years. Although the unexpected German attack on Russia soon after his return to Europe in 1941 upset his own plans of getting an immediate pledge of help from Germany, Subhas was able to contain his acute disappointment by passionately engaging himself in a massive propaganda campaign. He had once said that he envied the British most for their superb skill in propaganda, which they considered to be at times more powerful than howitzers.[196] Subhas now made it his mission to use propaganda in an organized fashion to undermine systematically the imperialist position and further the cause of Indian nationalism. As he explained, 'In fighting one's enemies, it is necessary not only to have a just cause, but also to convince the world that one's cause is just.'[197] Through daily radio broadcasts in several languages, and by making speeches, he used his persuasive skills to create awareness about India's developments. Through a secret radio station called the National Congress Radio, he was able to reach out to the Indian masses with a detailed programme of non-cooperation, which Gandhi had left unspecified since he had been incarcerated immediately after his Quit India call in 1942. To counter the activities of the Muslim League, he launched the Azad Muslim Radio to represent the views of the nationalist Muslims of India and to counter separatist views.[198]

Subhas also used his considerable skills of persuasiveness to raise an Indian Legion from among the prisoners of war of the Indian Army, to work in tandem with the Axis powers, but only in engagements aimed at securing India's freedom. Ultimately, however, although 'Mussolini allowed himself to be persuaded by Bose'[199] for a pledge supporting Indian independence, Subhas's meeting with Hitler was disastrous. India was low in Hitler's priorities and described by him as 'endlessly far'.[200] Subhas's continued stay in Germany became futile. Leaving Europe never to return, Subhas escaped yet again under dramatic circumstances, crossing turbulent seas after a change of submarines, to the Far Eastern sector where he spent the last phase of his career and life. He carried with him the experience of propaganda that he had acquired through broadcasts and the raising of Indian troops, and utilized this to the full while setting up the INA.

Although Subhas came to inherit the broad framework of the Indian National Army, which had already been set up by

Rashbihari Bose, he was able to revamp it, enthuse the ranks and make it operative with his persuasiveness, organization and propaganda skills. Even the Japanese leader, Prime Minister Tojo, sceptical of Rashbihari and cynical about the arrival of another Bose, was profoundly impressed by the personality of Subhas. Referring to the 'magnetic and almost hypnotic charm' of Subhas, Tatsuo Hayashida's observation was that 'Netaji won Tojo's heart or rather conquered him personally'.[201] Tojo not only pledged Japanese military cooperation for the INA initiative, but also made significant gestures such as recognizing Bose's provisional government, gifting it the Andaman and Nicobar islands which had a deep symbolical significance, and organizing an imperial audience for Bose.

Subhas also carried on vigorous propaganda through radio broadcasts and made extensive tours addressing large gatherings to win over the loyalties of the local Indians in Singapore, the Malay Peninsula, Indonesia, Burma and Thailand to the cause of Indian nationalism. His success in this endeavour was phenomenal, and often entire families of fairly traditional plantation workers pledged support, with the father joining the INA, the mother the Rani of Jhansi regiment, and the children the Balsena.[202] Subhas was very strict in instructing the veteran soldiers in the Azad Hind to treat the civilian recruits with the utmost respect and equality. He threatened severe punishment if anyone used terms with religious or caste connotations or terms of racial arrogance such as 'coolie' or 'rubber tapper' against them.[203] As Subhas's close associate, Shah Nawaz Khan, put it, 'It is seldom, if ever, that people sacrifice their all for the course of which the end is uncertain but Indians of all castes and creeds threw in their lot with Netaji.'[204] Not only was Subhas able to galvanize the diverse working classes of Indian origin to his cause, but the educated Indians, too, who had been sitting on the fence, suddenly became intensely patriotic and were swept off their feet by the intoxication of mass enthusiasm.[205] Within the ranks of the Azad Hind Army, Subhas laboured hard to get the military professionals to repose trust and faith in a civilian chief. Moreover, Subhas inspired a sustained education campaign through a series of platoon lectures to create greater awareness among the INA personnel about Japan's history and Japanese cultural traits, which could help them overlook Japanese military arrogance or condescension towards the all-women regiment in the INA while ensuring an efficient professional cooperation.[206]

Like Gandhi, Subhas's persuasiveness yielded phenomenal monetary contributions from across the board. Emilie Schenkl explained that Subhas had a certain hypnotic power with which he was able to exploit the emotional vulnerability of his audiences.[207] He declared dramatically to his Indian audiences in south-east Asia that their lives, wealth and property belonged to India, which was at war and in peril and should be unstintingly surrendered to the Azad Hind government, its representative.[208] While women readily parted with their jewellery, wealthy merchants such as Habib of Rangoon surrendered property worth a crore of rupees in lieu of a garland to Subhas,[209] and a poor labourer woman stood in a queue to contribute her sole possession of three rupees for the same cause.[210]

At the same time, a large part of Subhas's propaganda was aimed at India in the hope of sensitizing the public to the real aim of the INA so that in the eventuality of the Japanese making a military entry into the country along with the INA, there would be popular support from the population. He also counted on a shift in loyalties among the Indian component in the Indian Army, resulting not in a sporadic but a mass desertion of entire divisions. Unfortunately, the outreach of Subhas's propaganda programme in India remained woefully limited because the British were able to restrict the range of his radio broadcasts and also managed to capture many of the agents he had consistently sent across the border to carry the message of the INA. It was no wonder then that prior to the INA trials, most of India, including the Congress leadership, remained unaware about the real nature of the INA initiative.

The compulsive persuasiveness of Subhas never quite left him and even when Japan was conclusively defeated, the irrepressible Bose looked towards Russia in the hope of winning a new ally to come to the help of Indian nationalism. However, destiny willed otherwise and the plane crash in Taihoko, Taipei (Formosa) on 18 August 1945 put an end to Subhas's dreams. Keeping in mind the characteristic trait of persuasiveness in both Gandhi and Bose, it was a supreme irony that although they had been able to convince, cajole, emotionally blackmail, and bulldoze others over to their opinion, they could not work together for long as a team. But even so, there lurked in each a secret desire for the other's approbation. There had been considerable pathos, for instance, in Bose's appeal to Gandhi after he had won the Congress re-election bid in 1939 and found that Gandhi stood firm in his opposition to him. What good was it, he said, if he had converted the whole of India and yet not 'the greatest personality in India' to his cause.[211] While remaining adamant in his opposition, Gandhi, too, assured Subhas that he should follow his own path and if he obtained success, Gandhi's would be the first congratulatory telegram that he would receive.[212]

As Gandhi and Subhas were unconventional in the programmes that they enumerated for the realization of national freedom, so also they were flexible about their interpretation of different ideologies and judged them in the context of India. In the process, they absorbed diverse elements and combined them in unique formulae for application to India's peculiar condition. They also moved considerable ground as they periodically revised their own perspective. This caused ample confusion among observers who felt they were being unfaithful, uninformed and inconsistent. But Gandhi clearly declared that consistency is a hobgoblin of foolish minds, an expression that Bose also repeated. Gandhi explained that it was never his aim to be consistent with his previous statements on a given question but to be consistent with the truth as it appeared to him at a given moment so that he could grow from truth to truth.[213] Elaborating further, Gandhi said, 'I am not a visionary. I claim to be a practical idealist.'[214]

Socialism, for instance, was a major plank in the thinking of Gandhi and Bose. From an initial ideological position close to Nehru's, Subhas evolved to a stance that reflected his own changing perceptions and experiences and which became more reminiscent of the Gandhian approach. Thus, in the initial years of the national movement when Jawaharlal and Subhas headed the left-inclined elements in the Congress, they shared the same urgency in bringing about socially levelling changes which would bind people together across religious, economic and social barriers in a common cause against the exploitative forces in society. Indeed, Subhas was troubled by Gandhi's consensus politics, which drew under one umbrella peasant and landlord, worker and capitalist alike, and was convinced that a radical militant programme had to combine with the political movement to achieve a complete all-round freedom.[215] The Gandhian approach, guided more by his instinctive judgement of socio-economic realities rather than academic preferences, also caused considerable confusion among friends and critics alike. Romain Rolland, for instance, despaired that Gandhi was simplistically viewing the entire industrial class as the benign Ahmedabad mill owners who could be pressured and made to see reason.[216] Rolland stressed the need for Gandhi to read Marx and socialist literature and followed up on Gandhi's progress in his reading, with Madeleine Slade.[217] However, in truth, Gandhi relied on simple home-grown solutions, which in his perception would provide the answers to problems typical of India. For this he refused to be bound to any ideological framework. Gandhi found unacceptable the socialism which advocated the complete negation of the individual, as also the socialism which was adopted as a mere armchair philosophy. He called his own creed a harmonious blending of elements of socialism and communism.[218]

Subhas, too, increasingly came to have misgivings about imported ideology holding the key to a resolution of Indian problems. While impressed with the egalitarian content of Marxism, he questioned the proposition of the class struggle as the only means of socio-economic emancipation, sharing the scepticism of his mentor, C.R. Das, about the communist logic. For all his rhetoric, Subhas's self-professed 'left' label did not always make him espouse the cause of the peasant or tenant or worker on select issues where he felt the interests of his bhadralok constituency might be adversely affected. The formula of religious tolerance and harmony prescribed by Subhas, and earlier by Das, in his home state of Bengal, could not reduce the deep-rooted economic differences between the Hindu and Muslim communities. It was particularly awkward that the landlord–peasant divide in Bengal was also along communal lines. The Hindu political leadership in Bengal with a vested interest in land could not support radical programmes of land reform beneficial to the Muslim masses, largely peasant, without endangering their own vantage position of economic strength. Nor did the Bengal Congress's sympathies for revolutionary groups like the Karmi Sangha, which adopted Hindu imagery as its inspiration, help placate an alarmed Muslim opinion. It was ironic that the Krishak

Praja Party would emerge to protect the exclusive interests of Muslim workers and peasants.[219] Subhas was often a helpless observer of these developments and quite unable to intervene effectively to change their direction. The ground reality of Bengal politics made him tone down his rhetoric and adopt an almost Gandhian consensus logic.

At a philosophical level, echoing Gandhi, Subhas sought to situate liberal western values within an Indian context. Challenging the impression that by accepting democratic or semi-democratic institutions India was becoming westernized, Subhas stated that democracy was not a western but a human institution and cited the ancient Indian republics as an example. Communism, too, he pointed out, should not be claimed as a western institution as it had existed among the Khasis of Assam as a time-honoured tradition, with no particular clan having exclusive rights to land and private property.[220] Subhas wanted a value-based foundation for his envisioned state where the principles forming the basis of Indian collective life would be justice, equality, freedom, discipline and love. These would constitute the essence of *Samyavada* or his version of an Indian socialism, conditioned by India's peculiar environment, racial temperament and socio-economic conditions.[221] Reiterating the views of Das, Subhas declared that while seeking light and inspiration from abroad, there should be no blind imitation of any other people, but rather an assimilation of what was suited to Indian requirements and national genius.[222]

What weighed with Subhas most was 'realpolitik'—or considerations of practical importance for the independence movement. Since personal gain never ever figured in his calculations, Subhas was morally convinced of the correctness of his stand. He also convinced his collaborators, for instance the Italian authorities in Kabul, at the time of his escape in 1941, that he was the 'only realist among the Indian nationalist leaders'.[223] It was in this spirit of realism that he spoke of a synthesis between fascism and socialism being ideal for India, a comment which provoked an indignant and outraged reaction from critics. However, he genuinely felt that the discipline and efficiency of a Nazi state could be fruitfully incorporated with a set of socialist values to help the state make a smooth transition to progress and development. While approaching the Axis powers for help in India's struggle, he made a conscious decision to blot out the internal politics of the Nazi state and merely utilize their anti-British stance for furthering the cause of India's freedom. He argued that the 'internal politics of Germany or Italy or Japan do not concern us—they are the concern of the people of those countries'.[224] Not that Subhas was unaware of the deeply disturbing excesses of Hitler's regime but he decided to react only in so far as they impinged on India.

Thus, in the mid-1930s when Subhas was in Berlin, he publicly protested against the racism which affected the Indian community. Indeed, he himself experienced the humiliation of being called a 'nigger' in Munich.[225] He tried to get the Indian community to send a formal note to the German government protesting its racial attacks. He even explored the possibilities of using the weapon of trade boycott to make Germans realize the dire consequences of their racial attacks.[226] At a personal level he advised a friend, Kitty Kurti, who was pregnant, to flee to the United States as it would be dangerous to stay on in Berlin. She later wrote that Subhas did not disguise his deep contempt for the Nazis but justified seeking their help as the only available way and also because he had convinced himself that British imperialism was as intolerable.[227] In the years between 1933 and 1936, when Subhas was in Europe, he saw the meteoric rise of Hitler and was impressed by his nation-building measures which revived the country dramatically from the slump of the depression years. He sought to imbibe the lessons of discipline and nation making in the Indian context. In 1941, when Subhas made his way to Berlin following his dramatic escape from house arrest in India, the scenario had changed totally. With the rest of the world, he was equally surprised at Hitler's sudden attack on Russia in June 1941. The Indian communists never forgave Subhas for turning for help to Hitler, the perpetrator of an offensive against the Soviet Union and branded him a 'Quisling' or traitor.[228] However, in fairness to Subhas it must be said that he had no prior inkling about Hitler's motives, and at the first instance he made it known in a report to the German government how its attack on the Soviet Union would be most unwelcome in India.[229] When he finally met Hitler in May 1942, after a year's futile wait for German assurance of help which never came, Subhas showed a daredevil forthrightness in asking the Führer to remove sections in his *Mein Kampf* which made derogatory references to India.[230] It is important to note that after the conclusive defeat of Germany in July 1945, Subhas was once again quick to dissociate himself from these reversals and began to look to fresh pastures for help. He could separate the future of the Indian freedom movement from the misfortune of his allies in the war and could look to Russia in a new pan-Asian bloc of solidarity.[231]

Jawaharlal Nehru, too, evolved in his thinking and absorbed the diverse influences that were shaping contemporary world developments. Although the Russian example had moved him profoundly, his liberal core could not accept the negation of the individual that a typically socialist state required. As he put it, socialism was not about chasing out the whole tribe of landlords, capitalists and the like. Instead, socialism was about developing capitalism rather than combating it.[232] While cherishing socialist planning, he remained at the same time a fierce defender of individual rights. As Nehru candidly admitted, he was so deeply influenced by the 'humanist liberal tradition' that he disliked the dogmatism, regimentation and heresy that accompanied the writings of Marx or other texts.[233] However, Nehru's flexibility could never bring him to adopting a charitable view of fascism. Between communism and fascism, he stated unequivocally that he would much prefer communism because fascism to him was an unmitigated evil with which there could be no compromise and no selective acceptance.[234] Mussolini's nation-building measures in the early 1930s had impressed both Subhas and Gandhi, both of whom had met the Duce. Gandhi met him in 1931, ignoring Romain Rolland's deep reservations but earning Subhas's praise.[235] Subhas met Mussolini first in 1933 and subsequently presented him with a copy of his book, *The Indian Struggle*, in 1935. It was an association that was to continue over the years. Nehru, however, refused to meet Mussolini and successfully dodged the Italian dictator while transiting through Rome in 1936, although a meeting had been arranged by the Italian government.[236]

It is interesting to see how at the commencement of World War II, when the Congress had to formulate its position in response to the war situation, these contrasting opinions surfaced. Subhas and Gandhi did not unconditionally dismiss the fascist powers. The pacifist in Gandhi abhorred any war-like situation, and he was moved to tears imagining the destruction that war could bring to the much-loved buildings in London. He appealed to Hitler, imploring him in letters to desist from a violent course in the name of humanity.[237] Subhas made a fine distinction between the internal policies of the fascist governments, many aspects of which he was not comfortable with, and their external confrontational policy towards Britain, which he felt should be harnessed for the purpose of gaining India's freedom. Nehru, on the other hand, felt that while confronting the evil of fascism, Britain's war effort should not be unduly embarrassed or weakened by any Congress move. While the Congress in general felt let down at being dragged into the British war effort without any satisfactory assurance about India's independence in the immediate future, these differences of approach to the war within the Congress revealed the distinctive mindsets of its leaders.

Subhas had been clear from the beginning that the emerging war scenario should be exploited to India's advantage. Indeed, in March 1939, while embroiled in the Congress presidential election controversy, he had urged the Congress in his Tripuri address to give a six-month ultimatum to the British to grant the national demand for independence or face a civil disobedience campaign. Although the Congress did not respond, he felt his judgement had been partly vindicated when six months later, in September, war did actually break out. Although out of the Congress by then, Subhas was especially invited by the party as it deliberated on a suitable response to the war situation. He stuck to his original position, insisting that the situation should be utilized to press India's demands since fascism was no different from imperialism in its aggressive and grasping stance. Indeed, it was the British policy of appeasement and conciliation which had fed Hitler's appetite and led to his excesses.

Gandhi clearly judged the situation as being unripe for the start of a civil disobedience campaign, for the country lacked the resources just then for any such fight.[238] While sympathetic to the predicament of the Allies, he, too, felt like Bose that Hitler had been helped on his destructive course by British weakness and indulgence.

Nehru made a sharp distinction between democracy and fascism and believed that justice was on the side of Britain and France. But he recognized equally that these were imperialist countries and that the war had resulted from the inner contradictions of capitalism, which in its zeal to suppress communism had harboured the Nazi evil. Convinced that India could not take advantage of Britain's difficulties by launching an immediate struggle, he felt equally strongly that India could not be dragged into a war while she was denied her own freedom. Adopting Nehru's position, the Working Committee resolution, therefore, condemned Nazism while asking Britain to outline her war aims with regard to India's immediate future and claims of independence so that with such an assurance India could join Britain's struggle against fascism. Nehru followed this up with a personal request to Linlithgow, mentioning his personal keenness that the long conflict between India and England should be ended so that they could cooperate together against the war with all its horrors.[239] The stinging British reply—that there could be no statement of war aims—provoked a strong reaction from Gandhi, who said that the Congress had asked for bread and instead it had got a stone.[240] Subhas observed caustically, 'We shall continue to lick the feet of the British Government even though we have been kicked by them.'[241]

With Gandhi now in control of the Congress, the Congress ministries in the states where they had secured a majority were asked to resign, while moderates in the party, like C. Rajagopalachari who favoured unconditional support of British war efforts, made an exit. Although at the Ramgarh Congress session of March 1940, the official Congress policy—that British war aims should be stated—found repeated mention, at the parallel Forward Bloc session held in Ramgarh by Subhas, there was a pressing appeal to launch a mass struggle. Subhas never tired in his attempts to persuade the Mahatma, and at their last meeting in June 1940, he spoke of the need to abandon hopes of a British response and instead lead the

151

country to fresh agitation.[242] While Gandhi remained non-committal, he did ask Subhas to follow his own light. Within a couple of months, Gandhi initiated the limited measure of individual civil disobedience, which Subhas liked to believe had been partly influenced by his persuasiveness.[243] Actually, Gandhi was slowly getting tired of British insincerity and increasingly convinced that the war was gradually going in favour of the Axis powers. However, he sought to bide his time while handing over Congress matters formally to Jawaharlal, whom he had designated his successor in an AICC resolution dated 15 January 1942.[244] Events moved rapidly, and the sensational Japanese victories at Pearl Harbour (December 1941), Singapore (February 1942) and Rangoon (March 1942) made the British wake up to the reality of Japan's imminent appearance on India's eastern borders.

This sense of alarm lay behind British overtures to the Congress in the form of the Cripps Mission aimed at securing India's help in its war effort. While Gandhi watched carefully, Jawaharlal's hopes rose and he also sought to engage the offices of the US leader, President Roosevelt, so that Britain could be made to grant a meaningful assurance of independence to India. However, as events were to show, Cripps came with a limited mandate, and the reiteration of dominion status for India, with the suggestion of Pakistan, proved once again British insincerity. Nehru agonized and through the offices of Louis Johnson, Roosevelt's personal representative in India, he tried to get the United States to intercede with Churchill, but in vain. Gandhi was convinced that the will of the country had been sorely tested. Dismissing the Cripps offer as a post-dated cheque, Gandhi was determined to move the Congress along the path of positive action and was willing, if necessary, to go it alone. As he wrote to Nehru, 'The time has come when everyone of us has to choose his own course.'[245] He was unimpressed with

Jawaharlal's continued assertion that the Congress should continue its policy of non-embarrassment to the British so as not to impede war production. He forced Nehru to abandon his decision to publicly announce that if the Japanese invaded India they would be met with guerrilla warfare and a scorched earth policy.[246] In a draft resolution for the Congress, Gandhi stated that Japan's quarrel was not with India but the British Empire, and that the first step of a free India would, therefore, be to negotiate with Japan as India bore no enmity to Japan or any other nation. Nehru vehemently disagreed. Not only did he declare that he would continue to resist the Japanese, and in the process oppose even Subhas Chandra Bose and the Indian troops if they appeared on the north-eastern border of India,[247] but he also proceeded to redraft the Congress resolution and drop all Gandhi's references to Japan. The carefully worded resolution declared that the Congress was opposed to Nazism and fascism as well as imperialism, and that any attack on India would be resisted by non-violent non-cooperation. At the same time, in desperation, he wrote directly to Roosevelt asking him to intercede so that in a joint statement with Britain the Pacific war aims could include an assurance of freedom to India and resolve to defend India at all costs. Nehru's efforts were in vain. Equally unsuccessful were Subhas Bose's attempts, carried on at the same time in Germany, to persuade Hitler to declare as a war aim a pledge promising Indian independence, as Mussolini had agreed. Gandhi was left to follow his own light, and in a step which marked a pronounced change from his previous stand of non-negotiable non-violence he gave a 'Quit India' call to the British and a 'Do or die' call to his countrymen in August 1942.

What marked this change in Gandhi's approach? Feeling the pulse of the nation and sensing a deep unrest, Gandhi had judged that it was the right time to embark on another mass agitation. Also, he was increasingly coming around to believing that the Allies were going to lose the war.[248] By a coincidence, just about the time of the arrival of Cripps in March 1942, a news flash reported Subhas Bose's death in an air crash. Gandhi among others was deeply moved, and in a condolence message to Probhabati Debi, Subhas's mother, spoke about her son with considerable affection.[249] Later it turned out that the report was untrue, but even Cripps was surprised to see Gandhi speaking in such glowing terms about Subhas.[250]

From this time, a change in the attitude of Gandhi towards Subhas may be seen. Azad noted that the courage and resourcefulness displayed by Subhas in his daring escape from house arrest had earned the admiration of Gandhi, and had 'unconsciously coloured his views about the war situation and clouded discussions during the Cripps mission'.[251] Louis Fischer, in his book, *A Week with Gandhi* (1942), recalled how Subhas figured prominently in the conversation of Gandhi and everyone in his Ashram.[252] Kiron Shankar Roy, a Bengal Congress leader, recalled how at the time of formulating the Quit India resolution, Gandhi remembered Subhas and wished for his support.[253]

From Berlin, Subhas noted with satisfaction that the Quit India resolution had 'brought the Congress fundamentally near the stand always taken' by him.[254] He applauded Gandhi for once again rising to the occasion and firmly voicing his protest against the hypocritical moves of the British.[255] He declared that British imperialism, hand in glove with Yankee imperialism, stood unmasked before the world.[256] In a scathing attack on Nehru, Subhas pointed out that in his one-track anti-Axis stance Nehru had proved to be an ideological fanatic, far removed from the realism of Gandhi, adding that 'platitudes do not make a foreign policy'.[257] Regretting his inability to participate in this last campaign, Subhas felt that in the absence of the Congress leadership, which was behind bars, it was his duty to work in tandem with the Gandhian call, albeit from afar, and give substance to the Quit India call through detailed instructions. To keep up the momentum of an impending 'guerrilla war', which he predicted would end only in freedom, Subhas charted out a thorough programme which was aired in a series of broadcasts from Berlin Radio. In this, Subhas also included slightly absurd details, such as exhorting servants working for Englishmen to sabotage and strike and 'cook bad food or mix undesirable things with food and drink so that living in India will be impossible for Englishmen'.[258] Subhas's message did reach scattered corners, and pockets of resistance were created such as in Tamluk, Midnapore in Bengal, which spoke of a parallel national government at the end of 1942, to be kept in readiness for Subhas Bose when he arrived in India with victorious forces.[259] The forces unleashed in the Quit India movement were militant and disdained compromise, in a pronounced shift from the traditional Gandhian line of moderation.

From an objective distance in Europe, Subhas was to analyse that it was Gandhi who was displaying more political maturity and flexibility than Nehru. He acknowledged that in giving the Quit India call, Gandhi had travelled 'a long way' from his previous position. He understood that Gandhi could never openly adopt a pro-Axis policy since he was 'caught in the wheels of his own non-violent machine, which prevents his adopting such a policy'.[260] It was from this period of time that one can see a thawing in the relationship between Gandhi and Subhas. Separated from each other, they probably came to slowly recognize traits in their own personality in each other. Once outside the country, Subhas realized the indispensability of Gandhi. The Gandhian leadership of the Indian freedom movement was well acknowledged outside the country, and the respect he commanded gave legitimacy to the movement for independence, under the Congress. By being pushed out of the Congress, Subhas seemed to lose that legitimacy in the eyes of analysts of Indian affairs abroad. This may have been partly responsible for the delay in Hitler meeting him and in his decision to finally withhold German declaration of support for the Indian movement.[261] In Singapore, Subhas realized that the unprecedented support he secured from the Indian population in terms of money and recruitment into the ranks of the INA was for the cause of India's freedom struggle. There was an understanding that the INA initiative was working in tandem with the Gandhian movement as a supplementary and complementary exercise for the broader objective of securing freedom. It was this knowledge that made it imperative for Subhas to curb his caustic comments on Gandhi. In the major propaganda campaign that he began through radio broadcasts in order to familiarize his listeners with the Indian struggle, he had to accord primacy of place to Gandhi. Anything less caused a revolt not only among those Indians who worked with him, but it was also unacceptable to the Japanese.[262] Second, he had to try his level best to defeat any move of Gandhi that might lead to a compromise with the British authorities. The raison d'être of the INA initiative was based on its ability to work along with the Gandhian movement and, therefore, any understanding that Gandhi could bring about with the British government would rob the INA of its purpose. This is why, from the Cripps offer of 1942 to the Wavell Plan of 1945, Subhas used his customary persuasiveness through radio broadcasts to dissuade any temporizing move. Referring to the characteristic British insincerity behind the Wavell offer, he cautioned against the danger of unduly raising the importance of the Muslim League, adding, 'Even if the Pakistan plan is given assent to, the communal question will still remain unsolved.'[263] Indicating his disappointment at Nehru's lack of political realism, he expressed greater confidence in Gandhi's attitude of reserve and scepticism towards the Wavell offer. His ultimate appeal was to the Mahatma, whom he addressed as the 'Father of the Nation'. Subhas appealed to Gandhi's sense of fairness for help in absolving himself of the disturbing label of traitor that had attached itself to him in spite of his lifelong dedication to the cause of India's freedom.[264]

Gandhi, too, in turn came to publicly acknowledge that Subhas's unwavering patriotism which had informed all his moves, howsoever controversial, was 'second to none'.[265] The year 1946 saw Gandhi pushed slowly towards a state of isolation. Events were moving beyond his control, and political forces were heading towards a finale which would see a divided India. Gandhi had fought with all his heart against this development, but the communal harmony that was dearest to him was sorely threatened. He could not but think of his 'other son', Subhas,[266] who had repeatedly raised his voice, loudly and clearly, against the mischievous British moves of divide and rule which could tear apart the multi-religious fabric of Indian society. In vain did Subhas cite the examples of Ireland and Palestine to prove British insincerity and hypocrisy. Subhas had spoken of the need to sufficiently humour Jinnah and the Muslim League so that any move by the British to raise them as a bargaining alternative to the Congress might be forestalled. Indeed, in one of his last acts before leaving the country, Subhas, in a move reminiscent of Gandhian generosity, had offered an intractable Jinnah the prime ministership of an undivided country if he held his peace.[267] Earlier in his own regional base, Bengal, Subhas had initiated a short-lived but bold move of entering into a coalition alliance with the Muslim League to defeat the extreme communal elements that threatened to disturb the harmony of the province.

In 1946, when all sanity and reason seemed lost and Gandhi felt defeated, the INA trials lifted the curtain to reveal the full picture of Subhas's last initiative, which the British had kept a closely guarded secret. Although militarily a disaster, the INA presented on a limited scale an unprecedented picture of integrated communal harmony, which proved to be unattainable at the all-India level. Gandhi was deeply impressed. He wrote that the lessons that Netaji and his army brought were those of self-sacrifice, unity and discipline, irrespective of class and community. 'My praise and admiration can go no further.'[268] Gandhi felt vindicated when told by INA veterans that Subhas, in one of his last messages, had instructed them on their return to India to work in a non-violent manner for the cause of national unity and cohesion under the direction of the Congress.[269]

Thus, we see that after a troubled relationship during most of their political lives, Subhas and Gandhi arrived at a greater appreciation and understanding of each other's position once circumstances came to distance them. This mellowing of attitudes and softening of stances can be explained not only as the pragmatic result of the pulls and pressures of an evolving political scenario but also as the outcome of a deeper and more intuitive understanding that each came to have of the other, without necessarily acknowledging it. Cast in the roles of a stern father and a rebel son, Gandhi and Subhas perhaps in the autumn of their lives recognized how they were hewn out of the same block and that despite their conflicting positions they had inherited the same foundational values and beliefs. In contrast, Jawaharlal, while closer to Bose in many superficial details of their lives, remained fundamentally different in mindset and conviction.

Nine years older than Subhas, Jawaharlal was viewed as an elder brother by Bose, to be emulated, followed and supported in the bid for an alternative challenge to Gandhi.[270] However, very soon he came to realize that although Jawaharlal might agonize over Gandhi's sudden calling off of the non-cooperation movement after Chauri Chaura, or be peeved by his reluctance to allow the Congress to declare complete independence as its political goal, Jawaharlal would never break with Gandhi. He would not be part of Subhas's bolder challenge to walk out of the Congress, fashioning an alternative strategy and setting up a separate party. Nor would he be comfortable in critically condemning Gandhi, as Subhas did. A confused Jawaharlal would withdraw and agonize alone, introspect, and finally make up with Gandhi.

In truth, Nehru could not afford to make a break with Gandhi. In the absence of an independent programme and ideology, and without any established power base, he needed Gandhi to channel his pent-up nationalism in a worthwhile direction.[271] He admitted as much when he wrote, 'I represent nobody but myself. I have not the politician's flair for forming groups and parties. My one attempt in this direction—the formation of the Independence for India League . . . was a hopeless failure.'[272] Besides, unlike Subhas, Nehru believed that Gandhi was indispensable for India's destiny. Although often critical of Gandhi's decisions, overall he acknowledged that in any national struggle Gandhi's full association and guidance were essential. As Nehru put it, 'The dominating position of Gandhiji must always be remembered . . . India cannot do without him.'[273] Gandhi, too, needed Nehru,[274] and Jawaharlal was to become Gandhi's link with the younger generation of politicians. Also, Gandhi allowed himself to be informed by Nehru's judgement and knowledge of international developments. This underlying bond of mutual need and trust was reinforced by an attachment of deep affection, which continued throughout the period of the national struggle.

Gandhi explained, 'I cannot think of myself as a rival to Jawaharlal or him to me. Or, if we are, we are rivals in making love to each other in the pursuit of the common goal.'[275] He knew that despite differences of opinion, it would be Jawaharlal who would continue his direction of the Congress. With considerable confidence, Gandhi nominated Jawaharlal as his successor at the AICC session in January 1942, declaring:

> He (Jawaharlal) says that he does not understand my language, and that he speaks a language foreign to me. This may or may not be true. But language is no bar to a union of hearts. And I know this—that when I am gone he will speak my language.[276]

This emotive factor was totally missing in the Gandhi–Bose relationship. Subhas's zeal to fashion an alternative leadership challenge to Gandhi, and Gandhi's lack of confidence in Subhas's political sense, tended to eclipse the underlying respect that each had for the other. Despite their contrasting styles of functioning, there was recognition of each other's respective strengths, conviction about each other's fierce patriotism, and admiration for each other's unique leadership qualities. In the years following Subhas's escape, this mutual regard surfaced and showed Gandhi and Subhas to be much closer in their thinking than they would ever have acknowledged.

Almost reminiscent of a typical Indian family scenario, the more Gandhi, as Bapu, gave license to Jawaharlal and declared his love for him, the more Subhas felt abandoned and let down. However, he had no leader other than Jawaharlal to fall back upon who could support him in his ideological bid to challenge Gandhi. He was himself ill, forced by circumstances to political exile in Europe, while Jawaharlal was selected by Gandhi repeatedly to wear the mantle of the Congress president.

Although disappointed that Bengal was not being represented at the level of Congress president because of Gandhi's indulgence of Jawaharlal, [277] it made sense for Subhas to keep the channels of communication open with Jawaharlal and exercise pressure through him on the Gandhian movement. Subhas was in constant touch with Jawaharlal in the days of Kamala Nehru's critical illness, visiting the couple in Badenweiler, Germany, despite his own ill health. He was present in Lausanne when Kamala died, and stood by Jawaharlal offering solace and making arrangements for the cremation.[278]

On the eve of Nehru's return to India to assume the office of Congress president in Lucknow, Subhas wrote to him how crucial it was for him to lead the Congress in a progressive direction since Gandhi would be more accommodating to him than to anyone else. During his term as Congress president at Haripura in 1938, Bose had enjoyed a productive period of working together with Nehru on their favourite project of national planning. The National Planning Committee, initiated by Bose with Nehru as its chairman, envisaged planning as a coordinated scheme of a large number of subjects, the separate reports of which would be integrated to form a Comprehensive National Plan. Although both took pains to emphasize that the envisaged industrial planning would not be in conflict with cottage industries and nor would they challenge existing socio-economic structures, Gandhi remained unimpressed. He dismissed the initiative saying, 'Much money and labour are being wasted on an effort which will bring forth little or no fruit.'[279]

The days of harmonious working between Subhas and Jawaharlal proved to be short lived as the Tripuri election crisis in 1939 brought out the bitterness in their relationship. Nehru's refusal to support Subhas in opposition to Gandhi led to Subhas's scathing attacks on Nehru, which were unfortunate in view of the fact that Nehru did earnestly try to mediate between Gandhi and Bose and failed miserably. For all the commonality in their ideological persuasions and their youthful assertion against the Gandhian leadership, Jawaharlal and Subhas were temperamentally very different. Jawaharlal was very British in his mental make-up, with a natural reticence and reserve and strong feelings of loyalty which made it difficult for him to make dramatic breaks with positions held. Gandhi explained, 'Indeed he (Jawaharlal) is more English than Indian in his thoughts and make-up. He is often more at home with Englishmen than with his own countrymen ... though he is an ardent nationalist.'[280] Subhas was a passionate, emotional Bengali with an obsessive focus on Indian independence, a goal for which he could adopt any means. Romain Rolland wrote in exasperation about Subhas, 'At one time to the right, at another to the left. Moscow, Berlin, Tokyo ... These Bengalis, violent, impulsive, never a politics of reason, they obey the somersaults of their passions, victims of their own vulnerability to jealousy, vanity, stung to the quick by flesh wounds.'[281]

Rooted in traditional values, with a deep spiritual sense, and with a pressing practical concern to extract the most from every situation, Subhas's approach to life and its problems was very different from that of Jawaharlal. Nehru's liberal education, scientific temperament, lack of a marked religious sense, and romantic disposition gave him a different perspective on life. He hotly contested Subhas's argument for turning to the Axis powers for help, declaring, 'The fact that a particular country is an enemy of Britain does not necessarily mean that the country is our friend.'[282] Neither could he turn a blind eye to the excesses of the fascist countries, as Bose advised, for the purpose of harnessing their help for the cause of Indian independence. It was not that Subhas was unaware of the excesses of the Nazi regime and their use of chemical warfare.

While philosophically wishing that its victims would be able to face the challenge with the soul-conquering matter,[283] Subhas studiously avoided getting drawn into any discussion or action showing support for the Jewish cause, lest the larger plans of getting German help be jeopardized. Reacting sharply to Nehru's suggestion that India could benefit from giving refuge to Jewish experts in science and industry, Subhas reiterated that sentiment should not determine foreign policy.[284]

It was with the same boy-scout attitude—to seize every opportunity for the advancement of national well-being—that Subhas approached the arts and music, missing in the process the finer nuances of artistic creation. Writing to his friend, Dilip Roy, in 1925 from Mandalay Prison in Burma, Subhas spoke of using music as a formula, 'a spiritual pabulum', so that it could reach the masses. He spoke of reviving some of the dying musical traditions of rural Bengal such as kirtan, kathakata and jatra and making them the life soul of the masses.[285] Dilip's reply was cautious.[286] The liberal in him agreed that art should be rescued from the elitist clutches of a few. However, the musician in Dilip wondered how this goal could be achieved. He had learnt the hard way that the music which brought about a divine ecstasy among a select few could sound meaningless to others. He recalled with deep gratitude how, in 1923, it had taken a sensitive person like Nehru to chide a talkative audience into paying more attention to his musical rendition.[287] His reply to Subhas was that although he agreed in principle, Subhas's suggestion was a generalization incapable of realization. Tagore entered this discourse on reading Subhas's letter which Dilip had shared with him. While agreeably surprised by Subhas's broad view that music should have a larger outreach, he agreed with Dilip that it would be disastrous to downgrade a higher art form in order to cater to the 'demands of the marketplace'.[288] As he put it, 'If the man without any aesthetic sense fails to even look at the *Bokul* blossoms, let the *Bokul* blossoms wait for him eternally; let them not in despair try to turn into fields of arum.'[289] Subhas, however, with his sense of mission would probably have directed each gaze to be on the blossoms. This conclusion seems unavoidable when one compares how the two men were to recall from memory their favourite lines from Wordsworth. While Nehru quoted thus, 'A primrose by a river's brim/ A yellow primrose was to him/ And it was nothing more',[290] Subhas recalled them as follows: 'A primrose by the river's brim/ A yellow primrose is to him/ And it is something more.'[291] While Nehru despaired of men who lost their sense of aesthetic appreciation in their zeal to be precise,[292] Subhas felt it important to consciously take in the lessons from nature lest they be neglected.[293]

The differences in the mindsets of the two men were most evident in the presentation of their autobiographies and memoirs, which appeared around the same time. *The Indian Struggle* of Subhas, published by Lawrence & Wishart in London in 1935, was a commentary on the politics of the national struggle from 1920 to 1934. In his analysis, he criticized the Gandhian leadership for being slow and having outlived its usefulness, and he also faulted Nehru for divided loyalties, with his head being with the left and his heart with Gandhi. Subhas spoke with confidence about an alternative stance which would force the pace of the movement without succumbing to any temporizing move at the behest of the British. It is interesting that Subhas should have shared his manuscript with Nehru in Europe, who, while correcting certain factual errors, maintained a studious silence regarding his criticisms and observations.[294] Subhas added a sequel to his story for the period between 1935 and 1942, when he was in Europe in 1943 during the war. In view of the acrimony surrounding the Tripuri crisis and the circumstances of his escape from India, in this section he was bitterly critical of the 'sentimental politics' of Nehru and the obduracy of Gandhi. Earlier, in 1937, during a short ten-day stint in Europe, Subhas had hurriedly put together an incomplete autobiography called *An Indian Pilgrim*, which traced the story of his childhood, schooling and family influences until his resignation from the Civil Service in 1921. It did not, however, match up to his *The Indian Struggle*, and Subhas found it hard to get publishers in London to be excited by it because in the meantime Nehru's *Autobiography* had become a great success.[295]

Nehru's *Autobiography* (1936), coming after *Glimpses of World History* (1934), was his first real literary venture. Although he traced in it his childhood, early education and family influences, the bulk of the writing was a commentary on the national struggle, the coming of Gandhi, and the changing national and international scenario. While the canvas was the same, the tone of Nehru's book was totally different from that of Bose's volume. With its matter-of-fact approach, Subhas's book had a prosaic and prescriptive quality which made it markedly different from the elegant and reflective prose of Nehru. S. Gopal, Nehru's biographer, commented that Bose's book revealed 'a muscular, sanguinary temperament, totally different to Jawaharlal's highly-strung personality, plagued by introspection'.[296] Without a single critical comment on Subhas and lacking the judgemental tone of Subhas's book, his *Autobiography* was Nehru's examination of the course of the national struggle and was full of the author's doubts, anxieties and concerns. The western-educated Nehru confessed frankly that he was unable to comprehend much of Gandhi's basic thinking, which was often anathema to him. Yet his recognition of the enormous power that Gandhi wielded over the Indian masses made him realize that the national movement could ill afford any break with him. Subhas, on the other hand, rooted strongly in Indian tradition and social thinking, could understand where much of Gandhi's thoughts came from, and even when he disagreed he was not unduly surprised. He was exasperated because Gandhi's phenomenal power over the masses was not being harnessed in more sustained movements, because truces and suspensions often called abrupt halts to them. Nehru's book, with its quality of introspection and self-criticism, lacked the 'spirit of aggressive certitude' that marked Subhas's book.[297] Nehru's *Autobiography* ran through ten printings in 1936 and not only thrilled the Indian intelligentsia, but its lucid prose also reached out to a British readership, which considered the prose of a Gandhi or Tagore stilted and daunting. C.F. Andrews complimented Nehru, 'You are the only one outstanding person who seems instinctively to know what the West can understand and follow easily.'[298]

The tremendous success of Nehru's *Autobiography* inadvertently triggered off the underlying and almost sibling rivalry that existed between Subhas and Jawaharlal. Dilip Kumar Roy was to detect that his own fascination for Jawaharlal and his *Autobiography* created a certain discomfort in Subhas.[299] Subhas was, however, very satisfied that his own book, *The Indian Struggle*, had been well received and shared with a friend how some considered it to be 'the best book on India by an Indian politician'.[300]

The seriousness and one-track zeal with which Subhas went about his life's mission, and his blinkered vision and humourless attitude to gender socialization, made him very different from Nehru's personality. Indeed, Nehru had problems accepting Gandhi's rather puritanical attitude to sexuality, which Subhas in his early years also shared. In private, Nehru joked with Padmaja Naidu about her apparently having turned Subhas's head, but added on a more serious note that it was important to 'soften him and make him more human' and cure him of 'certain mannerisms and affectations' which made people judge him harshly.[301] To his daughter, Nehru confided how 'terrible' he found 'the lack of awareness and sensitiveness' in Subhas.[302] After the Tripuri crisis when Subhas was on the warpath against the Gandhian Congress in general and him in particular, Jawaharlal felt that 'Subhas had gone off the rails and had been behaving badly in many ways'.[303] Finding it difficult to put up with the 'arrant nonsense'[304] that Subhas kept mouthing, Nehru refrained from any mention of him until the veil was lifted from the INA mystery and he found himself donning lawyer's robes once again to defend Subhas's lost and forgotten army in the historic trials held at the Red Fort in Delhi.

The INA trials in 1946 involving three veterans from the Hindu, Sikh and Muslim communities, naively selected by the British to stand trial, brought into public view Subhas's breadth of vision and the almost impossible feat that he had accomplished of knitting together men and women from different religious communities and socio-economic backgrounds into one force. Along with Bhulabhai Desai, Nehru, chose to defend the war veterans of the Azad Hind Army, and in the process they delved into extensive material which proved the extent of the organization and planning that had gone into the venture. Bhulabhai Desai later confessed to Dilip Kumar Roy how humbled he had felt when he realized the unique qualities of Subhas, who had dared to challenge British might by single-handedly raising a force that had come within an ace of success.[305] It was also a sobering thought for Nehru when he saw the unprecedented admiration for Subhas that had been generated throughout the country and among the armed forces. He wrote to General Claude Auchinleck, 'No political organisation, however strong and efficient could have produced this enormous reaction in India. It was one of those rare things which just fit into the mood of the people.'[306]

The complete communal unity and harmony that Subhas had been able to build up in the INA, the high level of military competence, and above all the sense of independence that the INA could maintain in resisting Japanese attempts at overlordship, impressed Nehru greatly.[307] He also acknowledged that the INA had broken down the barriers that existed between the public and the army and had effectively brought the armed forces into the larger project of the Indian freedom struggle.[308] The INA that Nehru had once pledged to resist now became a tremendous vote catcher, and Nehru lost no time in mainstreaming Subhas's efforts into the larger story of the national struggle as he canvassed for the Congress in the elections of 1946, a year prior to independence. There was a strange irony as Subhas's erstwhile detractors, the Gandhian politicians in the Congress, sat among an adulatory audience in Calcutta's Roxy cinema watching a play enacting Subhas's great escape.[309] It was journey's end, for independence was to come soon after to India, albeit a partitioned India, an eventuality which Nehru accepted with pragmatism but which Gandhi and Subhas had resisted till the end.

~

FOUR

ENVISIONING INDIA

In the days of the freedom struggle, the Indian leadership not only concentrated on devising strategies to win political independence from British colonial rule, but also reflected in varying degrees on a vision for India. Philosophers and political statesmen alike turned the mirror onto Indian society and polity and tried to fathom what Nehru charmingly described as 'the Idea of India'.[1] This exercise involved taking stock of Indian tradition, judging the impact of the so-called modernizing mission of the West, and visualizing a future for a free India. Analyses, however, differed sharply and through heightened debates and discussions there emerged an evolution of thought about India's own identity. Many among India's leaders wrote a great deal during their long stints in prison, or during lulls in political agitation, or they spoke often to large audiences. Many of these reflections and addresses were published, and often opened the doors to national debates through which the ideal of freedom came to be broadened to eventually project notions of federal polity, democracy, secularism and social justice.

It is important to note that none of these ideas was static and that over the years, as the focus was sharpened and ideas refined, the idea of India came to be projected onto a broader canvas. Also, the critical rhetoric of Indian leaders, who alternately denounced or valorized aspects of Indian tradition, has to be seen in the context of the ongoing and evolving dialogue in which the colonial masters were engaged while trying to assess India's traditional past. The colonial critique provided a ready reference point against which Indians could conceptualize and analyse their arguments regarding their traditional heritage and define and redefine their weaknesses and strengths.

Orientalists such as William Jones (1746–94) had glorified the Indian civilization of the ancient past, and in painting its Sanskrit heritage as an exotic chapter of history they had glossed over several unwelcome aspects of Indian society relating to inequality in caste, class and gender. Further, by valorizing ancient Hindus as the Athenians of Asia, brilliant in creativity, their decline came to be ascribed to the interaction with Muslims, the Asian equivalent of the barbarians of the dark ages in Europe. Following this Orientalist wave, there came a period of colonial writing dominated by Utilitarian, Evangelical and other Christian missionaries, who focused instead on the peculiarities of Hindu civilization and particularly the harsh treatment of women. Mill's monumental account of India, written in 1817, spoke of the moral lapses of Indian civilization, ignoring any preceding cultural high watermark. In this interpretation, British rule was seen as the resurrecting force, the equivalent of the European Renaissance. Justifying their rule in liberal rationalist terms, the British sought to undermine those foundations of Indian life which they considered irrational and superstition ridden. English education was intended to bring about a moral and social transformation by creating an access to modern science and technology and an English way of life which would bring up a whole generation of collaborators, Indian in features and English in thinking. Following the blow received to this fond hope by the Indian Mutiny of 1857, the British reorganized the Indian Army after the uprising according to a categorization of the so-called martial races, which included the manly Rajputs, Marathas and Sikhs. The Bengalis were excluded from this scheme as being weak in constitution, clerical in mentality and servile in attitude, a point of view that echoed the well-known diatribe of Macaulay, Law Member for India in the 1830s.[2]

The British critique of Indian society and its pedagogical sermonizing approach provoked a unique response in nationalist thought. A hitherto vague and diffused self-consciousness coalesced for the first time into the articulation of a position vis-à-vis imperialist rule. Thinking Indians felt challenged to prove something worthwhile in their heritage and improve their self-esteem through a process of self-definition while simultaneously taking stock of the impact of colonial rule.

There was at the same time a tendency, sometimes open but mostly implied, among early nationalist thinkers to lay the blame for the degeneration of Indian society at the door of the experience with Muslim rule.[3] Reinforced by the Orientalist logic, there was a general feeling that, with the possible exception of Akbar, Muslim rulers had been tyrannical and contemptuous of Hindu beliefs, pushing Hindus to perpetuate social practices like sati, purdah, child marriage and a rigid caste structure as a countering strategy. The divisive British policy of initially favouring Hindus and then Muslims did much to strengthen this impression. Over the years, the British land settlement policy, particularly in Bengal which benefited the former at the cost of the latter, uneven economic and social progress between Hindus and Muslims, lack of adequate Muslim participation in the political dialogue between the largely Hindu national leadership and the British authorities, undermined the possibilities of bringing about a better understanding between the two communities.

By and large, however, the nationalist leaders were deeply disturbed about the state of their society and looked for means to regenerate it. There were four broad strands in the nationalist approach to the imperialist challenge. One was a grudging acceptance of the colonial diagnosis of Indian physical weakness, with the resultant attempt to correct that impression through greater physical training and bodybuilding by promoting indigenous forms of martial arts and wrestling. Vivekananda's message that the Gita could be better understood with the biceps inspired many young nationalist minds. Second, there was an attempt by the English-educated classes to seek lessons from western Enlightenment liberal values and to attempt a critique of Indian traditional practices. This led to the third approach, namely that of initiating social reform programmes, such as those that Ram Mohan Roy (1772–1833) was to spearhead, to end certain social evils which had crept into Indian society. Finally, there was also an attempt to focus on the finer elements of Indian tradition and its underlying corpus of spiritual, ethical and moral values, in an attempt to increase national pride and self-esteem. None of these approaches excluded the others, and very often the leaders shifted from one position to the other, thus belying all simplistic attempts to categorize them.

In the Gandhian phase of the Indian freedom movement, a unique dialogue dominated the intellectual horizon of nationalist thinking, representing contrasting outlooks, which provided an important backdrop against which younger politicians such as Jawaharlal Nehru and Subhas Chandra Bose could clarify their own impressions in envisioning India. The senior-most voice was that of Rabindranath Tagore (1861–1941), the nation's poet and philosopher, generally respected as Gurudev. His queries were directed at the leader who had introduced a new idiom into Indian politics, Mohandas Karamchand Gandhi (1869–1948). Addressing him as the Mahatma, Tagore lauded his unique efforts for drawing the masses into the struggle while seriously disagreeing with several of Gandhi's prescriptions. The exchanges between the poet and the political leader, which sparked off lively debates and were published as a series of articles, brought several important issues to the foreground.

The encounter between modernity and tradition, at the various levels of India's social, political and economic existence, was the crucial focus of this discourse. Tagore—who had associated himself with the swadeshi movement during the partition of Bengal in 1905, spontaneously joining street protests, singing patriotic songs, tying rakhis on Muslim participants to strengthen communal harmony, and raising funds for encouraging national education—had been left unsure about the efficacy of programmes such as the boycott. Actively discouraging students who pledged to leave their schools and colleges, Tagore explained that 'the anarchy of emptiness never tempts me, even when it is resorted to as a temporary measure'.[4] It is no wonder, then, that he appeared unenthused by Gandhi's call for non-cooperation in 1921. Disputing the negative content of calls such as the boycott of educational institutions and non-cooperation with the British, Tagore explained that such rigours would merely lead to 'non-education' and evoke 'a fierce joy of annihilation'.[5] To him, it seemed most ironical that while the underlying message of his cherished university at Santiniketan was cultural cooperation between the East and the West, Gandhi's call was unnecessarily hurting that truth by appearing as narrow provincialism and 'spiritual suicide'.[6]

In vain did Gandhi try to persuade Tagore to join his fight for swaraj which, he explained, was the natural offspring of Tagore's own involvement with swadeshi. Explaining that all negatives were not necessarily signs of weakness, Gandhi reassured the poet that the ability to say 'no' to a foreign government would serve as the nation's notice that it was no longer satisfied to be under tutelage.[7]

An important subject of discussion that emerged from these debates was on the relative merits of English education. Countering the poet's concern that the non-cooperation call would lead students down a blind alley of frustration, Gandhi critiqued the existing education system for having turned a people into clerks and interpreters, making them helpless and godless in the process.[8] Adopting a functional and moral approach, Gandhi felt that true education should enhance character building and instil ethical values. To a peasant who earns his bread honestly, a mere knowledge of letters may not enhance his quality of life but might plant seeds of discontentment and frustration. Similarly, an emphasis on the knowledge of English to the total neglect of the vernaculars increased hypocrisy and enslaved people to a borrowed medium. Gandhi recommended that a universal language for India should be Hindi, with the option of writing it in Persian or Nagari characters which should be known to all so that a bond could be created between Hindus and Muslims.[9] Tagore also agreed that Hindi was 'the only possible national language' at the inter-provincial level, but a period of preparation was necessary to 'pave the way towards its general use by constant practice as a voluntary acceptance of a national obligation'.[10]

Perhaps the poet's most celebrated dissent from the Mahatma was regarding the call of the charkha. Gandhi's formula of compulsory spinning, which would be economically beneficial to India's masses, besides strengthening them spiritually to defy an industrially superior power, failed to convince the poet. Lamenting that the prescriptive tone of the call would suppress the free spirit of the individual, Tagore declared his inability to accept 'the terrible habit of blindly obeying orders'.[11] He felt that the logic of boycotting foreign cloth was essentially grounded on economic science and should not be made into 'a fictitious moral dictum'[12] with a magical formula that foreign cloth is impure and should be burnt.

Gandhi, in his well-reasoned response to Tagore, whom he addressed as 'The Great Sentinel',[13] argued that the charkha had been adopted not from blind faith but keeping in mind the economic reality of the villages where the majority of Indians lived. By 'employing their enforced idleness'[14] through spinning, he was promoting their self-determination and growth as well as enhancing their spiritual freedom. Confessing that he did not draw any sharp distinction between economics and ethics, Gandhi declared that he considered it a 'sin' to wear foreign cloth because the material civilization of the West with its attendant greed had exploited the weak.

As this debate took place when the non-cooperation movement was at its height, nationalist public opinion was incensed by Tagore's critique of Gandhi. Staunch Gandhians in Bengal such as Acharya Prafulla Ray openly disagreed with Tagore,[15] while writers of newspaper articles wondered at the volte-face of the poet, who in the swadeshi era, inspired by a new nationalism or patriotism, had led the country and was now putting all his force against it.[16]

A powerful voice to join this debate was that of Chittaranjan Das, the astute Bengal leader. While politically Das was to chart out a path independent of the Gandhian line, he shared several of the Mahatma's thoughts while openly disagreeing with certain aspects of Tagore's thinking. Sceptical of Tagore's plea for universalism, which he traced to the influence of the poet's visit to the United States,[17] Das felt that before trying to assimilate western culture, Indians had to first discover their own national ethos and identity without which there could only be a slavish imitation.[18] He feared that a meeting of the East and the West would result in sections of society aping western ways and neglecting their own cultural distinctiveness.

The younger Das had pleaded in the poem 'Harlot', in his collection *Malancha*, for greater compassion for and rehabilitation of prostitutes, thereby provoking sufficient unpopularity in the Brahmo Samaj for many to boycott his wedding with Basantidebi in 1897.[19] But the older Das was now deeply uncomfortable with Tagore's message to women urging them to chart out an independent identity, defying, if necessary, stereotypical expectations of them by society. In the Bengali weekly, *Narayana*, he repeatedly attacked Tagore for importing ideas from the West, which he claimed threatened the national genius and individual culture of Bengal. Declaring that 'we should not suffer to be led by the glamour of the west', Das criticized Tagore's celebrated short story '*Strir Patro*' (The Wife's Letter), and urged the writing of a counter story as a rejoinder.[20] Das also shared Gandhi's contempt for English education, which he said churned out graduates from the university mills much like buttons and pinheads, filled with ideas of superiority, dismissing those who did not receive it as illiterate and uneducated. He pleaded instead for vernacular education.[21]

Although Tagore and Gandhi had taken sharply contrasting positions with regard to particular issues and programmes, interestingly enough they evolved from different premises and arrived at a common ground where they both refused to envision India in terms of a monocultural nation state and accept the western idea of nationalism as the inevitable universal of the times.[22] Their fierce patriotism and commitment to anti-imperialism did not take them in the direction of what Gandhi called 'exclusive nationalism'. Rather, both came to share a certain degree of anarchistic thinking.

At a time when the idea of nationalism was clubbed in the minds of ordinary people with the concepts of patriotism and anti-imperialism, it is remarkable that both Tagore and Gandhi were able to dissociate their passionate opposition to imperialism from the project of nationalism which they saw as being alien to Indian tradition. Gandhi was convinced that India's salvation would come only by invoking the society's conscience and working through an indigenous model. Introduction of western institutions in an Indian milieu, he feared, would merely create an 'Englistan' without the English, and he was certain that 'this is not the Swaraj I want'.[23] Gandhi, no believer in the sole value of the impersonal ballot box, sought to involve society's conscience in the process of nation building.

It is true that over the years Gandhi had moved away from the rigid anti-western position of his *Hind Swaraj* (1909) days when he had said, 'India has nothing to learn from anybody else and this is as it should be.'[24] In 1921, he was prepared to admit some of the benefits of western civilization and the strides made by western science. On a more philosophical plane, he was to make his celebrated comment, 'I do not want my house to be walled in all sides and my windows to be stuffed. I want the culture of all the lands to be blown about my house as freely as possible. But I refuse to be blown off my feet by any.'[25]

But even so, Gandhi envisioned India not as a modern nation state, but as a village swaraj, providing citizens with minimum necessities, completely independent of its neighbours for vital needs while interdependent for certain other exchanges, and run by a panchayat of five on a cooperative basis, a system of local self-government which would ensure a perfect democracy, based upon individual freedom. Ideally based on truth, non-violence and pacifism, and sustained by faith in an all-knowing living force, all religions would find in this village swaraj a full and equal place. By placing full confidence in the individual's social commitment and faith in his sense of responsibility, the need for an overseeing and controlling state would slowly become redundant. There would be instead 'a state of enlightened anarchy in which each person will become his own ruler'.[26] This vision of Gandhi found resonance in Tagore's celebrated song, 'We are all kings in our reign of kings'.[27]

Tagore, too, although a great advocate of the meeting of the East and the West, evolved in his attitude towards the West. Towards the end of his life, he became bitter about the deep hypocrisy of the British in mouthing liberal notions of freedom and justice and consistently denying these to the subject people of the empire, thus betraying a lack of moral force.[28] He debunked the notion justifying the reign of an external state on a society such as India, a 'world in miniature', arguing that 'the looseness of its diversity and the feebleness of its unity' made it impossible to fit it into the straitjacket of a nation.[29]

Tagore, however, did make a distinction between the 'Nation of the West', which he considered a mechanical and soulless entity, and the 'Spirit of the West',[30] which he felt represented some of the Enlightenment values of equality, reason and scientific progress. He pleaded for this 'Spirit of the West', which could be invoked for reforming certain inherent social weaknesses in India such as caste divisions which had become fixed over time, ignoring the law of mutability, the life breath of progress.[31] Tagore's free spirit found it objectionable that in the traditional *varnashram*, occupations with their hierarchical positions were supposedly predetermined at birth, thus denying individuals freedom of choice and opportunities for social mobility and improvement.

The real obstacle to meaningful reform, Tagore argued, lay in the habit of mind which, on the one hand, resisted any proposal for fundamental attitudinal change while being, on the other hand, easily attracted to external solutions, which could never be deep rooted. Tagore applied this analysis in particular to the question of the communal divide. He bluntly stated, 'The real difficulty is for Hindus and Moslems to give up their respective prejudices which keep them apart. That is where the problem now rests. To the Hindu, the Mussalman is impure: for the Mussalman, the Hindu is a kafir.'[32] Without removing this deeply ingrained intolerance, he feared pacts and ententes could only offer the 'imaginary easy prospect of Hindu-Muslim unity'.[33] So greatly bothered was he by the ugliness of communal violence that he declared that 'straightforward atheism' was 'preferable to this terrible thing, delusion of religiosity ... the satanic bestiality which wears the garb of religion'.[34]

Although Gandhi, too, passionately worked for Hindu–Muslim harmony, he continued to be rooted in his Hindu identity. For him, religion was important and his complaint was that under the impact of modern civilization India was becoming irreligious. To support his arguments Gandhi used Hindu imagery in his discourses. He justified the *varnashram* of caste sanctioned by the shastras, saying that they existed all over the world as four classes. The problem, he felt, lay in the erosion of equality and sense of purpose underlying the caste structure, which had, therefore, become mongrelized. Gandhi also held out as his model the ideal of Ramrajya, which he defined simply as 'the kingdom of God on Earth'.[35] In this perfect world, there would be political freedom where the country would be independent of the British, economic freedom where the humblest would feel equal to the tallest, and a moral freedom where pacifism would reign and there would be no need to rely on armed strength.

Despite his Hindu rhetoric, however, Gandhi's religion embraced the essence of all other faiths. He advised, 'Those who do not wish to misunderstand things may read up the Koran and they will find therein hundreds of passages acceptable to the Hindus; and the Bhagvat Gita contains passages to which not a Mohamedan can take exception.'[36] Gandhi believed in the great necessity of the different communities to understand each other. As he wrote, 'Hindu Muslim unity is not less important than the spinning wheel. It is the breath of our life.'[37]

Gandhi approached the question of gender equality with the same principle of equality with which he had approached the question of *varnashram*. As he put it, 'I would have no use for that swaraj to which women have not made their full contribution.'[38] It was Gandhi who brought women into the mainstream of the national movement, encouraging them to participate along with men in the mass campaigns. He believed women, with their innate moral strength, capacity for suffering and inborn compassion, would be the natural advocates of his principles of ahimsa and satyagraha. However, he ensured that their participation was restricted to the parameters of non-violent pickets and marches. Although a believer in full gender equality, Gandhi felt that separate roles had been apportioned to men as breadwinners and women as homemakers, and he was unwilling to see women going beyond their prescribed role. As he put it, 'In trying to ride the horse that man rides, she brings herself and him down. There is as much bravery in keeping one's home in good order and condition as there is in defending it against attack from without.'[39] Indeed, he felt there was something degrading and vulgar about women being called to shoulder the rifle for the protection of the hearth.[40]

In prescribing an ideal society where there would be full equality, Gandhi was, however, careful not to advocate any programme which would be socially and economically disruptive. He stated that the western ideals of socialism or communism could be adopted in India only if based on non-violence, and called for the harmonious cooperation of labourer and capitalist, landlord and tenant.[41] He advocated the highly philosophical concept that the propertied classes should hold their property in trust for the welfare of their tenants since he (Gandhi) would definitely not be party to dispossessing them forcefully.

At the root of Gandhi's philosophy lay his abiding belief in the law of authentic moral living. It was this conviction that made him challenge ecological or environmental damage whether by machinery or medicines or an industrialized life, all of which he associated with the excesses of modern civilization. Tagore, too, while welcoming the advances of western science for improving the general quality of human life, was very apprehensive of allowing the machine to curb man's spirit of independence. The tyranny of the *yantra danav* or the machine monster was a recurring theme in his poetry; Tagore also focused in his plays on the exploitative role of technology which he depicted as enslaving its users.[42]

Intensely spiritual, both men felt the need to direct the country's gaze to the reservoir of inner strength and draw on the wealth of moral and ethical values in the struggle against imperialism. However, the free spirit of Tagore could not be bound down to the form and structure of religion, while Gandhi, on the other hand, relied on it for giving discipline and focus to the anti-imperialist struggle at hand. In essence, the poet and the statesman operated in different mediums. While Tagore, as a philosopher, could intellectually rise above the differences with the West and turn instead to ideologically and mutual enriching dialogue and interaction, Gandhi, the practical leader on the ground, had to be brutally persistent in pressing his non-cooperation agenda at all levels. As the well-articulated thoughts of a poet were countered by the incisive logic of a lawyer, younger politicians such as Jawaharlal Nehru and Subhas Bose came to be deeply influenced. Afforded with a reference point against which they could sharpen and refine their own ideas, they evolved considerably in their own individual ways of envisioning the future of India.

Nehru later recalled:

> Tagore and Gandhi have undoubtedly been the two outstanding and dominating figures of India in this first half of the twentieth century. It is instructive to compare and contrast them. No two persons could be so different from one another in their make up or temperaments. Tagore, the aristocratic artist, turned democrat with proletarian sympathies, represented essentially the cultural tradition of India, the tradition of accepting life in the fullness thereof and going through it with song and dance. Gandhi, more a man of the people, almost the embodiment of the Indian peasant, represented the other ancient tradition of India, that of renunciation and asceticism. And yet Tagore was primarily the man of thought, Gandhi of concentrated and ceaseless activity. Both in their different ways had a world outlook, and both were at the same time wholly Indian. They seemed to present different but harmonious aspects of India and to complement one another.[43]

Nehru remarked that Tagore's concept of universalism, however attractive, was in itself 'an airy nothing' without nationalism, while nationalism, in turn, was 'a narrow creed' without the wider concept. A chauvinistic nationalism made one overplay and exaggerate one's heritage while an internationalism which overlooked the deep-seated springs of nationalist consciousness was unrealistic. The challenge was to find the equilibrium for fitting in the two, and achieving a harmony between the outer and the inner life.[44] Although he disliked nationalism per se for being essentially anti-foreign and, therefore, limited in scope,[45] he felt that in the India of his day nationalism was an 'inevitable' and 'healthy growth'.[46] Nehru strove hard to understand India's rich heritage. Sometimes he despaired that the dead weight of superstition, ritual and prejudice would prevent the country from going forward. In such a frame of mind, he wrote to Frances Gunther what a joy it would be to write on a clean slate unencumbered by the burden of the past.[47] In other moments, he envisioned India as a palimpsest which acquired various influences and rarely sloughed off anything.[48] In trying to cross the chasm between tradition and modernity, Nehru's resolution was, 'Let us not say we are old, but that the old belongs to us, which suggests that we can with our heritage go forward to tomorrow.'[49] In attempting to understand the distinctive layered character of Indianness, Nehru shied away from using religion as the defining index of cultural identity. Convinced that religious preferences should be respected as strictly personal choices, he felt that only secularism could guarantee religious freedom. To him, the rich body of epic narratives, folklore and mythological stories that existed throughout the country with regional variations, or the wealth of architectural, artistic and religious motifs that showed a cohesive pattern despite nuanced varieties, all pointed towards a deep civilizational bond.[50] In the midst of this diversity, it was, however, important to build India's identity around certain broad liberal values of justice, equality, democracy and secularism.

A self-confessed socialist and republican, Nehru envisioned India through the levelling lens of social equity. However, he realized soon enough that in the Gandhi-led national movement all classes and vested interests would have to be accommodated on a common platform of anti-imperialism. Nevertheless, it remained important for him to secure the admission of the principles of socio-economic and gender equity in Congress policy and planning statements so that subsequent initiatives in free India could draw on the foundations laid and the precedents established. It was in keeping with this belief that he welcomed the declaration of Fundamental Rights and Economic Policy that was passed at the Karachi Congress of 1931. Nehru worked with Gandhi on the resolution, which went beyond the customary nationalist programme to hold an economic promise reflecting 'a new outlook in the Congress'.[51] The resolution combined general democratic demands (civil liberties, legal equality, adult suffrage, free primary education, state policy of religious neutrality) with basic promises to labour (end of forced labour, living wages, trade union rights, etc.), a clause about state control of key industries and mineral resources, and a moderate programme of agrarian change which would include substantial reductions in land revenue and rent, but with no mention of rural indebtedness or land redistribution or landlord elimination. As Nehru was to admit, 'A capitalist State could easily accept almost everything contained in that resolution.'[52] Gandhi explained that the zamindars and the maharajas could rest assured that the Congress did not seek to destroy them since all that the resolution sought was to 'indicate to the poor inarticulate Indian the broad features of Swaraj or Ramrajya'.[53] Although Bose regarded the resolution as an attempt to placate the socialist elements in the Congress,[54] and the British felt it was Gandhi's concession in lieu of securing Congress support for his Pact with Irwin in 1931, there was nothing dramatic or sensational about it. Its actual importance, however, lay in committing the Congress organization to provide, in any future constitution, for not only basic civil liberties, but also the essence of economic freedom.[55]

Nehru's endeavour to secure a Congress commitment for

planning initiatives continued. As chairman of the National Planning Committee in 1938, he was able to engage in preparing a bold and pioneering policy declaration, which was novel because it was articulated at a time when India had not yet secured independence. Conscious that planning could not be for the present but for an unascertained future, Nehru was careful to ensure that the process involved the widest cross section of people, ranging from hard-headed big businessmen to idealists and doctrinaires, socialists and near communists to technical experts and directors of industries from the provincial Congress governments. This 'strange assortment of different types' made it imperative that the focus should be on specific programmes rather than on articulating a common philosophy, which would be difficult to chart out between the contrasting approaches of socialism, seeking profit elimination, on the one hand, and capitalism, striving to retain free enterprise, on the other.[56]

Nehru characteristically chose to elaborate on the ideal of the Congress in deliberately imprecise and vague terms. He spoke of the need to establish a free and democratic state in India, with an egalitarian society where equal opportunities were provided for every member for self-expression and self-fulfilment and an adequate minimum was assured for securing a civilized standard of life.[57] While adhering to the spirit of the 1931 resolution on Fundamental Rights, that the state should own or control key industries and services, private enterprise was not ruled out either, though it would have to be strictly controlled and coordinated in accordance with the general plan. Conscious of the need to allay the apprehensions of big business, Nehru spoke of the need to adapt socialism to Indian conditions so that it did not combat capitalism but instead developed it. It would be absurd to chase out and put an end to the 'tribe of landlords, capitalists and the rest'. Instead, the introduction of socialism in India would be contingent on understanding the country's cultural conditions and the genius of the Indian people.[58]

Further, Gandhi's apprehension and concern regarding the possible threat that planning posed to his project of khaddar and cottage industries had to be dealt with. In the comprehensive scheme of planning, therefore, industries were grouped into heavy, medium and cottage, emphasizing their equal importance and stressing that they could all equally coexist. It was accepted that the charkha and khaddar created self-reliance and gainfully employed the wasted manpower of India.[59] By outlining all the broad options of planning, Nehru hoped that blueprints would be created and when the time came for giving effect to the plan, the then existing government could choose what basic policy they wished to adopt.[60] In the meantime, he was content to focus on non-controversial steps, such as a plan over the next ten years for improved nutrition, more clothing and better housing for every Indian, the introduction of compulsory programmes of physical fitness for boys and girls at every stage of education, and social and labour services for young people in projects of national utility. Twenty-nine sub-committees, specializing in a wide range of subjects—from agriculture, industry, commerce and finance to transport, education, public welfare, demographic relations and women's role in the planned economy—were set up to investigate and analyse the responses to a formidable questionnaire which had been widely distributed. By the summer of 1940, despite serious disadvantages posed by lack of a common viewpoint among planners, a paucity of data, and the knowledge that there would be no immediate implementation, seventeen sub-committees had presented final or interim reports, on the basis of which a comprehensive report began taking shape. The sub-committee on which Nehru placed the most importance, and which he acknowledged had done the most work, was that on women.[61] The report produced by the sub-committee was a comprehensive document whose recommendations were surprisingly modern and advanced.[62]

With the arrest of Nehru in October 1940, and Gandhi's veto against publishing the sub-committee reports, the entire planning project languished. However, it was not all in vain. As Nehru recalled, it was a vastly educative and path-breaking exercise.[63] Although Gandhi was to remain totally unconvinced about the need for the planning exercise, which he held was a waste of money and effort,[64] Nehru received full support from Subhas Bose, who as Congress president at Haripura in 1938 had initiated the National Planning Committee of which Nehru had been nominated chairman. The preoccupations of Subhas as Congress president, and later his involvement in the Congress presidential re-election crisis, left him with little time to personally pursue the planning initiative. However, both Bose and Nehru shared a keen interest and commitment to the planning process through which they could project their respective visions of a free and independent India.

To Tagore, Bose and Nehru were the only two 'modernists' who could be entrusted with the responsibility of drawing up a map of the future direction of India.[65] Unconvinced that Gandhi's programmes provided the only answer, Tagore was willing to recognize and support, from a distance, any personality that might emerge within the Congress with a legitimate alternative to the hitherto accepted Congress direction.[66] Hailing Subhas as Deshnayak, or the nation's leader, Tagore observed how he had followed the evolution of Subhas from an unsure, impetuous young man to an individual of considerable maturity and responsibility. He was confident that if there was a change in the direction and momentum of the movement for freedom, Subhas would prove equal to the task

187

of assuming the mantle of leadership.[67]

Tagore had certainly revised his opinion of the young man with whom he had returned on the same boat from England in 1921. An unimpressed Tagore had not responded favourably to Subhas's suggestion several years later that he request Bernard Shaw to write a foreword to Subhas's book, *Indian Struggle*.[68] However, over time Tagore came to believe in the need for fresh blood to enter the public arena and rescue politics in general, and Bengal politics in particular, from a sense of despondency and lack of purpose. He particularly agonized over the factionalism and intrigue indulged in by Bengal politicians and was deeply uncomfortable with Gandhi's Communal Award decision of 1932.[69] Tagore regarded the Award as having the potential to vitiate the communal atmosphere of Bengal by giving an electoral edge to the Muslims, where they were in any case in a majority, causing thereby considerable heartburn among a predominantly Hindu political elite. In vain did Tagore plead with Gandhi,[70] who, however, remained unconvinced and instead urged Tagore to persuade others in Bengal to accept his arguments.[71] Nor was Gandhi willing to consider Tagore's intercession on behalf of Subhas when he was pushed out of the Congress as a fallout of the Tripuri Congress debacle. Gandhi sent a message to Tagore through C.F. Andrews, saying that he should stay out of the controversy as Subhas had been acting like a 'spoilt child'.[72]

Subhas, too, over the years had evolved in his assessment of Tagore, who had not been his favourite early author; he had shared instead the passion of his mentor, C.R. Das, for Bankim Chandra Chattopadhyay. Subhas did not agree with Tagore that India had never been a nation. In the nationalism–internationalism debate, Subhas refuted charges that nationalism was narrow, selfish and aggressive, declaring instead that in India nationalism was inspired by the highest ideals of *Satyam* (the true), *Shivam* (the good) and *Sundaram* (the beautiful).[73] Emphasizing that the nation was no western concept, he referred to the extensive Indian empire under the Maurya emperor Asoka in the third century BC, which went beyond the existing boundaries of the country to include Afghanistan and a part of Persia.[74] However, over time he came to appreciate Tagore's world view and receptivity to international cultural influences which, Subhas felt, made him markedly different from Gandhi, who had generally an antagonistic view of western civilization. Initially out of tune with the points of view of both Gandhi and Tagore, which he clubbed together as the opinions of an older generation, over the years Subhas came to detect different strands in their thinking and identified with aspects of both.[75]

Among the Indian leadership, circumstances perhaps afforded Subhas the greatest opportunity not merely to contemplate India's potential prospects but also to try out, on a limited scale, the blueprint of his future vision. Out of the twenty-four years since 1921, when he returned from England, until his death in 1945, Subhas spent more than fourteen years either in captivity or in exile. This period, when he was not in the thick of political agitation, provided him with unique opportunities to reflect deeply on India's multilayered identity, envision a future for the country, and give effect to certain programmes during his Azad Hind initiative which could be continued in a post-colonial state. None of the other protagonists in this study were provided with opportunities before independence to try out the ideas they had envisioned about India's future.

This section, therefore, dwells longest on Subhas in particular, if only to focus on some of his thoughts and the programmes he had initiated. The innovativeness and considerable

significance of these initiatives have remained largely
unrecognized in view of the overall failure of the military
initiative. First, the overall thinking of Subhas on matters of
polity and socio-economic policy has been traced as it evolved
from a purely academic level to a reflective one. Subhas strove
hard to correlate his theoretical positions with the practical
realities of an India poised as it was between tradition and
modernity. The compulsions of ground realities and regional
requirements often made him alter or modify his stands on
important issues such as socialism, democracy or secularism.
Next, the concrete programmes envisaged by Subhas for India's
development at multiple levels, whether municipal or national,
have been elaborated. From various public platforms, he voiced
his thoughts on the details of planning, industrial growth, gender
equality and the development of a common lingua franca.
Finally, some of the programmes he was able to actually initiate
during his two stints, first with the Indian Legion in Germany
and then with the Azad Hind in south-east Asia, have been
examined. Although failures as military initiatives, these
provided a novel opportunity to test out many of his cherished
ideas and programmes for nation building. Subhas believed
that the leadership which led the country in a struggle for
liberty also had the responsibility to envisage a post-war
reconstruction programme. Kemal Ataturk remained his ideal
for having combined the roles of a revolutionary on the
battlefield with that of a nation maker.[76]

Subhas declared that perhaps his natural inclination was to
be a thinker first, though circumstances had forced him into a
life of hectic politics. He claimed to have 'certain definite ideas
on philosophic, social, economic and political problems', which
he wished 'to be amplified and worked out by the generation
that follows ours'.[77] With an academic interest in political
ideologies and social thought, which had begun with his study

of philosophy at university, he enjoyed interpreting the unfolding scenario of India in the context of changing international developments. Recalling his INA days, Captain Prem Sahgal commented that Subhas was a natural teacher or guru and enjoyed exchanges with his colleagues, which helped him to sharpen and fine-tune his own views.[78] Over the years, his thinking shed some of its fixed notions, making him more flexible and accepting of different points of view. Calling himself primarily a man of action, Subhas realized the need to manoeuvre around various theoretical stances and adopt positions which were dictated by India's own peculiar needs and the compulsions of the hour.

The quest to grasp 'what is India in reality',[79] particularly in the context of the discourse of tradition and modernity, which troubled Nehru deeply, was more confidently addressed by Subhas. During frequent bouts of forced exile abroad, Subhas felt compelled to defend India's traditional past and valorize it sufficiently so as to debunk the self-appointed colonial mission of civilizing and reforming. During his stay in various European countries, he was appalled to see the general ignorance about India and made it a mission to encourage local Indians to set up Indian associations where they could act as India's many ambassadors, presenting comprehensive information on India's past and speaking on the various dimensions of her national struggle for freedom against imperialism. To Subhas, this propaganda was very important for winning potential allies and supporters abroad for the Indian struggle, while earning for the Indians greater local respect and sympathy. Enthused by this assignment, he often tended to gloss over many of India's social ills while attempting to situate liberal western values within an Indian context. Conscious of the need to steer public opinion abroad, between the widely held impressions that India was either the land of snakes, fakirs and maharajas or that it was a land of mystics and philosophers, Subhas emphasized the unique sense of cultural and historical continuity present in India from ancient times to the present. As he put it, 'India of the past is not dead. India of the past lives in the present and will live on in the future.'[80] The cultural influences which entered India at different moments of her history had all been assimilated and absorbed into the country's national life. Subhas tried to cite indigenous equivalents of several of the western institutions which were to emerge later. Thus, the principle of democracy, he pointed out, was by no means unique to the West, as it had existed in India in the form of several ancient republics and self-governing village councils. In a similar vein, he referred to communities in India such as the Khasis of Assam whose tradition of joint ownership of property anticipated, in essence, the principle of communism.[81] Often such an exercise led Subhas to simplify India's complexities and make rather sweeping generalizations, such as when discussing India's religion at Tokyo University, he commented that in modern India there was no caste problem since intermarriages and interchangeable professions had taken away the problems posed by caste distinctions.[82]

Similarly, despite his impassioned rhetoric emphasizing the need to usher in an egalitarian society through 'a radical militant programme'[83] breaking down socio-economic divisions, he was to discover soon enough the hazards of supporting programmes with divisive consequences. Subhas had been scathing in his attacks on Gandhi for having held together in a coalition all the warring elements—landlord and peasant, capitalist and labour, rich and poor—through a policy of adjustment. Declaring that such a 'queer mixture' of political democracy and social conservatism[84] would surely be the 'ultimate cause of his (Gandhi's) failure',[85] Subhas had spoken loudly of the need to conduct the political struggle and the social struggle simultaneously. However, when faced with contentious issues concerning both labour and peasants in his own state, Bengal, he betrayed the same ambivalence as Gandhi. The gap, therefore, between the powerfully articulated positions of Subhas and his actual stands taken on specific issues, which made him appear as being impetuous and somewhat inconsistent, showed him to be ultimately much closer to Gandhi than perhaps he would ever have admitted.[86]

Confronted with the ground realities, Subhas gradually came to emphasize that the labour problem was irrevocably linked with the political question and that 'unless India wins her freedom . . . no ameliorative programme for the benefit of labour can be given effect to'.[87] Making a distinction between two phases of the Indian movement, Subhas said in an address to the Indian Political Conference in London in 1933,[88] that in the first phase there would be an anti-imperialist struggle with an all-inclusive alliance between the various constituents on the Congress platform. In the second phase, there would inevitably be an inter-class struggle to end all privileges, distinctions and vested interests. The socialist phase of the movement would begin with national reconstruction, after freedom was won.

While remaining an advocate of socialism as the perfect solution for India, Subhas's definition of socialism did not follow any western model and progressed in response to his perceptions of India's changing scenario and needs. He was quite definite that Marxist principles, which had given birth to Bolshevism in Russia, would not apply to India, which would instead have to forge an 'Indian socialism' which would suit our 'national requirements as well as our national genius'.[89] Subhas envisioned an ideal state or society where there would be complete economic emancipation, state control of the means of production and distribution of wealth, and social equality, where there would be no castes, no depressed classes, no inequality between the sexes either in social status or in law, and where women would be the equal partners of men.[90] Despite the economic appeal of many communist ideas, Subhas was convinced that the materialistic interpretation of history would not find unqualified acceptance in India and nor would the 'anti religious and atheistic ethos of Russia' be appropriate in India, with its deep spiritual character.[91] In a country of considerable religious and cultural pluralism, Subhas instead advocated 'a dose of secular and scientific training' leading to informed coexistence, where different religious groups could become acquainted with the traditions, ideals and history of one another, paving the way for 'cultural intimacy' and 'communal peace and harmony'[92] along the lines that Gandhi had recommended. Elaborating on this thought a decade later, Subhas spoke of the need to 'live and let live—a policy of complete non-interference in matters of conscience, religion and culture as well as of cultural autonomy for the different linguistic areas'.[93]

Inspired by the Vedantic thoughts of Vivekananda and Sri Aurobindo as also the Vaishnava ideals of C.R. Das, the socialism of Subhas echoed Gandhian feelings of compassion and tolerance. For Subhas, the principles constituting the essence of socialism were not only justice, equality and freedom but also equally love, as in compassion, and also discipline.[94] Disagreeing with Gandhi's view that after independence the Congress Party should wither away, Subhas felt instead that the Congress Working Committee, operating during the national movement as 'the directing brain' of the national army of freedom fighters, should take on the role of the 'Shadow Cabinet of Independent India'.[95] Once the goal of winning freedom had been achieved, freedom fighters, who were 'morally prepared men and women', should form the nucleus of a centralized and well-disciplined All India Party, to be called the Samyavadi Sangh,[96] which would then, in a 'scientific' manner, engage in the task of national reconstruction. The Sangh would have representatives in the National Congress, the Trade Union Congress, organizations of peasants, women, students, depressed classes, and sectarian and communal groups, and work throughout the country under the control of a central committee.

While consistently committed to *samya* or equality as the ultimate goal, Subhas moved considerable ground in envisioning the political structure that the India of the future should assume. From his initial commitment to democracy, he changed dramatically to supporting a totalitarian state. In 1928, Subhas had pleaded for sovereignty of the people in the true sense of democracy and had spoken of the need for a constitution to be drafted which would guarantee the elementary rights of citizenship.[97] In 1933, he reiterated, 'Free India will be a social and a political democracy.'[98] In his years in Europe from 1933 to 1936, however, he was sufficiently impressed with the discipline and efficiency of the Nazi state to write in his *Indian Struggle* about a synthesis between fascism and socialism as being ideal for India.[99] He genuinely felt that the discipline and efficiency of a Nazi state could be fruitfully incorporated with a set of socialist values to help a new India make a smooth transition to progress and development. Later, facing outraged critics such as the noted socialist R.P. Dutt, Subhas admitted that perhaps his choice of words had not been a happy one, but he had made his observations at a time when Germany had not embarked on its imperialist expedition.[100] Subhas remained convinced of the need for 'a strong central government' which would be directed by a responsible party run on a 'democratic basis', unlike the Nazi party based on the 'leadership principle'.[101] He was much influenced by the logic of Kemal Ataturk, the founder of modern Turkey, who, while declaring a democracy, had felt the need to put certain preventive restrictions on the people, lest early political crises shake the foundations of the new state.[102]

In the context of India, with its religious and cultural pluralism, Subhas envisaged that only a strong and centralized government in the first decades of its existence could ensure its happy transition into a successful polity. He wanted Muslims and other minority groups in India to be assured that they had 'nothing to fear on India winning her freedom', for 'a policy of complete non-interference in matters of conscience, religion and culture as well as of cultural autonomy for the different linguistic areas' would make them feel they had indeed 'everything to gain'. He felt it was necessary to underscore the importance of the minorities being fully 'entitled' to keep their 'personal law' without 'any change in this respect being imposed by the majority'.[103] The brief experience of the Congress in ministry making (1937–39), observed closely by Subhas during his Congress presidentship, disillusioned him considerably, and during his Tripuri address in 1939 he spoke forcefully of the need to 'ruthlessly remove whatever corruption or weakness has entered our ranks largely due to the lure of power'.[104] To Subhas, the only way to do so was by enforcing discipline, necessary as 'a basis of life', which could ensure that freedom did not regress into license and the absence of law.[105] The bitter experiences of Subhas during the infighting within the Congress, precipitated by his re-election as Congress president in 1939, defying Gandhi's candidate, doubtless strengthened this belief. Contemplating on *Free India and Its Problems* while in exile, Subhas was to repeat the need for a 'strong central government' behind which would stand 'a well-organised, disciplined all-Indian party'.[106] After taking up the military option and forming the Azad Hind Fauj, his firm belief in the efficacy of a strong government deepened, and in informal discussions with colleagues he spoke of his preference for a presidential form of government.[107] Gradually, democracy found no more mention in his speeches. Speaking in July 1944 over Rangoon Radio,[108] he said that he had no personal objection to dictatorship provided it was for the right cause. A few months later, he declared unequivocally that a democratic system could not solve the problems of free India. He felt India needed a 'State of an authoritarian character, which will work as an organ, or as the servant of the masses, and not of a clique or of a few rich individuals'.[109]

From the early years of his political leadership, whenever afforded an opportunity, Subhas would dwell on details of national planning and specific projects of reconstruction. His brief experience with the Calcutta Municipality, first as chief executive officer in 1923 under the stewardship of the mayor, C.R. Das, and later as mayor in 1930, gave him a first-hand feel for the task of civic administration. While jailed in Mandalay, Burma, he thought at great length about how to popularize home industries, and shared detailed ideas of improving rural skills, such as making buttons out of shells, moulding clay dolls, and utilizing the knowledge of women, particularly the widows of Bengal, in making crispies, pickles and chutneys so that these items could become commercially viable.[110] He also tried to follow up on several municipal ideas such as the cold storage scheme for perishable food, the reorganization of Calcutta's Hogg Market according to a modern vision of a marketplace, the introduction of the study of municipal government in the faculty of political science in Calcutta University, and the introduction of a health examination for students so as to monitor and improve their physique.[111] As mayor, Subhas spoke of the need to infuse programmes of civic improvement, such as better schools, housing, drainage, medical care, lighting and roads, with a genuine concern about the real needs of all sections of society, which C.R. Das called the spiritual equivalent of what modern Europe regarded as socialism. In an early reference to what he was to reiterate later, Subhas spoke of the need to combine 'justice, equality and love, which is the basis of socialism, with the efficiency and discipline of Fascism as it stands in Europe today'.[112] Quoting Bryce that the real school of democracy was local self-government, he welcomed the general global trend towards 'municipal socialism', which was 'a collective effort for the service of the entire community'.[113] Forced into political exile in Europe in 1933, Subhas secured help from the mayor of Vienna to visit a range of municipal institutions, from electric, gas and water works to drainage and sewage works, and also to learn about road making and road clearing.[114]

His experiences in Europe also convinced Subhas of the need to harness the advances of science and technology for the purpose of taking India on the road to national reconstruction. He emphasized that for the economic revival of the country, improvement only in the agricultural sector was not enough and that a comprehensive scheme of industrial development under state ownership and state control was also indispensable. During the course of his prolonged periods of stay in Europe, Subhas had systematically studied the patterns of industrialism in various countries and drawn lessons from them. In Ireland, in 1933, for instance, he discussed with the ministers of de Valera's government aspects of their industrial policy and learnt of their experiences with the abolition of landlordism.[115] Even later, while exiled in war-torn Europe, Subhas continued his interest in this matter and visited several chemical and armament factories in Czechoslovakia.[116] Despite Gandhian apprehensions of modern industrialism, Subhas firmly believed that India could not go back to the pre-industrial age. Although rooted in tradition, he was receptive to the gains of science and technology and declared the need for India to adapt to living in a modern world despite its ancient culture and tradition. Convinced that India having missed the Industrial Revolution needed 'a forced march',[117] Subhas felt it necessary to map out economic planning without waiting for the actual arrival of independence.

It was in this spirit that Subhas, as Congress president in Haripura in 1938, initiated the National Planning Commission in which he found a ready partnership with Nehru, whom he selected as the chairman of the Planning Committee. Regarding as imperative the need to initiate an industrial process along with the systematic and organized exploitation of the country's abundant natural resources and mineral wealth, Subhas classified industries into heavy, medium and cottage. Heavy industries formed the backbone of the national economy, while mother industries such as power supply, metal production and the manufacture of essential chemicals were vital for providing the basic infrastructure on which the entire development process depended. While admitting that any significant development in this sector could only be possible after central power was captured, Subhas spoke of the need, in the meantime, to encourage indigenous business leaders to begin medium-scale industries with government cooperation and help. All along he was careful to point out that cottage industries did not face any threat from heavy industries and should be encouraged to develop for they served an important historical, social and economic purpose, thereby allaying the fears of the Gandhian leadership. As an essential part of the planning initiative, Subhas sought to promote scientific and technical research, recommended training programmes abroad for students, and encouraged the formation of a permanent

Council for National Research. Although the national planning process, which was interrupted by the resignation of the ministries following the outbreak of war, proved to be very short lived, it was to remain a cherished ideal of Subhas. Even after his dramatic escape from India he continued to be interested in the various reports put together by the planning committees.[118]

The need to forge national unity on the basis of the advances made by scientific progress was a constant preoccupation with Subhas. With a restless zeal and inspired by the example of Russia, which in a short while had progressed from being a country of half-starved peasants to well-clothed industrial workers, Subhas envisaged an India where industrial progress could improve 'the standard of living of the people at large'.[119] While 'such modern scientific contrivances as aeroplanes, telephone, radio, films, television' would help knit together the scattered parts of the country, a common educational policy could infuse the population with a common spirit.[120] Recognizing that the problem of unity was largely 'psychological', Subhas felt that people needed to be 'drilled' to feel the 'will to be one nation and to hold together as one nation, when foreign domination ceases'.[121] However, while some of his suggestions for promoting national solidarity such as introducing a common dress or a common diet were rather extreme,[122] his idea of forging a common lingua franca found some favour with Nehru.

Endorsing the Congress view that the most natural lingua franca would be a mixture of Hindi and Urdu, he differed from Gandhi's recommendation that the language should be written in both the Nagari and Urdu scripts in order to create a bond between Hindus and Muslims. Instead, Subhas felt that the best solution would be to adopt the roman script which would bring India in line with the rest of the world. In India, where the vast majority was illiterate, with no knowledge of any script, it might be more practical to introduce them to a common roman script.[123] Subhas had given considerable thought to this issue and had held long discussions with the noted scholar and linguist, Suniti Kumar Chatterjee, on the subject.[124] Aware that his suggestion might sound 'anti-national' to some, who would 'gape with horror', he explained that his visit to Turkey in 1934 had demonstrated the advantages that had emerged from Kemal Ataturk's introduction of the roman script in that country.[125] Indeed, Nehru, too, had been greatly impressed by the success of the Latin script in Turkey and Central Asia and had taken the innovative step of issuing invitation cards for the wedding of his sister, Krishna, in Hindustani but written in the Latin script. However, to his disappointment, this was unfavourably received, particularly by Gandhi, which made him believe that despite his personal conviction the idea could never be accepted in India, where the script had an intimate and inalienable link with traditional language and literature.[126] Although Nehru was to abandon the idea of popularizing the Latin script, Subhas was afforded an opportunity to try out his linguistic experiment with considerable success in the INA.

In envisioning the future of India, both Nehru and Bose placed considerable importance on the position of women and sought to initiate measures by which they could be brought into the mainstream of the development process. One of the most comprehensive reports prepared under the aegis of the National Planning Committee was on women and their future in the planned economy of India. Proceeding along the guidelines suggested in the Fundamental Rights Resolution adopted by the Karachi Congress in 1931, the women's report in the National Planning Committee spelt out in detail the existing social, economic and legal obstacles to the achievement of equal status and opportunity and advocated ameliorative measures, which were surprisingly modern and advanced. While Nehru, as chairman of the National Planning Committee, was actively involved in its preparation, Subhas shared most of its recommendations, without, however, being directly involved because of his preoccupations as Congress president.

Over the years, at different platforms, Subhas had voiced specific concerns with regard to women's emancipation, many of which were now to find mention in the report. He had spoken strongly about the need to abolish socially backward customs such as child marriage, purdah and the dowry system,[127] and had expressed concern about women's education and their need to be economically self-supporting. He had also spoken about women's right of choice, the right to remain unmarried, and had stressed the importance of training them for self-defence. Anticipating the opposition that women might face, he urged young people to brace themselves to defy parents and relatives, if need be, with Arjuna's steadfastness.[128] Another issue that also preoccupied Subhas was India's increasing population which, he felt, needed to be urgently addressed by scientific methods of population control.[129] Confiding to a friend that Gandhi's formula of self-control might not find much favour, he spoke of the 'absolutely essential' need to control population.[130] The final report of the women's sub-committee proposed, among other things, important changes in personal law regarding property, inheritance and marriage, which would remove the disadvantages that women faced. Recognizing the crux of the problem to be the economic position of women, the report recommended various measures for providing the same opportunities to women for carrying on any trade or profession and accepting remunerative employment for such. It spoke of the need for women to be taught the art of self-defence through physical culture and suggested that every young man and woman of a certain age should contribute one year to national disciplined service. It also spoke of the need, from the national point of view, for men and women to have knowledge of scientific methods of birth control so that families could be limited and the rates of infant and maternal mortality could be brought down.

Apart from promoting the cause of women through long-term planning, Subhas more immediately sought to engage them actively in the national movement. While it was Gandhi who had for the first time introduced mass participation in the national movement and involved women, he had been prescriptive about the nature of women's participation. With Sita as his role model, he had stressed the innate propensity of women for non-violent suffering and felt that they would be the ideal satyagrahis for his campaigns of picketing, boycott and civil disobedience. However, Subhas did not envision women's participation along any such exclusive lines. He was keen to create a cadre of Indian women equal to men in valour and efficiency. It was in this spirit that he created a separate cadre of women to be part of the Bengal Volunteers, formed by him at the time of the Calcutta Congress in 1928. Although largely ceremonial, the sight of a 200-strong contingent of women marching in military uniform on the streets of Calcutta was a novel experience. While detractors dismissed this effort of Subhas as being largely theatrical,[131] the experience of networking and recruiting women from various women's revolutionary groups, mahila samitis and women's colleges, initiating them into self-defence training, and giving them a sense of participation and self-confidence, had momentous lessons for the future. Drawing on this experience, Subhas went on in 1943 to launch a plan for a more ambitious and large-scale involvement of Indian women in a patriotic military exercise directed from outside India. The desire to induct women into the service of the nation was not a mere symbolical gesture for Subhas. His dream was that after independence this committed cadre of women would be pressed into action to combat the more real war against inequality and social and economic deprivation. He was genuinely convinced that if half of India's population was not engaged in the country's development efforts, there could be no progress. He felt that educated women had a mission to spread the message of development among the uneducated.[132] As Congress president, he had initiated talks for the creation of a women's department within the AICC office to help increase women's membership in the Congress, to improve the working of local self-government bodies for constructive work like khadi, and to function as an information and enquiry bureau to supply information regarding international women's movements.

A dramatic chain of events followed Subhas's unsuccessful bid in 1939 to remain in the office of Congress president despite his victory in the election against the Gandhian candidate. Unfurling his flag of revolt, he was to form an alternative Forward Bloc Party. However, his arrest shortly after and then his sensational escape from house arrest in January 1941 saw Subhas leaving India and embarking on the last and most eventful chapter of his life. Taking up the military option, he sought intervention first from Germany and, when that proved impossible, from Japan. Although his bid to harness help from the Axis powers to defeat the British in India proved disastrous, this period did provide him with a unique opportunity to try out some of the most cherished programmes that he had envisioned for the future of India.

While Germany extended to Subhas the formal trappings of a government in exile, providing him with a residence, office, funds and the support of a special department on India in the

Foreign Office, it became painfully evident to him that German help would not be forthcoming.[133] Months after he arrived in Berlin, Germany unexpectedly attacked Soviet Russia in June 1941, dealing a severe blow to Subhas's dream of enlisting German help for advancing the cause of India's freedom.

Confronted with this disturbing realization and recognizing that he could never return to India, Subhas dedicated himself to the Free India Centre, set up in November 1941 with German help, meticulously planning its programmes and functioning. He also concentrated on forming an Indian Legion from among the captured soldiers of the British Indian Army, which he specified could only be used in the anti-British engagements of the Germans. While this concept was not unique,[134] Subhas put all his passion into infusing the Indian Legion with some of his distinctive programmes of cohesion and integration. Essential to his plans was the element of propaganda and persuasion, with which he hoped to enthuse alike Indian soldiers in the Legion and Indian civilians involved in the Centre. In many ways, he saw his initiatives as a hands-on experience for many of the programmes which could be introduced in the larger mission of India's post-colonial reconstruction.

Involving himself personally in the recruitment drive, Subhas visited the Annaberg camp in Germany in December 1941, where practically all the Indian prisoners of war had been assembled by the German authorities. Addressing the prisoners individually and in gatherings, Subhas, with characteristic enthusiasm, appealed to their patriotism as he attempted to knit together a cadre overcoming the differences of class, caste and religion, an experiment which he was to later carry to his Azad Hind initiative. Although many of the junior officers were sceptical, hundreds of prisoners of war volunteered to join the Legion. The success of Subhas lay in the uniqueness of his appeal. He promised that advancement in the Legion would depend only on ability and proof of aptitude, independent of birth or former grade. His close associate, N.G. Ganpuley, observed that the experiment to form Hindus, Sikhs, Muslims, Punjabis, Marathas, Bengalis and members of other religious communities into mixed military units was crowned with success. 'The intellectual basis for the growth and success of the Legion was created by Subhas Bose.'[135] By the autumn of 1942, members of the Indian Legion, numbering around 3,000, took their oath as soldiers of free India.[136]

In the functioning of the Free India Centre, Subhas drew on his previous experiences, and set up a Planning Commission, hoping to introduce on a small scale several initiatives which could be replicated later. Keen that the work of the Centre be taken seriously, he sought to promote its ceremonial aspect by creating a flag in the Congress tricolour with an embossed springing tiger as the insignia of the Azad Hind movement, and by adopting as its national anthem Rabindranath Tagore's song *Jana gana mana*. Hindustani in roman script was declared to be the official national language, while 'Jai Hind' was introduced as a common and universal Indian form of greeting.

One of the main purposes of the Free India Centre was to carry out extensive dissemination of news on India's national struggle through the regular publication of the periodical *Azad Hind* and by carrying out extensive broadcasts on the Azad Hind Radio. While technical support for the broadcasts was arranged by the Foreign Office with the German Radio, Subhas was able to enlist a committed group of young Indian students and journalists to help with his broadcasting initiative. Making clear that the broadcasts would be on Indo–British relations, Subhas was able to prevent any censoring by the Germans.[137] These broadcasts were the only means for Subhas, in exile from his country, to keep alive his involvement with the national movement. During the Quit India movement, when the Congress leadership was behind bars, he took upon himself the responsibility of giving a direction to his countrymen, through the broadcasts, to keep the movement alive. Initially slotted for forty-five minutes, the broadcasts slowly extended to over three hours daily, and consisted of bulletins in several Indian languages such as Hindi, Bengali, Pushto, Telugu, Tamil, Gujarati and Marathi, in addition to English. To represent the nationalist Muslim opinion, and counter the separatist claims of the Muslim League, he also initiated the Azad Muslim Radio. Tapping the diverse linguistic talents available among a dedicated coterie of friends and supporters, Subhas was able to forge a feeling of commitment for a common cause. It was the inspiration provided by him that made the motley group[138] stick together, functioning like a team through the war years, moving from place to place to escape Allied bombings. Alexander Werth, who was with the special division on India at the German Foreign Office and closely associated with Subhas during these years, assessed the impact that Subhas had on his associates. He wrote:

Bose succeeded in achieving in a miniature form in Europe what he did in a bigger way later in South-east Asia with the Indian National Army; namely to inspire every member with the idea of national unity irrespective of any consideration for race, caste, religious and regional beliefs. In Hilversum (a base for the Azad Hind broadcasts), all of them, regardless of their provincial origin or caste, lived together under one roof, ate the same food under the same conditions. Hindus, Muslims, Sikhs, Christians and Parsis all together, worked for one, united and free India.[139]

Realizing the futility of remaining indefinitely in Germany, Subhas, with Nazi help, left in March 1943, taking a German submarine from Kiel and changing into a Japanese one on the open seas off southern Africa; he reached the furthest point of Indonesia in July. Abid Hasan, who accompanied him, recalled that throughout the difficult voyage Subhas concentrated completely on India, its present challenges and his plans for the future of the country. Unfazed by some very anxious moments caused by Allied bombing, he continued to dictate notes to Hasan, to the amazement of all. Among the many ideas that Subhas tossed around in his mind during this momentous voyage, one in particular related to the unique concept of forming an all-women contingent as part of the Indian National Army that he was on his way to resurrecting.[140]

The First Indian National Army had been formed from among the Indian prisoners of war captured by the Japanese after their sensational victories over the British in 1941–42, in the Far Eastern sector. Encouraged by the Japanese, the INA leadership had been provided first by General Kiani and later by the Indian nationalist leader Rashbihari Bose, who had been in political exile for several years. However, although the idea had caught on, the initiative was not successful because of the simmering tensions that lay between the various constituents of the army, accentuated by communal feelings and heightened by the conflicting personalities of the leaders. Despite his efficiency, General Kiani found himself unpopular even among the Japanese, who ordered his arrest. The advanced age of Rashbihari Bose made it impossible for him to assume leadership. There was, therefore, a sense of great anticipation and apprehension not only among the Indian population in south-east Asia and the defunct INA, but also among the Japanese leadership, when Subhas appeared on the scene.

The task facing Subhas was tough. Due to his enforced halt

in Germany, he had missed the high point of Japan's successes, which he had hoped to use to India's advantage. Already in 1943, the tide was turning in the military fortunes of the Axis powers. The INA leadership that he took over had a troubled past. Subhas's task was to convince the wary Japanese, encourage the uncertain Indian population in south-east Asia and inspire the Indian military prisoners of war, suspicious of a civilian leader, of the credibility of his calling. The infectious enthusiasm of Subhas, his total belief and conviction in a dearly held cause, and the sincerity of purpose that he exuded, achieved the impossible. His phenomenal success on all counts, however, remained largely unnoticed because of the ultimate failure of the military mission.

The importance of Subhas's INA venture lay in his ability to find a practical application for some of his cherished ideas of nation building. The concepts of equality, justice, love and discipline that he had spoken of time and again were now to find practical application as he attempted to build up a cohesive fighting force from among diverse participants. The Japanese leadership, which had been apprehensive of his assuming leadership of the INA even before he actually arrived on the scene, underwent a sea change after Prime Minister Tojo met him in July 1943.[141] As in Germany, in Japan too, Subhas was able to secure the honour and prestige of an Indian government in exile with the commitment that the Indian forces would not be used for any Axis imperialist aims but would be reserved exclusively for an impending attack on the British position in India. While the Japanese demonstrated their sincerity by gifting the Andaman and Nicobar islands to the Azad Hind government, Subhas in a demonstrative gesture of equality gifted the Japanese the funds he had raised, to purchase a war plane. Committed to returning the German loans incurred on the Free India initiative, Subhas periodically sent remittances from the large amounts of funds he raised in south-east Asia. Keen to follow protocol so that the credibility of his initiative could not be underestimated, Subhas kept the Japanese ambassador designate to the Azad Hind government waiting in Singapore because his papers were not in order. Determined not to be bypassed in the military programme, Subhas kept up his insistence that the INA be an advance guard in any Japanese offensive and not be regarded as a mere symbolical presence or an add-on.[142] Similarly, he demanded that the Japanese overcome their cultural reservations and treat with seriousness and respect the all-women Rani of Jhansi regiment that he had initiated within the INA. Subhas's earnest attempts to demand equal treatment from the Japanese, even while seeking their help, raised him in the estimation of not only the local Indian population in south-east Asia but also among the Indian prisoners of war.

The majority of Indians in the Malay peninsula were principally workers on rubber plantations who had left their country of origin in large numbers at the beginning of the twentieth century, lured by better financial prospects. Though many married locals, complete social integration had proved elusive for both the coolie labour as also for those in more successful business operations. Subhas's open call to them to join or financially support a national army for the independence of India, which would work in tandem with Gandhi's movement, gave them an opportunity to redeem their national pride. Subhas's phenomenal powers of persuasion, accompanied by extensive tours, led to large-scale recruitment in the INA as also generous monetary contributions. In return for participation, Subhas promised equality of treatment, justice and fair play in the INA so that a camaraderie could be built up ignoring the traditional divides of caste, class and gender. Women responded in large numbers to Subhas's call, with the full support of the male members of their families. They joined the Rani of Jhansi regiment where their lives took an unprecedented turn. Donning trousers, cutting their hair short, learning how to wield guns, these essentially unlettered women from plantation labour families now found a new reason to assert their identity. Their lives on the plantation had often meant hard work in the fields and homes as also surrendering to the demands made on their bodies by their employers.[143] In his call, Subhas spoke not merely of the women's involvement in a struggle which would free their mother country from colonization but also spoke of the women's own emancipation and freedom to demand equal rights and no longer be the exploited sex.[144] This initiative of Subhas to integrate women into the military as a fighting force was probably one of the first conscious attempts ever to do so.

Among the Indian prisoners of war, Subhas's call carried an equally persuasive appeal. While there was an initial disbelief among some of the Sandhurst-trained officers regarding the authority of a civilian leader, there was a gradual recognition of his grasp of military detail as also an appreciation of his ability to lucidly present to them a cogent picture of India's history, tradition and the exploitative role of British colonialism. Recalling the impact of Subhas, Shah Nawaz Khan observed, 'I was hypnotised by his personality and his speeches. He placed the true picture of India before us and for the first time in my life I saw India through the eyes of an Indian.'[145] The prospect of serving in an army where promotions could no longer be denied by the white rulers, and where there was a promise to the ranks that there would be no discrimination along caste, class or religious lines, seemed a most encouraging prospect. In addition, Subhas pledged that the INA would ultimately form the nucleus of an Indian Army in free India, which proved to be a great incentive. In the 40,000-strong INA, with a women's contingent of 1,000, Subhas was able to introduce some of his concepts of justice, equality and discipline while instilling a love which endured in the form of a fierce loyalty long after the battle was lost and their leader dead.

One of the great successes of Subhas was to introduce Hindi in the romanized script as the language of the INA. Despite strong roots in his own regional language, Subhas, perhaps more than most politicians from Bengal, realized the importance of using a common language to knit together a people as diverse as Indians. Always addressing large gatherings of Indian military men, whether in Germany or Asia, in Hindustani, Subhas constantly tried to improve his own knowledge by being attentive to the various nuances of the language. Captain Prem Sahgal has humorously recalled his painstaking attempts to acquire a precision in the language.[146] Subhas firmly believed that the Hindustani taught should not be merely a working knowledge of Hindi but should also include the full complement of Urdu words. The INA watchwords of unity, faith and sacrifice were thus rendered as *ittefaq*, *itmad* and *kurbani* rather than *ekta*, *viswas* and *balidan* as the pure Hindi version would have been.[147] He was convinced that in a country with high rates of illiteracy, it would be useful to introduce one language in a common roman script which could later help in learning the English language and comprehending scientific terms. Recording the phenomenal success of this intervention, Captain Lakshmi Sahgal wrote, 'Within three months illiterate recruits to the INA, those whose mother tongue was Tamil, Malayalam or Hindi, were able to read and write Roman Hindustani. It also proved to be a boon to the signaller who could train new recruits in the Morse code.'[148] Gripped with this idea of engendering a feeling of oneness through a common language, Subhas encouraged the composition of a series of patriotic songs in Hindustani to build up the INA morale.

Tagore's *Jana gana mana*, which he had adopted as the national anthem for the Free India Centre in Germany, was given a dramatically different Hindustani version while being sung to the original tune.[149]

Another cherished ideal of Subhas was to promote a deep-seated understanding and tolerance among the various religious and ethnic groups in India. An informed coexistence between communities, he felt, would work better for a country with a deep religious ethos rather than a strict relegation of religion to the private realm as implied in the notion of secularism. Accordingly, Subhas encouraged common participation in religious festivities while keeping the observance of beliefs a strictly private matter. On Diwali, for instance, Muslim officers organized a *bada khana* or feast, while on Id Hindus organized the same for their Muslim colleagues.[150] On Christmas there was carol singing, and though there were very few Indian Christians in the regiment, the women in the Rani of Jhansi regiment organized an occasion of musical celebration. Subhas firmly believed that religious identities should be kept intact while there should be an informed tolerance for one another. While advocating the abolition of separate caste kitchens, he did not welcome, for instance, an initiative among the Indian Legion in the Koenigsbrueck camp in Germany to compose a common prayer for Indians of all regions and religions addressing God as 'Malik' in the bhakti tradition of Kabir. Dismissing this initiative as a 'stunt', Subhas explained that if the religious idiom was used as a strategy for unifying people, it could be used as a divisive tool as well. He encouraged Indians of different religions to use the separate congregational centres for prayers but while together, to cherish unifying national sentiments.[151] Subhas also made it a point to have Muslim officers in visible positions of importance in the INA structure to bring about a more meaningful cooperation. A Muslim colleague commented that by making Muslims in the INA feel that they were ambassadors working for their country's cause, Subhas had worked like 'a wizard's wand on their confidence'.[152]

At the same time, Subhas worked hard to break the divisive caste barriers of ritual and tradition which had stood in the way of a closer integration. By ordering soldiers and civilians to share a common kitchen, he initiated what his INA colleague General J.K. Bhonsle called 'a social revolution'. 'Men who had clung all their lives to their orthodoxy became cosmopolitans overnight.'[153] However, while ordering the men of the Azad Hind Fauj to drink water and tea from common containers and sit together for meals, he was careful to respect their sensitivities by forbidding beef and pork in the kitchen. With a basically vegetarian meal, mutton was served only on request. Subhas also took the initiative to challenge certain discriminatory Hindu religious practices with a tenacity that recalled Gandhi's perseverance during the temple entry agitation. Abid Hasan recalled the response of Subhas to a local Hindu temple in Singapore, known for its rigid denial of access to non-caste Hindus, which had promised contributions for the Azad Hind fund provided Subhas visited it. Knowing the temple's record, Subhas in characteristic style took up the offer to visit the temple, accompanied, however, by officers and men carefully chosen to represent all the major religions. Abid Hasan wrote that when he found himself in the temple's sanctuary, 'I did what Netaji did, submitting the offerings already prepared for us and being blessed in turn by a *tilak* on the forehead put there, with a reverent smile on his face, by the high priest himself.'[154] Subhas followed this up with an impassioned speech to the temple where he spoke of universal brotherhood, which brought 'a glow in the faces of all'.[155]

Keen to preserve the feeling of equality and fairness that he had so assiduously cultivated in the INA, Subhas emphasized the need to discipline those who were found insensitive to communal, caste or gender issues. Strong orders were issued, therefore, that use of socially derisive terms such as 'coolie' or 'rubber tapper' in reference to labour recruits into the INA would be severely punished.[156] Concerned about the all-women Rani of Jhansi regiment that he had initiated, Subhas issued comprehensive instructions that its members were to be treated with respect like sisters while being given training and defended from the overall scepticism with which the Japanese had viewed their formation. He went to the extent of issuing orders to the INA that in the case of any Japanese maltreatment of an Indian woman, they were at liberty to use force, or even shoot, in a preventive action.[157] Discipline remained an important watchword with Subhas, and he was prepared to be quite ruthless in dealing with offenders or deserters.

While organizing the INA, Subhas was constantly aware that he was drawing up a blueprint which could later be introduced in India. While planning the various ministries of his Provisional Government, he, therefore, placed importance not only on departments which would manage the war effort but he also created other departments, such as women's affairs and publicity and propaganda, which could form the nucleus of similar initiatives in independent India. It was in the same spirit that he created the National Bank of Azad Hind in 1944. Captain Lakshmi Sahgal, who helped create the Rani of Jhansi regiment and was selected to head the Provisional Government's ministry on women, observed that it was Subhas's idea that after independence the dedicated band of women in the Rani of Jhansi regiment would be useful role models to inspire confidence and bring about development, education, and self-sufficiency among unlettered rural women in India. Subhas had also hoped that the INA would form the nucleus of the Indian armed forces after independence, and herald a new trend with its proven values of communal harmony and peaceful coexistence among men of various regional backgrounds.[158] He emphasized the importance of the INA entering India with perfect unity, so that they could form a new government and maintain law and order.[159] After independence, however, Nehru, as India's first prime minister, failed to be persuaded that the Ranis had any particular role to play in the advancement of rural women since the general development plans of the country were already in place.[160] Nor did the INA become integrated into the armed forces of independent India, largely due to political considerations. Many of Subhas's dreams remained unrealized.

Both Subhas and Nehru had an international outlook and saw India's problems against the bigger picture. Convinced that the country could never progress in isolation, they both sought to correlate its growth with international developments. However, the lessons they drew from their analyses were strikingly different. Nehru found an intellectual affinity with democracies upholding liberal principles and regarded them as vital to check the naked imperialism of the fascist powers. He also had an abiding faith in international bodies such as the United Nations and placed his trust in their ability to stand guarantee for greater justice and fair play in the post-war world. Subhas, on the other hand, was above all a realist and tended to view the international scenario principally with a view to manipulating it in India's favour. It was this logic that made him wilfully close his eyes to the internal developments in fascist states like Germany, Italy and Japan while seeking their collaboration in a military intervention against British imperialism. While this gamble of his proved futile, and the INA participation in a Japanese military offensive in the north-east of India ended in disaster, many other assessments of Subhas regarding an emerging world order in a post-war scenario seem in retrospect to be very insightful.

Subhas was convinced that the USA would manipulate its involvement on the Allied side to ultimately establish world domination. Without mincing words, Subhas declared in a hard-hitting radio address, 'In my opinion, world enemy number one is America—and if America were to succeed by any chance, we would have American hegemony in this world. Spokesmen of America's Dollar Imperialism have been openly talking of the American Century and make no secret of their ambitions to dominate the world.'[161] Subhas foresaw that the massive US military help to Britain would deplete British assets and securities, reducing her to 'a colony of Roosevelt's New Empire'.[162] He predicted that Britain's predicament would be that of 'the British Lion metamorphosed into a tame lamb by the master of the White House'.[163]

Subhas envisaged a special role for India in the world scenario. Its unique geographical position between the East and the West gave it a natural geopolitical importance. In order to reverse the disadvantages suffered from years of isolation, India had to wake up to modern-day reality recognizing that frontiers, in a way, had been obliterated and the world was one unit. An active foreign policy establishing international contact would stand India in good stead as 'India has something original to contribute to the culture and civilisation of the world in almost every department of human life'. Subhas dreamt of a time and day in the 'near future' when India would be 'called upon to play an important role in world history'. Drawing from examples in history, he recalled how the seventeenth century had seen England making remarkable contributions to world civilization with ideas of constitutional and democratic government; the eighteenth century had seen the momentous lessons of the Revolution in France; the nineteenth century had seen Germany's remarkable gift of Marxist philosophy; and the twentieth century had seen Russian achievements with the proletarian revolution. The next century would be for India to contribute to the culture and civilization of the world.[164]

~

NOTES

Chapter One
1. Atal Bihari Vajpayee, 'My Musings from Kumarakom', 2 January 2001.
2. Subhas Chandra Bose, February 1938, The Haripura Address, *Netaji Collected Works*, vol. 9, New Delhi: OUP, 1995, pp. 10–11.
3. Vajpayee, 'My Musings from Kumarakom'.
4. *Selected Works of Jawaharlal Nehru* [henceforth referred to as *SWJN*], Advisory board: M. Chalapathi Rau, H.Y. Sharada Prasad, and B.R. Nanda; general editor: S. Gopal. New Delhi: Orient Longman, 1972, vol. 6, p. 2.

Chapter Two
1. Speech at a rally at Padang, 9 July 1943, File No. 199, Indian National Army [henceforth referred to as INA], National Archives of India [henceforth referred to as NAI], New Delhi.
2. Leonard Gordon, *Brothers against the Raj: A Biography of Sarat and Subhas Chandra Bose*, New Delhi: Viking Penguin, 1990, p. 304.
3. In 1940, Subhas sent Lal Shankar Lal, general secretary of the Forward Bloc, to Japan, where he met Rashbihari Bose and Japanese officials, but was caught by the British and his mission revealed. See Gordon, *Brothers against the Raj*, op. cit., p. 416.
4. Subhas's nephew, Amiya Bose, then a student in England, took messages from his uncle to Comintern officials in Europe.
5. Gandhi to Subhas, 29 December 1940, in *The Alternative Leadership: Speeches, articles, statements and letters, June 1939–January 1941 / Subhas Chandra Bose: Netaji Collected Works*, vol. 10, edited by Sisir Kumar Bose and Sugata Bose, New Delhi: OUP, 1985, p. 155.
6. This was the view of J.H. Broomfield, *Elite Conflict in a Plural Society:*

        Twentieth Century Bengal, Berkeley: University of California Press, 1968. For an analytical account, see Rajat Kanta Ray, *Social Conflict and Political Unrest in Bengal 1875–1927*, New Delhi: OUP, 1984.

7.   *Netaji Collected Works, Vol. 2, 1920–42*, Calcutta: Netaji Research Bureau, 1980, pp. 57–60.

8.   M.K. Gandhi, *Autobiography*, in *Collected Works of Mahatma Gandhi* [henceforth referred to as *CWMG*], Publications Division, Ministry of Information and Broadcasting, Government of India, vol. 39, p. 190.

9.   See Mario Prayer, *The Gandhians of Bengal: Nationalism, Social Reconstruction and Cultural Orientations 1920–1942*, Istituti Editoriali e Poligrafici Internazionali, Roma, 2001, p. 245.

10. N.C. Chaudhuri, *Thy Hand Great Anarch! India 1921–1952*, London: 1987, p. 435.

11. Quoted in Mukund Ramrao Jayakar, *The Story of My Life*, vol. I, Bombay: Asia Publishing House, 1958, p. 509.

12. Bose, *Netaji Collected Works: Vol. 2, The Indian Struggle, 1920–1942*. Published for the Netaji Research Bureau, by Sisir Kumar Bose, Calcutta, 1981.

13. Jawaharlal Nehru, *An Autobiography: With musings on recent events in India*, New Delhi: Allied Publishers, 1962, p. 81.

14. Ibid., p. 104.

15. Ibid., p. 166.

16. To Rangaswamy Iyengar, General Secretary of the Congress, 25 January 1927, *SWJN*, vol. 2, pp. 258–59.

17. To Gandhi, 11 January 1928, *SWJN*, vol. 3, p. 12.

18. Bose, *Netaji Collected Works, Vol. 2, Indian Struggle*, Calcutta: Netaji Research Bureau, 1981, pp. 205–06.

19. Ibid.

20. 'The National Congress', *Young India*, 5 January 1928, *CWMG*, vol. 35, p. 438.

21. Gandhi to Nehru, 4 January 1928, *CWMG*, vol. 35, pp. 432–33.

22. Nehru to Gandhi, 11 January 1928, *SWJN*, vol. 3, pp. 10–15.

23. Gandhi to Nehru, 17 January 1928, *CWMG*, vol. 35, pp. 469–70.

24. Nehru to Gandhi, 23 January 1928, *SWJN*, vol. 3, pp. 18–19.

25. 16 January 1928, Jawaharlal Nehru MSS, vol. 22, NMML.

26. Speech at the All Parties Conference, *SWJN*, vol. 3, p. 60.

27. Nehru to Gandhi, 30 June 1928, *SWJN*, vol. 3, p. 50.

28. Interview to the Press, 16 November 1928, *SWJN*, vol. 3, p. 77.
29. See Reba Som, *Differences within Consensus: The Left–Right Divide in the Congress 1929–1939*, New Delhi: Orient Longman, 1995, p. 88.
30. Gandhi to Nehru, 4 January 1928, *CWMG*, vol. 35, p. 433.
31. 'What's in a name?', 29 December 1928, *CWMG*, vol. 38, p. 296.
32. Gandhi's speech on resolution on Nehru Report, Calcutta Congress, 26 December 1928, *CWMG*, vol. 38, p. 271.
33. Rajendra Prasad, *Autobiography*, Bombay: Asia Publishing House, 1957, p. 289.
34. Jawaharlal Nehru, Calcutta Congress 1928, in *Indian Annual Register*, II, July–December 1928.
35. Gandhi's speech on resolution on Nehru Report, Calcutta Congress, 31 December 1928, *CWMG*, vol. 38, p. 307.
36. Nehru, *An Autobiography*, op. cit., p. 173.
37. 'My Notes: Gujarat's Diary', 24 November 1929, *CWMG*, vol. 42, p. 209.
38. Jawaharlal Nehru to Gandhi, 13 July 1929, *SWJN*, vol. 4, p. 156.
39. Speech at Lahore Congress, December 1929, *Select Speeches of Subhas Chandra Bose*, Delhi, 1962, p. 61.
40. 'Speech at Congress Session, Lahore, 31 December 1929', *CWMG*, vol. 42, p. 356.
41. Gandhi to Nehru, 1 July 1929, *CWMG*, vol. 41, p. 153.
42. Subhas Bose, *The Indian Struggle*, op. cit., p. 180.
43. Telegram from Lahore, File No. G-126/1930, AICC Papers, NMML.
44. Nehru to Abdur Rahim, 7 January 1939, File No.G-126/1930, AICC Papers, NMML.
45. 'Clearing the Issue', *Young India*, 30 January 1930, *CWMG*, vol. 42, pp. 434–35.
46. Subhas Bose, *The Indian Struggle*, op. cit., p. 245.
47. Gandhi to Purushottamdas Thakurdas, 9 February 1930, *CWMG*, vol. 42, p. 465.
48. Nehru, *An Autobiography*, op. cit., p. 210.
49. Subhas Bose, *The Indian Struggle*, op. cit., p. 199.
50. *Liberty*, 20 August 1929.
51. 24 August 1929, Mahatma Gandhi, *Collected Works*, vol. XLI, p. 276.
52. *Amrita Bazar Patrika*, 10 March 1931.
53. Subhas Bose, *The Indian Struggle*, op. cit., p. 280.
54. Nehru, *An Autobiography*, op. cit., p. 257.

55. Bose, *Select Speeches*, op. cit., *Liberty*, 28 and 29 March 1931.
56. Patel to Nehru, 21 July 1931, File No. G-60/1931, AICC Papers, NMML.
57. 'Alone, yet not alone', *Young India*, 28 August 1931, *CWMG*, vol. 47, p. 369.
58. Government of India, Home Political, File No. 143/1931, NAI.
59. In a speech at Shraddhananda Park, Calcutta, mid December 1931. See Gordon, *Brothers against the Raj*, op. cit., p. 253.
60. File No. G-120/1931, Part 1, AICC Papers, NMML.
61. See Dilip Kumar Roy, *The Subhash I Knew*, Bombay: Nalanda Publications, 1946, and Dilip Kumar Roy, *Netaji, the Man: Reminiscences*, Bombay: Bharatiya Vidya Bhavan, 1966.
62. Mentioned by Sisir Bose in conversation with the author, September 1998, Netaji Research Bureau, Calcutta.
63. Nathalal D. Parikh, 'Reminiscences', in *Life and Work of Netaji Subhas Chandra Bose: A nation's homage*, edited by P.D. Saggi, Bombay: Overseas Publishing House, no date, p. 38.
64. Personal interview of Mrs Vetter with Gordon. See Gordon, *Brothers against the Raj*, op. cit., pp. 283–84.
65. Bose to Nehru, 4 March 1936, in *Netaji Collected Works*, vol. 8, Netaji Research Bureau, edited by Sisir Kumar Bose and Sugata Bose, New Delhi: OUP, 1994, p. 144.
66. Nehru to Bose, 26 March 1936, *SWJN*, vol. 7, p. 407.
67. Gandhi to Ramsay MacDonald, 18 August 1932, *CWMG*, vol. 50, p. 383.
68. Nehru, *An Autobiography*, op. cit., p. 370.
69. Note dated August 1934, *SWJN*, vol. 6, pp. 270–73.
70. Nehru to Gandhi, 13 August 1934, Jawaharlal Nehru MSS, vol. 24, NMML.
71. *Bombay Chronicle*, 19 July 1934.
72. Nehru, *An Autobiography*, op. cit., p. 546.
73. Gandhi to Vallabhbhai Patel, 18 April 1934, *Letters to Sardar Vallabhbhai Patel*, Ahmedabad; Navajivan Publishing House, 1957.
74. Presidential Address, Lucknow Congress, 12 April 1936, *SWJN*, vol. 7, pp. 170 et seq.
75. Nehru to Gandhi, 25 May 1936, File No. II/36, Col. 1, Rajendra Prasad MSS, NAI.
76. Circular to Pradesh Congress Committees, 22 April 1936, File No.

CPIII/36, Col 1, Rajendra Prasad MSS, NAI.

77. 'The Role of Big Business', Speech in Bombay, 20 May 1936, *SWJN*, vol. 7, p. 244.
78. 'Manifesto of the 21', *Tribune*, 20 May 1936.
79. Letter from Prasad, Patel, Rajagopalachari, etc. to Nehru, 29 June 1936, vol. 85, Part 1, Jawaharlal Nehru MSS, NMML.
80. Patel to Prasad, 29 May 1936, *CWMG*, vol. 62, Appendix V, p. 476.
81. Nehru to Gandhi, 5 July 1936, vol. 24, Jawaharlal Nehru MSS, NMML.
82. Gandhi to Nehru, 15 July 1936, *CWMG*, vol. 63, p. 144.
83. Ibid.
84. Gandhi to Nehru, 30 July 1936, vol. 24, Jawaharlal Nehru MSS, NMML.
85. 11 April 1936, *SWJN*, vol. 7, p. 167.
86. Birla to Thakurdas, 20 April 1936, File No. 177, Sir Purushottamdas Thakurdas MSS, NMML.
87. Speech at Gandhi Seva Sangh Meeting, 17 April 1937, *CWMG*, vol. 65, pp. 99–100.
88. *Mahratta*, File No. III/35, Rajendra Prasad MSS, NAI.
89. Gandhi to Amrit Kaur, 19 July 1937, *CWMG*, vol. 65, p. 380.
90. Prasad to Patel, 6 December 1937, File No. 1/R.P., PSF (1) 1937, Rajendra Prasad MSS, NAI.
91. Translated from Gujarati by Mahadev Desai, 26 August 1936, File No. 9-85 (1) of 1936, AICC Papers, NMML.
92. Gandhi to Patel, 1 November 1937, *Letters to Sardar Vallabhbhai Patel*, Ahmedabad, 1957.
93. 'Telegram to Subhas Chandra Bose, January 23, 1938', *CWMG*, vol. 66, p. 346.
94. See Chapter Four, 'Envisioning India'.
95. Nehru to Subhas Bose, 4 February 1939, *SWJN*, vol. 9, pp. 482–83.
96. Nehru, Press Statement, 26 January 1939, *SWJN*, vol. 9, p. 477.
97. Statement of 25 January 1939, Bose, *Crossroads*, Calcutta: Netaji Research Bureau, 1981, p. 91.
98. Statement of Subhas Bose, 27 January 1939, in *Netaji Collected Works*, vol. 9, pp. 83–84.
99. *Indian Annual Register*, 1939, vol. 1, pp. 314–15.
100. Patel to Gandhi, 24 December 1938, Jawaharlal Nehru MSS, vol. 81, NMML.
101. Nehru to Bose, 3 April 1939, *SWJN*, vol. 9, pp. 538–39.

102. See Nirad C. Chaudhuri, *Thy Hand, Great Anarch*, Chapter 4, Gandhi–Bose Feud, p. 510.
103. 'Nehru's interview to Amrita Bazar Patrika, London, 5/9/38', *SWJN*, vol. 9, p. 130.
104. K.M. Munshi, Law Minister in the Bombay Government, was given the information by the Raj's Director of Central Intelligence, which he passed on to Gandhi. See Rajmohan Gandhi, *The Good Boatman: A Portrait of Gandhi*, New Delhi:Viking Penguin, 1995, pp. 364–65.
105. Mihir Bose, *The Lost Hero: A Biography of Subhas Bose*, London; New York: Quartet Books, 1982, p. 136.
106. Gordon, *Brothers against the Raj*, op. cit., p. 368.
107. 'Statement to the Press', *CWMG*, vol. 68, pp. 359–60. Originally published in *Harijan*, 4 February 1939.
108. M.N. Roy, letter of 1 February 1939, in file 'Bose and Forward Bloc', M.N. Roy Papers, Dehra Dun.
109. Gandhi to Bose, 4 February 1939, *A Bunch of Old Letters*, p. 317.
110. R.K. Dalmia to Rajendra Prasad, 15 March 1939, File 4M/39, Col. 1, Rajendra Prasad MSS, NAI.
111. Gordon, *Brothers against the Raj*, op. cit., p. 376.
112. 'Where are we?', 28 February 1939, *SWJN*, vol. 9, p. 490.
113. Nehru to Subhas, 3 April 1939, *A Bunch of Old Letters*, Bombay:Asia Publishing House, 1960, p. 355.
114. Subhas to Amiya Nath Bose, 17 April 1939, *Crossroads*, op. cit., p. 113.
115. Subhas to Gandhi, 29 March 1939, in *Netaji Collected Works*, vol. 9, p. 133.
116. Subhas to Gandhi, 25 March 1939, in *Netaji Collected Works*, vol. 9, p. 129.
117. Subhas to Gandhi, 25 March 1939, File No. 2G/39, Col 1, Rajendra Prasad MSS, NAI.
118. 'Statement of resignation from Congress Presidentship', May 1939, *Crossroads*, op. cit., p. 171.
119. Nehru to Gandhi, 17 April 1939, Jawaharlal Nehru MSS, vol. 25, NMML.
120. 'The AICC and After', 24 May 1939, *SWJN*, vol. 9, pp. 577–79.
121. Tagore's telegram to Gandhi, *CWMG*, vol. 71, p. 50, footnote 2.
122. Letter to C.F. Andrews, 15 January 1940, *CWMG*, vol. 71, pp. 113–14.
123. 'The Charkha', *Harijan*, 13 January 1940, *CWMG*, vol. 71.
124. Letter to C.F. Andrews, 15 January 1940, *CWMG*, vol. 71, pp. 113–14.

125. Gordon, *Brothers against the Raj*, op. cit., p. 401.
126. Bose, *Crossroads*, op. cit., p. 229.
127. Letter of 2 March 1940, *SWJN*, vol. 10, pp. 345–46.
128. Gandhi to Subhas, 29 December 1940, *Crossroads*, op. cit., pp. 405–06.
129. Ibid.

Chapter Three

1. Bhikhu Parekh, *Colonialism, Tradition and Religion: An Analysis of Gandhi's Political Discourse*, New Delhi: Sage Publications, 1989, p. 64.
2. Leonard Gordon, *Brothers against the Raj: A Biography of Sarat and Subhas Chandra Bose*, New Delhi: Viking Penguin, 1990, p. 385.
3. Special Order of the Day, 1 January 1945 by Subhas Chandra Bose, Supreme Commander, Azad Hind Fauj, File No. 199, INA, INA Papers, NAI.
4. Nirad C. Chaudhuri, *Thy Hand, Great Anarch*, London, 1987, p. 501.
5. Calcutta, September 1921, in Krishna Datta and Andrew Robinson, *Rabindranath Tagore: The myriad minded man*, Delhi: Rupa & Co., 1997, p. 237. Also see Tagore's essay, 'The Cult of the Charkha', September 1925, in *The Mahatma and the Poet*, edited by Sabyasachi Bhattacharya, New Delhi: National Book Trust, 1997, pp. 99–112.
6. Subhas Chandra Bose, *The Indian Struggle, Netaji Collected Works, Vol. 2*, Calcutta: Netaji Research Bureau, 1981, pp. 328–29.
7. Ibid., p. 375.
8. 'The Role of Mahatma Gandhi in Indian History', in *The Essential Writings of Netaji Subhas Chandra Bose*, edited by Sisir Bose and Sugata Bose, New Delhi: OUP, 1998, p. 149.
9. Nirad C. Chaudhuri, *Thy Hand, Great Anarch*, p. 513.
10. 'Speech at all-India Naujawan Bharat Sabha, Karachi, 5 April 1931', in *The Essential Writings of Netaji Subhas Chandra Bose*, pp. 113–14.
11. 'Forward Bloc: Its Justification, Feb–March 1941', ibid., p. 270.
12. *Selected Works of Jawaharlal Nehru* [henceforth referred to as *SWJN*, Advisory board: M. Chalapathi Rau, H.Y. Sharada Prasad, B.R. Nanda; general editor: S. Gopal. New Delhi: Orient Longman, 1972, vol. 9, p. 123.
13. Gandhi to Subhas Bose, 5.2.1939, File 2-G/39, Col 1, Rajendra Prasad MSS, NAI.
14. 'Forward Bloc: Its Justification, thesis written in Kabul, March 1941', in *The Essential Writings of Netaji Subhas Chandra Bose*, p. 271.

15. 'The Doctrine of the Sword', 11 August 1920, in *The Penguin Gandhi Reader*, edited by Rudrangshu Mukherjee, New Delhi:Viking Penguin, 1993, p. 99.
16. Ibid.
17. 'An Indian Pilgrim', *Netaji Collected Works*, vol. I, Calcutta: Netaji Research Bureau, 1980.
18. Ibid., p. 19.
19. Subhas to Bivabati Bose, 11 September 1925, in *The Essential Writings of Netaji Subhas Chandra Bose*, p. 54.
20. 'My strange illness', *Modern Review*, April 1939, in *The Essential Writings of Netaji Subhas Chandra Bose*, p. 235.
21. Subhas Bose, 'An Indian Pilgrim', *Netaji Collected Works*, vol. I, Calcutta: Netaji Research Bureau, 1980.
22. Subhas to Sarat Bose, 23 April 1921, *Netaji Collected Works*, vol. I, Calcutta: Netaji Research Bureau, 1980, p. 233.
23. Ibid., pp. 70–71.
24. Subhas Chandra Bose, A poem written in 1947 by Oaten in Appendix 7, *Netaji Collected Works*, vol. I, Calcutta: Netaji Research Bureau, 1980, p. 269.
25. 'An Indian Pilgrim', *Netaji Collected Works*, vol. I, Calcutta: Netaji Research Bureau, 1980, pp. 72-73.
26. Lord Macaulay, *Critical, Historical and Miscellaneous Essays*, Boston, 1860, V, pp. 19–20.
27. Kumkum Sangari and Sudesh Vaid (eds.), *Recasting Women: Essays in Colonial History*, New Delhi: Kali for Women, 1989.
28. 'An Indian Pilgrim, *Netaji Collected Works*, vol. 1, Calcutta: Netaji Research Bureau, 1980, p. 38.
29. Ibid., p. 30.
30. 11.5.1926, *Netaji Collected Works*, vol. 5, 1985, p. 16.
31. Ibid., p. 15.
32. Ibid., p. 8.
33. 'An Indian Pilgrim', *Netaji Collected Works*, vol. I, Calcutta: Netaji Research Bureau, 1980, p. 92.
34. Ibid., pp. 89–90.
35. Ibid., p. 170.
36. Ibid.
37. Dilip Kumar Roy, *Netaji, the Man: Reminiscences*, Bombay: Bharatiya Vidya Bhavan, 1966, pp. 38–39.

38. 'An Indian Pilgrim', in *Netaji Collected Works,* vol. 1, p. 98.
39. 'At Cambridge', in *The Essential Writings of Netaji Subhas Chandra Bose*, p. 36.
40. Upendra Nath Banerjee, 'Subhas', in *Masik Basumati*, Magh 1352, January 1945.
41. Subhas to Sarat Chandra Chattopadhyay, 12 August 1925, in *The Essential Writings of Netaji Subhas Chandra Bose*, p. 50.
42. Subhas to Hemendranath Dasgupta, 20 February 1926, in *The Essential Writings of Netaji Subhas Chandra Bose*, p. 73.
43. Ibid.
44. Ibid., p. 65.
45. Ibid.
46. 'Why Forward Bloc', signed editorial, in *Forward Bloc*, 5 August 1939, in *The Alternative Leadership, Netaji Collected Works*, vol. 10, 1998, p. 1.
47. *Netaji Collected Works*, vol. 8, 1994, p. 262.
48. Subhas to Amita Purakayastha (Guha), 3 September 1938, in *Netaji Collected Works*, vol. 9, 1995, pp. 270–71.
49. 'An Indian Pilgrim', in *Netaji Collected Works*, vol. 1, Calcutta, 1980, Netaji Research Bureau, p. 34.
50. Ibid.
51. Ibid., p. 141.
52. Subhas to Basantidebi, 17 July 1927, in *Netaji Collected Works*, vol. 4, Netaji Research Bureau, 1982, pp. 238–39.
53. Dilip Kumar Roy, *The Subhash I Knew*, Bombay: Nalanda Publications, 1946, p. 19.
54. Ibid., p. 26.
55. Ibid., p. 38.
56. Mentioned by Emilie Schenkl privately to Leonard Gordon on 14 October 1978. See Leonard Gordon, *Brothers against the Raj*, New Delhi: Viking Penguin, 1990, p. 344.
57. Nirad Chaudhuri, 'Subhas Chandra Bose: One among Six Prominent Bengalis', *Desh*, 13 January 1996, pp. 106–09.
58. Sharmila Bose, 'Husband, father and leader', *Desh*, 13 January 1996, p. 92.
59. Subhas to Emilie Schenkl, March 1936, in *The Essential Writings of Netaji Subhas Chandra Bose*, pp. 160–61.
60. 'An Indian Pilgrim', *Netaji Collected Works*, vol. I, Calcutta: Netaji Research Bureau, 1980, pp. 54–56.

61. See his letters to Kitty Kurti, 25 July 1936 and 17 March 1937, in *Netaji Collected Works*, vol. 8, New Delhi: OUP, 1994, p. 179 and p. 194.

62. Asoke Nath Bose, *My Uncle Netaji*, Calcutta: Esem Publications, 1977, pp. 161–62.

63. Leonard Gordon, *Brothers against the Raj*, p. 520.

64. Subhas Chandra Bose, *Letters to Emilie Schenkl 1934–1942, Netaji Collected Works*, vol. 7, Netaji Research Bureau, 1994, pp. 21–22; pp. 32–33.

65. Ibid., Subhas to Emilie, 11 February 1936.

66. Ibid., Subhas to Emilie, 17 June 1937.

67. A.C.N. Nambiar recalled drinking Dubonet with Netaji at a cafeteria in Paris in 1941. Subhas explained that when he returned to Europe he decided to do away with inhibitions so as not to seem very conspicuous. A.C.N. Nambiar, Oral History Transcript, NMML.

68. Hugh Toye, *The Springing Tiger: A Study of Subhas Chandra Bose*, 1959.

69. Reba Som, *Subhas Chandra Bose and the 'Resolution of the Women's Question', Ideas and Ideologies*, Monograph II, Centre for Women's Studies, New Delhi, 2002.

70. Louis Fischer, *The Life of Mahatma Gandhi*, New York: Harper & Row, 1983, p. 15.

71. Ibid., p. 17.

72. Ibid., p. 18.

73. Ibid.

74. Ibid., p. 60.

75. Ibid., p. 20.

76. Ibid.

77. Ibid. p. 41.

78. Ibid, p. 117.

79. Ibid., p. 69.

80. B.R. Nanda, *Mahatma Gandhi: A Biography*, London: George Allen & Unwin Ltd., 1958, p. 68.

81. Louis Fischer, *The Life of Mahatma Gandhi*, p. 35.

82. Ibid., p. 69.

83. Ibid., p. 89.

84. Tolstoy to Gandhi, 7 September 1910, Fischer, p. 99.

85. *Hind Swaraj*, Chapter VII 'Why was India Lost', in *The Penguin Gandhi Reader*, edited by Rudrangshu Mukherjee, 1993, p. 19.

86. *Collected Works of Mahatma Gandhi*, vol. 66, p. 245.

87. *Hind Swaraj*, Chapter VI 'Civilisation', in *The Penguin Gandhi Reader*, p. 18.
88. *Hind Swaraj*, Chapter VIII 'The Condition of India', in *The Penguin Gandhi Reader*, p. 22.
89. Ibid., p. 58.
90. *Hind Swaraj*, Chapter V 'The Condition of England', in *The Penguin Gandhi Reader*, p. 13.
91. *Hind Swaraj*, Chapter XVII 'Passive Resistance', in *The Penguin Gandhi Reader*, p.46.
92. *Hind Swaraj*, Chapter XX 'Conclusion', in *The Penguin Gandhi Reader*, p. 66.
93. Speech at Tanjore, 16 September 1927, in *The Penguin Gandhi Reader*, p. 207.
94. See Judith M. Brown, *Gandhi's Rise to Power: Indian Politics 1915–22*, Cambridge: Cambridge University Press, 1972.
95. Speech at Women's Conference, Sojitra, 16 January 1925, in *The Penguin Gandhi Reader*, p. 181.
96. Nehru, *An Autobiography*, p. 8.
97. Ibid., p. 20.
98. Ibid., p. 25.
99. Ibid., p. 26.
100. Ibid., p. 601.
101. To Harsha Hutheesingh, 26 August 1959, Jawaharlal Nehru MSS, NMML.
102. Narendra Dev, 'Favourite of Fortune', in *Nehru Abhinandan Grantha*, New Delhi, 1949, p. 108.
103. Nehru, *An Autobiography*, p. 35.
104. Ibid., p. 64.
105. Ibid., p. 49.
106. Ibid., p. 81.
107. Ibid., p. 104.
108. S. Gopal, *Jawaharlal Nehru, Vol. 1 (1889–1947)*, New Delhi: OUP, 1976, p. 109.
109. Nehru, *An Autobiography*, p. 490.
110. Ibid., p. 372.
111. Ibid.
112. Ibid., p. 379.
113. Ibid., p. 510.

114. Ibid., p. 515.

115. Ibid., p. 549.

116. Ibid., p. 539.

117. Extract from Romain Rolland's Diary, 22 October 1935, in *Romain Rolland and Gandhi Correspondence*, New Delhi, 1976.

118. Nehru, *An Autobiography*, p. 512.

119. Jawaharlal Nehru to Gandhi, 24 July 1941, *SWJN*, vol, 11, pp. 658–59.

120. Ibid.

121. Quoted in Aruna Asaf Ali in association with G.N.S. Raghavan, *The Private Face of a Public Person: A Study of Jawaharlal Nehru*, New Delhi: Radiant Publisher, 1989, p. 86.

122. Ibid.

123. Reba Som, 'Chitrangada, Not Sita: Jawaharlal Nehru's Model for Gender Equation in Gender and Nation', NMML, 2001, pp. 357–87.

124. Jawaharlal Nehru, *The Discovery of India*: New Delhi: OUP, 1982, p. 41.

125. Speech during debate on the Third Reading of the Hindu Marriage Bill, 5 May 1955, *Lok Sabha Debates*, 1995, 1V, Pt. II.

126. Reba Som, 'Jawaharlal Nehru and the Hindu Code: A Victory of Symbol over Substance', *Occasional Papers on Perspectives in Indian Development, Number XXX, April 1992*, Centre for Contemporary Studies, NMML, New Delhi. This article also appeared in *Modern Asian Studies*, vol. 28, Part I, February 1994, Cambridge University Press.

127. Nehru, *An Autobiography*, p. 254.

128. Subhas Bose, 'The Indian Struggle', in *Netaji Collected Works, Vol. 2*, 1981, p. 327.

129. See p. 81.

130. Ibid., p. 253.

131. Ibid., pp. 523–24.

132. Ibid., p. 28.

133. Erik H. Erikson, *Gandhi's Truth: On the Origins of Militant Non violence*, New York: Norton, 1969, p. 108.

134. 'Smriticharan', in *Rachanagraha: Dilip Kumar Roy*, Calcutta, 1997, p. 639.

135. Dilip Roy to Subhas Bose, 27 September 1925, in *Netaji Collected Works*, vol. 3, 1981, p. 88.

136. 'The call of the motherland', December 1925, in *Netaji Collected Works*, vol. 5, 1985, p. 223.

137. Gandhi to Subhas Bose, 2 April 1939, in *Netaji Collected Works*, vol. 9, 1995, p. 145.

138. *Harijan*, 20 March 1937, in M.K. Gandhi, *Non Violence in Peace and War*, vol. 1, Ahmedabad: Navajivan Publishing House, 1942, p. 138.

139. Nehru, *An Autobiography*, pp. 194–95.

140. See Reba Som, *Differences within Consensus: The Left and Right in the Congress 1929–1939*, New Delhi: Orient Longman, 1995.

141. Subhas Bose to Mrs Kitty Kurti, 23 February 1934, in Kitty Kurti, *Subhas Chandra Bose as I Knew Him*, Calcutta: Firma K.L. Mukhopadhyay, 1966, p. 59.

142. 'The Rashtrapati', *SWJN*, vol. 8, pp. 520–23.

143. Dilip Kumar Roy, *The Subhash I Knew*, Bombay: Nalanda Publications, 1946, p. 144.

144. 'The Rashtrapati', *SWJN*, vol. 8, p. 523.

145. 'My Health and other thoughts: Letter to a friend, 16 April, 1932', *Netaji Collected Works*, vol. 6, p. 246.

146. *Deshnayak*, Tagore to Subhas Bose, 27 January 1939, in *Netaji Collected Works*, vol. 9, p. 247.

147. M.K. Gandhi, *Non-violence in Peace and War*, vol. 1, Ahmedabad: Navajivan Publishing House, 1942, p. 4.

148. Subhas Bose to Satyendranath Majumdar, 28 April 1933, in *Netaji Collected Works*, vol. 8, 1994, p. 9.

149. 'An Indian Pilgrim', in *Netaji Collected Works*, vol. I, Calcutta: Netaji Research Bureau, 1980.

150. Subhas to his mother, 1912, in *The Essential Writings of Netaji Subhas Chandra Bose*, pp. 21–22.

151. Subhas to his mother, 1912, in *The Essential Writings of Netaji Subhas Chandra Bose*, pp. 21–22.

152. *Hind Swaraj*, Chapter XVIII 'Education', in *The Penguin Gandhi Reader*, p. 57.

153. Romain Rolland's Diary, December 1931, in *Romain Rolland and Gandhi Correspondence*, New Delhi, 1976.

154. *Hind Swaraj*, Chapter VIII 'The Condition of India', in *The Penguin Gandhi Reader*, p. 21.

155. Subhas Bose to the Superintendent Presidency Jail, 30 October 1940, in *The Alternative Leadership*, *Netaji Collected Works, Vol. 10*, 1998, p. 189.

156. In conversation with the late Dr Sisir Bose, in Calcutta, 20 September 1999.

157. Dilip Kumar Roy, *The Subhash I Knew*, Bombay: Nalanda Publications, 1946, p. 98.
158. 'My Faith Philosophical', in *The Essential Writings of Netaji Subhas Chandra Bose*, pp. 191–96.
159. Subhas to Anil Ganguly, 8 August 1937, in *Netaji Collected Works*, vol. 8, 1994, p. 216.
160. Subhas Bose, speech in Berlin, 26 January 1943, in *Netaji Collected Works*, vol. 11, *Azad Hind, Writings and Speeches 1941–1943*, edited by Sisir and Sugata Bose, Netaji Research Bureau and New Delhi: Permanent Black, 2002, p. 11.
161. 'My Faith Philosophical', in *The Essential Writings of Netaji Subhas Chandra Bose*, p. 195.
162. Presidential address at the Maharashtra Provincial Conference, Poona, 3 May 1928, in *The Essential Writings of Netaji Subhas Chandra Bose*, p. 86.
163. 'My Faith Philosophical', in *The Essential Writings of Netaji Subhas Chandra Bose*, p. 193.
164. Presidential address at the Maharashtra Provincial Conference, Poona, 3 May 1928, in *The Essential Writings of Netaji Subhas Chandra Bose*, p. 86.
165. Ibid.
166. Gandhi in *Young India*, quoted in Thomas Pantham, 'Gandhi, Nehru and Modernity', in *Crisis and Change in Contemporary India*, edited by Upendra Baxi and Bhikhu Parekh, New Delhi: Sage, 1995.
167. 'Free India and its Problems', August 1942, in *The Essential Writings of Netaji Subhas Chandra Bose*, p. 291.
168. Broadcast over Azad Hind Radio (Germany), 25 March 1942, in *Netaji Collected Works*, vol. 11, New Delhi, 2002.
169. 'Free India and its Problems', August 1942, in *The Essential Writings of Netaji Subhas Chandra Bose*, p. 291.
170. Subhas Bose to Bhatnagar, Dalhousie, 6 August 1937, in Subhas Chandra Bose Papers, Group IV, Misc. Acc. No. 262, NAI.
171. Radio talk, 21 October 1944, File No. 199, INA Papers, NAI.
172. Nehru, *An Autobiography*, 1962, p. 536.
173. Dilip Kumar Roy, *The Subhash I Knew*, Bombay: Nalanda Publications, 1946, p. 116.
174. Gandhi's foreword to the *Collected Speeches of Gopal Krishna Gokhale*, quoted in Thomas Pantham, 'Gandhi, Nehru and Modernity', p. 109 in *Crisis and Change in Contemporary India*, New Delhi: Sage, 1998,

edited by Upendra Baxi and Bhikhu Parekh.

175. Dilip Kumar Roy, *The Subhash I Knew*, p. 155.

176. Romain Roland to Subhas Bose, 22 February 1935, in *Netaji Collected Works*, vol. 8, 1994, p. 303.

177. Diary, March 1928, in *Romain Rolland and Gandhi Correspondence*, New Delhi, Publications Division, Government of India, 1976.

178. Gandhi to Subhas, 29 December 1940, in *The Alternative Leadership, Netaji Collected Works*, vol. 10, 1998, p. 155.

179. Presidential address at the Maharashtra Provincial Conference, Poona, 3 May 1928, in *The Essential Writings of Netaji Subhas Chandra Bose*, p. 91.

180. N.G. Jog, 'The Alternative Leadership 1936–41', in *A Beacon Across Asia*, edited by Sisir Bose and Alexander Werth, 1996, p. 87.

181. M.K. Gandhi, *Non Violence in Peace and War*, vol. I, Ahmedabad: Navajivan Publishing House, 1942, p. 164.

182. See Chapter Two, 'Sailing in Different Boats'.

183. Nehru to Bose, 4 February 1939, in Jawaharlal Nehru, *A Bunch of Old Letters*, Bombay: Asia Publishing House, 1960, p. 321.

184. The telegram from Prasad to Bose, 14 August 1939, was drafted by Gandhi but the word 'cheerfully' included by him was dropped by Prasad in the final version sent. File 2-G/39, Col. 1, Rajendra Prasad MSS, NAI.

185. See *A Bunch of Old Letters*, Bombay: Asia Publishing House, 1960.

186. See Hiren Mukerjee, *The Gentle Colossus: A study of Jawaharlal Nehru*, Calcutta: Manisha Granthalaya, 1964.

187. INA Memorial Parade, Rangoon, 11 July 1944, File No. 199, INA Papers, NAI.

188. Subhas Bose, *The Indian Struggle 1920–42*, in *Netaji Collected Works, Vol. 2*, Netaji Research Bureau, 1981, p. 180.

189. Nehru, *An Autobiography*, pp. 129–30.

190. *Romain Rolland and Gandhi Correspondence: Letters, Diary Extracts, Articles, etc.*, Publications Division, Government of India, New Delhi, 1976.

191. Girija K. Mookerjee, *Subhas Chandra Bose*, Publications Division, Ministry of Information and Broadcasting, Government of India, New Delhi, 1975, p. 94.

192. M. Sivaram, *The Road to Delhi*, Tokyo: Charles T. Turtle, 1966, p. 140.

193. Lakshmi Sahgal, *A Revolutionary Life: Memoirs of a Political Activist*, New Delhi: Kali for Women, 1997, p. 50.

194. *Times of India*, 28 December 1936, File No. 800109 II, 1937, Home Dept. Special, Maharashtra Archives, Mumbai.

195. See B.R. Nanda, *Mahatma Gandhi: A Biography*, London: George Allen & Unwin, 1958, p. 355.

196. Presidential Address at the Third Indian Political Conference, London, 10 June 1933, in *The Essential Writings of Netaji Subhas Chandra Bose*, p. 141.

197. Speech, Berlin, 26 January 1943, in *Netaji Collected Works, Vol. 11, Azad Hind, Writings and Speeches 1941–1943*, edited by Sisir and Sugata Bose, Netaji Research Bureau and New Delhi: Permanent Black, 2002, p. 183.

198. Alexander Werth, 'Planning for Revolution 1941–43', in *A Beacon Across Asia: A Biography of Subhas Chandra Bose*, edited by Sisir Bose and others, Orient Longman, 1996, pp. 110–11.

199. 4 May 1942, Count Ciano's Diary (1939–43), edited by Malcolm Muggeridge, London, 1947, in *Forgotten Images: Reflections and Reminiscences of Subhas Chandra Bose*, edited by T.R. Sareen, Delhi: S.S. Publishers, 1997, p. 88.

200. Hitler's meeting with Subhas Bose, 29 May 1942, Record of the Conference, in *A Beacon Across Asia: A Biography of Subhas Chandra Bose*, edited by Sisir Bose and others, Orient Longman, 1996, p. 105.

201. Fred Saito and Tatsuo Hayashida, 'To Delhi! To Delhi! 1943–1945', ibid., pp. 139–41.

202. Shah Nawaz Khan, 'Netaji as I saw him', in *Forgotten Images: Reflections and Reminiscences of Subhas Chandra Bose*, edited by T.R. Sareen, Delhi: S.S. Publishers, 1997, p. 155.

203. Special instructions to officers and men, 11 February 1944, File No. 199, INA Papers, NAI

204. Ibid.

205. Chin' Kee Onn, 'Malaya Upside Down, Kuala Lumpur, 1946', in *Forgotten Images: Reflections and Reminiscences of Subhas Chandra Bose*, edited by T.R. Sareen, Delhi: S.S. Publishers, 1997, p. 185.

206. Platoon Lectures, INA Papers, NAI.

207. Emilie Schenkl, Oral History Transcript, NMML.

208. See Peter Ward Fay, *The Forgotten Army: India's Armed Struggle for Independence, 1942-1945*, New Delhi: Rupa & Co., 1994, p. 215.

209. Shah Nawaz Khan, 'Netaji as I saw him', in *Forgotten Images: Reflections*

and Reminiscences of Subhas Chandra Bose, edited by T.R. Sareen, Delhi: S.S. Publishers, 1997, p. 152.

210. Ibid.

211. Subhas Bose to Gandhi, 6 April 1939, in *Netaji Collected Works*, vol. 9, New Delhi: OUP, 1995, p. 153.

212. The Indian Struggle 1920–1942, *Netaji Collected Works*, vol. 2, Calcutta: Netaji Research Bureau, 1981, p. 384.

213. Louis Fischer, *The Life of Mahatma Gandhi*, New York: Harper & Row, 1983, p. 352.

214. M.K. Gandhi, *Non-violence in Peace and War*, Vol. 1, Ahmedabad: Navajivan Publishing House, 1942, p. 9.

215. Speech at All India Naujawan Bharat Sabha, Karachi, 5 April 1931, in *The Essential Writings of Netaji Subhas Chandra Bose*, pp. 113–14.

216. Romain Rolland to Edmond Privat, 5 May 1931, in *Romain Rolland and Gandhi correspondence: letters, diary extracts, articles, etc.* / foreword by Jawaharlal Nehru. New Delhi: Publications Division, Ministry of Information and Broadcasting, Government of India, 1976.

217. Ibid.

218. Gandhi to Louis Fischer, in M.K. Gandhi, *Non-violence in Peace and War, Vol. 2*, Ahmedabad: Navajivan Publishing House, 1949, p. 111.

219. See Bidyut Chakrabarty, *Subhas Chandra Bose and Middle Class Radicalism: A Study in Indian Nationalism 1928–1940*, New Delhi: OUP, 1990.

220. Democracy in India, Presidential address at Poona, Maharashtra Provincial Conference, 3 May 1928, in *The Essential Writings of Netaji Subhas Chandra Bose*, p. 83.

221. The Anti Imperialist Struggle and Samyavada, London, 10 June 1933, speech of Subhas Bose delivered in absentia, in *The Essential Writings of Netaji Subhas Chandra Bose*, p. 145.

222. The Fundamental Problems of India, November 1944, in *The Essential Writings of Netaji Subhas Chandra Bose*, p. 317.

223. Report of an interview with Subhas Bose by Alberto Quaroni, Italian Minister to Kabul, in March 1941, in *Netaji Collected Works, Vol. 11, Azad Hind, Writings and Speeches 1941–1943*, edited by Sisir and Sugata Bose, Netaji Research Bureau and New Delhi: Permanent Black, 2002, p. 36.

224. Radio broadcast from Berlin, 17 June 1942, in *Netaji Collected Works, Vol. 11, Azad Hind, Writings and Speeches 1941–1943*, edited by Sisir

Bose and Sugata Bose, Netaji Research Bureau and New Delhi: Permanent Black, 2002, p. 120.

225. Subhas Bose to C.R. Prufer, Berlin, 5 April 1934, in *Netaji Collected Works*, vol. 8, 1994, p. 63.

226. Subhas Bose to Amiya Chakravarti, 11 March 1936, in *The Essential Writings of Netaji Subhas Chandra Bose*, p. 154.

227. Kitty Kurti, *Subhas Chandra Bose as I Knew Him*, Calcutta: Firma K.L. Mukhopadhyay, 1966, p. 46.

228. J.P. Narayan, *Towards Struggle: Selected manifestoes, speeches and writings*, edited by Yusuf Meherally, Bombay: Padma Publications, 1946, p. 44.

229. Orlando Mazzota (alias Subhas Bose) to Dr Woermann of the German Foreign Office, 5 July 1941, in *Netaji Collected Works, Vol. 11, Azad Hind, Writings and Speeches 1941-1943*, edited by Sisir Bose and Sugata Bose, Netaji Research Bureau and New Delhi: Permanent Black, 2002, p. 59.

230. Record of the Conference between Hitler and Subhas Bose, 29 May 1942, in ibid., p. 102.

231. See Lothar Frank, 'Epilogue', in *A Beacon Across Asia: A Biography of Subhas Chandra Bose*, edited by Sisir Bose and others, New Delhi: Orient Longman, 1996, p. 205.

232. Speech in Madras, 8 October 1936, in *SWJN*, vol. 7, p. 517.

233. Nehru, *An Autobiography*, p. 591.

234. Ibid.

235. Subhas Chandra Bose, *The Indian Struggle*, in *Netaji Collected Works*, vol. II, p. 231.

236. Nehru, *An Autobiography*, p. 600.

237. Gandhi to Hitler, 23 July 1939, *Harijan*, 9 September 1939, in M.K. Gandhi, *Non-violence in Peace and War*, vol. I, Ahmedabad: Navajivan Publishing House, 1942, pp. 226–27; Gandhi to Hitler, 24 December 1940, in D.G. Tendulkar, *Mahatma*, vol. 6, 1962, pp. 34–36.

238. Bipan Chandra, *India's Struggle for Independence 1857–1947*, New Delhi: Viking, 1988, p. 446.

239. Nehru to Linlithgow, 6 October 1939, in S. Gopal, *Jawaharlal Nehru, A Biography, Vol. 1 (1889–1947)*, New Delhi: OUP, 1976, p. 255.

240. Bipan Chandra, *India's Struggle for Independence 1857–1947*, New Delhi: Viking, 1988, p. 450.

241. 'The Correct Line', signed editorial in *Forward Bloc*, 26 December 1939, in *The Alternative Leadership, Netaji Collected Works*, vol. 10, 1998, p. 53.

242. Subhas Chandra Bose, *Indian Struggle*, in *Netaji Collected Works*, vol. II, p. 384.
243. Ibid., p. 386.
244. D.G. Tendulkar, *Mahatma: Life of Mohandas Karamchand Gandhi*, Illus. collected and arranged by Vithalbhai K. Jhaveri; foreword by Jawaharlal Nehru, Bombay: Publications Division, Government of India, 1951–54, vol. 6, p. 43.
245. Gandhi to Nehru, 24 April 1942, in Jawaharlal Nehru, *A Bunch of Old Letters*, 1960, p. 484.
246. Gandhi in *Harijan*, 26 April 1942.
247. Interview to the Press, Gauhati, 24 April 1942, in *SWJN*, vol. 12, p. 262.
248. Maulana Abul Kalam Azad, *India Wins Freedom*, Delhi: Sangam Books, Orient Longman, 1978, p. 41.
249. *The Selected Works of Subhas Chandra Bose*, vol. 1, edited by Ravindra Kumar, New Delhi: Allied Publishers, 1992, Document No. 86, p. 134.
250. Maulana Abul Kalam Azad, *India Wins Freedom*, Delhi: Orient Longman, 1978, p. 41.
251. Ibid.
252. See Samar Guha, *The Mahatma and the Netaji: Two Men in the Destiny of India*, New Delhi: Sterling Publishers, 1986, p. 83.
253. Ibid., p. 87.
254. Subhas Bose, *Indian Struggle*, in *Netaji Collected Works*, vol. II, p. 391.
255. Berlin broadcast, 17 June 1942, in *Azad Hind: Writings and Speeches 1941–1943*, *Netaji Collected Works*, vol. 11, New Delhi: Permanent Black, 2002, p. 118.
256. Ibid., p.138.
257. Ibid., p. 130.
258. Ibid., p. 137.
259. See Hitesranjan Sanyal, 'The Quit India Movement in Medinipur District', in *The Indian Nation in 1942*, edited by Gyanendra Pandey, Calcutta: Published for Centre for Studies in Social Sciences, Calcutta by K.P. Bagchi, 1988, p. 26.
260. Article by Subhas Bose, early August 1942, in *Azad Hind, Netaji Collected Works*, Vol. 11, 2002, p. 131.
261. See Christopher Sykes, *Troubled Loyalty: A Biography of Adam von Trott zu Zolz*, London: Collins, 1968.
262. See M. Sivaraman, *The Road to Delhi*, Tokyo: Charles E. Turtle Co. Publishers, 1967, pp. 208–17.

263. Broadcasting Speech of Subhas Bose, 21/22 July 1945, File No. 16, INA Papers, NAI.

264. Address to Mahatma Gandhi over the Rangoon Radio, 6 July 1944, in *The Essential Writings* of *Netaji Subhas Chandra Bose*, p. 304.

265. M.K. Gandhi, *Non-violence in Peace and War*, vol. II, Ahmedabad: Navajivan Publishing House, 1942, p. 38.

266. *Harijan*, 14 April 1946.

267. Subhas Bose, *Indian Struggle*, in *Netaji Collected Works*, vol. II, p. 384.

268. *Harijan*, 24 February 1946.

269. *Harijan*, 14 April 1946.

270. Subhas Bose to Jawaharlal Nehru, 28 March 1939, in *A Bunch of Old Letters*, 1960, p. 329.

271. See Judith M. Brown, *Nehru*, London: Longman, 1999.

272. Nehru to Gandhi, 13 July 1929, in *SWJN*, vol. 4.

273. 'India can't do without him', *SWJN*, vol. 9, p. 513.

274. See B.R. Nanda, *Jawaharlal Nehru: Rebel and Statesman*, New Delhi: OUP, 1998, p. 48.

275. *Harijan*, 25 July 1936.

276. 'Jawaharlal my Successor', 15 January 1942, Tendulkar, *Mahatma*, vol. 6, p. 43.

277. Subhas Bose to Sunil Mohan Ghosh Moulik, 20 December 1935, in *Netaji Collected Works*, vol. 8, New Delhi: OUP, 1994, p. 123.

278. Subhas Bose to Mrs Woods, Badgastein, 5 March 1936, in *Netaji Collected Works*, vol. 8, New Delhi: OUP, 1994, p. 149.

279. Gandhi to Nehru, 11 August 1939, in *CWMG*, vol. 69

280. M.K. Gandhi, *Non-violence in Peace and War*, vol. I, Ahmedabad: Navajivan Publishing House, 1942, p. 237.

281. Romain Rolland, *Inde: Journal (1915–1943)*, Paris: Éditions A. Michel, 1960, pp. 513–14.

282. Interview to *Amrita Bazar Patrika*, London, 5 September 1938, in *SWJN*, vol. 9, p. 130.

283. 'After Paris', signed editorial in *Forward Bloc*, in *The Alternative Leadership, Netaji Collected Works*, vol. 10, 1998, p. 113.

284. Subhas Bose to Jawaharlal Nehru, 28 March 1939, in *A Bunch of Old Letters*, 1960, p. 334.

285. Subhas Bose to Dilip Roy, 9 October 1925, in *Netaji Collected Works*, vol. 3, 1981, p. 130.

286. Dilip Roy to Subhas Bose, 21 November 1925, in ibid., p. 136.

287. Dilip Kumar Roy, *Netaji, the Man: Reminiscences*, Bombay: Bharatiya Vidya Bhavan, 1966, p. 85.

288. Tagore to Dilip Roy, in Appendix of *Netaji Collected Works*, vol. 3, 1981, p. 346.

289. Ibid. See Reba Som, 'Art of the Matter: No short cuts', *Indian Express*, New Delhi, 26 July 2002.

290. 'Speech at Centenary Celebrations of Government Museum, Madras, 27 November 1951', in *Foundations of Education For Free India: Toward a New Quality of Life: Selections from writings and speeches of Abul Kalam Azad, Jawaharlal Nehru, Sarvepalli Radhakrishnan*, 1989, edited by Prem Kirpal and Reba Shome, New Delhi: Allied Publishers, 1989, p. 119.

291. *Netaji Collected Works*, vol. 1, 1980, p. 35.

292. 'Speech at Centenary Celebrations of Government Museum, Madras, 27 November 1951', in *Foundations of Education For Free India*, p. 119.

293. *Netaji Collected Works*, vol. 1, 1980, p. 35.

294. Subhas Bose to Jawaharlal Nehru, 4 October 1935, in *Netaji Collected Works*, vol. 8, New Delhi: OUP, 1994, p. 109

295. See Mihir Bose, *The Lost Hero*, 1982, p. 117.

296. S. Gopal, *Jawaharlal Nehru: A Biography, Vol. I: 1889–1947*, New Delhi: OUP, 1976, p. 245.

297. B.R. Nanda, *Jawaharlal Nehru: Rebel and Statesman*, New Delhi: OUP, 1998, p. 280.

298. 6 November 1935, Jawaharlal Nehru MSS, NMML.

299. Dilip Kumar Roy, *Netaji, the Man: Reminiscences*, Bombay: Bharatiya Vidya Bhavan, 1966, p. 85.

300. Subhas Bose to Dr Curt Prufer, 2 February 1935, in *Netaji Collected Works*, vol. 8, New Delhi: OUP Press, 1994, p. 89.

301. Jawaharlal Nehru to Padmaja Naidu, 2 March 1938, in *SWJN*, vol. 13, pp. 695–96.

302. Jawaharlal Nehru to Indira Nehru, 22 April 1939, in *SWJN*, vol. 9.

303. Jawaharlal Nehru to V.K. Krishna Menon, 22 February 1939, in *SWJN*, vol. 13, p. 711.

304. Jawaharlal Nehru to V.K. Krishna Menon, 2 March 1940, in *SWJN*, vol. 10, p. 345.

305. Dilip Kumar Roy, *Netaji, the Man: Reminiscences*, Bombay: Bharatiya Vidya Bhavan, 1966, Appendix X, pp. 199–202.

306. Nehru to Auchinleck, 4 May 1946, in *SWJN*, vol. 15, p. 90.

307. Speech, *Hindustan Times*, 24 January 1946, in *SWJN*, vol. 14, p. 373.

308. Nehru at Bihar Students' Conference, 4 January 1946, File No. 802, INA Papers, NAI.
309. 11 December 1945, File No. 802, INA Papers, vol. I, NAI.

Chapter Four

1. *Selected Works of Jawaharlal Nehru* [henceforth *SWJN*], vol. 11, p. 785.
2. In 1841 Macaulay wrote, 'The physical organisation of the Bengalee is feeble even to effeminacy. His pursuits are sedentary, his limbs delicate, his movements languid. During many ages he has been trampled upon by men of bolder and more hardy breeds.' Thomas Babington Macaulay, *Critical, Historical and Miscellaneous Essays*, New York: Sheldon & Company; Boston: Gould & Lincoln, 1860, vol. V, pp. 19–20.
3. The tendency to blame Muslim rule is evident in the writings of most of the early nationalist Hindu thinkers, from Ram Mohun Roy to Bankim Chandra Chattopadhyay, Romesh Dutt to Gokhale and Tilak.
4. Tagore to C.F. Andrews, *Modern Review*, May 1921, *The Mahatma and the Poet: Letters and Debates between Gandhi and Tagore, 1915–1941*, compiled and edited with an introduction by Sabyasachi Bhattacharya, New Delhi: National Book Trust, 1997, p. 58.
5. Tagore to C.F. Andrews, *Modern Review*, May 1921, in Sabyasachi Bhattacharya, ed., *The Mahatma and the Poet*, p. 57.
6. Ibid., p. 61.
7. Gandhi, *Young India*, 1 June 1921, in Sabyasachi Bhattacharya, ed., *The Mahatma and the Poet*, pp. 65–67.
8. Ibid., p. 66.
9. Gandhi, *Hind Swaraj*, Chapter XVIII Critique of Modern Civilisation, in *The Penguin Gandhi Reader*, edited by Rudrangshu Mukherjee, New Delhi: Penguin, 1993, p. 57.
10. Tagore to Gandhi, 24 January 1918, in Sabyasachi Bhattacharya, ed., *The Mahatma and the Poet*, p. 45.
11. Tagore, 'The Call of Truth', *Modern Review*, in ibid., p. 84.
12. Ibid., p. 83.
13. Gandhi, 'The Great Sentinel', *Young India*, 13 October 1921, in ibid., pp. 87–92.
14. Ibid., p. 89.
15. Tagore, 'The Cult of the Charkha', *Modern Review*, September 1925, in ibid., p. 99.

16. Editorial, *Ananda Bazar Patrika*, 5 June 1923, in ibid., p. 29.
17. C.R. Das, Speech at Bengal Provincial Congress, Calcutta, April 1917, in *Deshbandhu Chitta Ranjan: Brief Survey of Life and Work: Provincial Conference & Congress Speeches*, Calcutta: Sen, 1927.
18. C.R. Das, Undelivered Presidential Address for Congress Session, Ahmedabad, December 1921, ibid.
19. Ibid.
20. Hemendranath Dasgupta, 'C.R. Das', in *Political Thinkers of Modern India, vol. 22*, edited by V.N. Grover, New Delhi: Deep & Deep Publications, 1993.
21. C.R. Das, Speech at Bengal Provincial Congress, Calcutta, April 1917.
22. See Ashis Nandy, *The Illegitimacy of Nationalism: Rabindranath Tagore and the Politics of Self*, New Delhi: OUP, 1994.
23. Gandhi, *Hind Swaraj*, Chapter IV, 'What is Swaraj?', in *The Penguin Gandhi Reader*, pp. 11–13.
24. Gandhi, *Hind Swaraj*, Chapter XIII, 'What is True Civilisation?', in *The Penguin Gandhi Reader*, pp. 34–36.
25. Gandhi, 'The Great Sentinel', *Young India*, 1 June 1921, in *The Penguin Gandhi Reader*, p. 64.
26. Gandhi, 'Enlightened Anarchy', January 1939, in *The Penguin Gandhi Reader*, p. 79.
27. Tagore, 'Amra shabayi raja amader ei rajar rajotye', *Gitobitan* (Collected volume of Tagore's Songs), Calcutta: Visva-Bharati, 1960, p. 247.
28. Tagore, *Crisis in Civilization*, Calcutta: Visva-Bharati, 1961.
29. Tagore, 'Nationalism in India', Speech in America, in *The English Writings of Rabindranath Tagore*, vol. 2, edited by Sisir Kumar Das, New Delhi: Sahitya Akademi, 1996, pp. 453–65.
30. Ibid.
31. Ibid.
32. Ibid., p. 116.
33. Tagore, 'The Cult of the Charkha', *Modern Review*, September 1925, ibid., p. 102.
34. Sermon at Santiniketan, recorded by Kshitimohan Sen in 1926, translated by Sabyasachi Bhattacharya (ed.), in *The Mahatma and the Poet*, p. 16.
35. Gandhi on Independence, 29 April 1946, in *The Penguin Gandhi Reader*, op. cit., p. 82.
36. *Hind Swaraj*, Chapter X, 'The Condition of the Hindus and the Mahomedans', ibid., p. 29.

37. Gandhi on Hindu Muslim unity, 26 December 1924, ibid., p. 266.
38. Gandhi at Women's Conference, Sojitra, 16 January 1925, ibid., p. 181.
39. Gandhi, 'What is women's role?', 12 February 1940, ibid., p. 195.
40. Ibid.
41. On socialism and trusteeship, interview to Nirmal Kumar Bose, 9 November 1934, ibid., pp. 241–43.
42. *Rakta Karabi* (1926); *Muktadhara* (1922).
43. Jawaharlal Nehru, *The Discovery of India*, New Delhi: OUP, 1989, pp. 340–41.
44. Jawaharlal Nehru, Visvabharati Convocation Address, 24 December 1945, in *SWJN*, vol. 14.
45. Speech in Madras, 8 October 1936, in *SWJN*, vol. 7, p. 517.
46. Jawaharlal Nehru, *The Discovery of India*, New Delhi: OUP, 1989, p. 53.
47. Jawaharlal Nehru to Frances Gunther, 5 May 1938, Frances Gunther MSS, NMML.
48. Jawaharlal Nehru, *The Discovery of India*, New Delhi: OUP, 1989, p. 59.
49. Jawaharlal Nehru, Visvabharati Convocation Address, 24 December 1945, in *SWJN*, vol. 14.
50. See Sunil Khilnani, *The Idea of India*, New Delhi: Penguin, 1999.
51. Jawaharlal Nehru, *An Autobiography: With musings on recent events in India*, New Delhi: Allied Publishers, 1962, p. 266.
52. Ibid., p. 266.
53. 'Speech on Fundamental Rights, Karachi Congress, 31 March 1931', *Complete Works of Mahatma Gandhi*, vol. 45, pp. 372–73.
54. Subhas Bose, *Collected Works*, vol. 2, p. 20.
55. The considerable faith that Nehru placed in the general commitment that had been secured for the cause of fundamental rights was to receive a severe jolt later, when as prime minister, he was opposed in Parliament trying to pass bills on personal laws, giving substance to what had already been agreed to in spirit in 1931.
56. Jawaharlal Nehru, *The Discovery of India*, New Delhi: OUP, 1989, p. 396.
57. Note to National Planning Committee, 30 August 1940.
58. Speech in Madras, 8 October 1936, in *SWJN*, vol. 7, p. 517.
59. Jawaharlal Nehru to Krishna Kripalani, 29 September 1939, *SWJN*, vol. 10.
60. Jawaharlal Nehru, *The Discovery of India*, New Delhi: OUP, 1989, pp. 396–97.

61. Jawaharlal Nehru, Address at AIWC, Allahabad, 28 January 1940, in *SWJN*, vol. 10.

62. See Reba Som, *Subhas Chandra Bose and the Resolution of the Women's Question: Ideas and Ideologies*, Monographs II, Centre for Women's Studies, New Delhi, 2002.

63. Jawaharlal Nehru, *The Discovery of India*, New Delhi: OUP, 1989, pp. 400–01.

64. Gandhi to Jawaharlal Nehru, 11 August 1939, in *A Bunch of Old Letters*, Bombay: Asia Publishing House, 1960, p. 388.

65. Jawaharlal Nehru to Anil Chanda, 1 December 1938, in *SWJN*, vol. 9, 1976, p. 357.

66. Tagore, 'The Congress', *Modern Review*, July 1939, in Sabyasachi Bhattacharya, ed., *The Mahatma and the Poet*, pp. 175–76.

67. *Rabindra Rachanabali*, Centenary Edition, West Bengal Government, Calcutta, 1961, vol. 13, pp. 387–90.

68. Nepal Majumdar, *Rabindranath O Subhaschandra*, Calcutta, 1998.

69. Gandhi had begun a fast unto death in September 1932 in protest against MacDonald's Communal Award of August 1932, which created separate electorates for untouchables. In the Poona agreement that Gandhi secured and which made him break his fast, the Hindu joint electorate was retained with reserved seats for untouchables, who were now given greater representation than they had been by MacDonald.

70. Tagore to Gandhi, 8 August 1933, in Sabyasachi Bhattacharya, ed., *The Mahatma and the Poet*, p. 149.

71. Gandhi to Tagore, 27 July 1933, ibid., p. 147.

72. Gandhi to Andrews, 15 January 1940, ibid., p. 18.

73. Bose, 'Presidential Address to the Maharashtra Provincial Conference, Poona, 3 May 1928', in *The Essential Writings of Netaji Subhas Chandra Bose*, edited by Sisir Bose and Sugata Bose, New Delhi: OUP, 1998, pp. 83–84.

74. Bose, 'Fundamental Problems of India, November 1944', in *The Essential Writings of Netaji Subhas Chandra Bose*, op. cit., p. 311.

75. Bose, 'The Fundamental Problems of India, Address to Tokyo University, November 1944', in *The Essential Writings of Netaji Subhas Chandra Bose*, edited by Sisir and Sugata Bose, New Delhi: OUP, 1998, pp. 315–17.

76. 'On Kemal Ataturk, Tribute by Subhas Bose on his death, November 1938', in *Netaji Collected Works*, vol. 9, edited by Sisir and Sugata Bose, New Delhi: OUP, 1995, p. 61.

77. Subhas Chandra Bose, 'My Personal Testament, 29 November 1940', in *Alternative Leadership*, p. 140.
78. Prem Sahgal, Oral History Transcript, NMML, New Delhi.
79. Bose, 'The Fundamental Problems of India, November 1944', in *The Essential Writings of Netaji Subhas Chandra Bose*, op. cit., p. 310.
80. Ibid., p. 311.
81. Bose, 'Democracy in India, Address in Poona, 3 May 1928', ibid., p. 83.
82. Bose, 'Address to Tokyo University, November 1944', ibid., p. 320.
83. Bose, 'Speech at all-India Naujawan Bharat Sabha, Karachi, 5 April 1931', ibid., p. 114.
84. Bose, 'Democracy in India, Address in Poona, 3 May 1928', ibid., p. 86.
85. 'The Role of Mahatma Gandhi in Indian History', Chapter 16, *The Indian Struggle*, ibid., p. 152.
86. In a significant address in Poona in 1928, Subhas, as president of the Maharashtra Provincial Conference, had spoken of the need to mobilize into the national movement sections of society, particularly peasantry and labour, which he felt had hitherto not been sufficiently addressed. He spoke of the intrinsic bonds created among these groups by common economic ties, which belied the division of religion. The demography of Bengal, however, was such that although it had a majority of Muslims, most of them actually worked on the land as cultivators, while the landholding classes were largely Hindu, who also held political importance. Subhas himself was supported by the clique of the Big Five (a name given by a Calcutta journalist to a group consisting of Nalini Ranjan Sarkar, Tulsi Goswami, Nirmal Chandra Chunder, Sarat Bose and Dr Bidhan Roy), most of whom were from this Hindu, landlord, economically well-off and politically important class. Thus, later that year, when the Bengal Tenancy Amendment Bill, 1928 was proposed in order to regularize the rights acquired by a large chunk of Muslim sharecroppers to land bought from defaulting landlords, a bitter debate ensued with the Hindu landlords, who demanded a *salami* or transfer fee. Although there was strong opposition to the fee from the largely Muslim pro-tenant group, the bill was passed with the support of the Swarajist Party which, despite their pledge to pursue non-cooperation from within, came to actively support the landlord lobby, with which Subhas, too, cast his vote. This directly led to the Muslims breaking away from the Congress to form their own peasant party, which later became the Krishak Praja Party.

The same ambivalence was displayed again by Subhas when he confronted the widespread labour strikes in 1928. Determined to induct workers into the momentum of the nationalist movement, Subhas became involved that year in three major strikes in Bengal. In two of the strikes, against the railway authorities and the jute mills, Subhas supported, with radical rhetoric, the cause of the workers since the opponent, as in the larger anti-imperialist struggle, was represented by the British government and foreign capital. However, in the third strike, this one against the Tata management in the Jamshedpur Iron and Steel factory, Subhas's stance was more guarded. Adopting the role of a mediator, he tried to work out a mutually satisfactory agreement between Indian labour and Indian capital but failed to completely satisfy either.

87. Presidential address at the All India Trade Union Congress Session, Calcutta, 4 July 1931, in *The Essential Writings of Netaji Subhas Chandra Bose*, op. cit., p. 125.
88. Read in absentia, London, 10 June 1933, ibid., p. 139.
89. Bose, Speech at all-India Naujawan Bharat Sabha, Karachi, 5 April 1931, ibid., p. 112.
90. Ibid.
91. Bose, *The Indian Struggle, 1920-42, Netaji Collected Works*, vol. 2, Calcutta: Netaji Research Bureau, 1981, pp. 352–53.
92. Bose, Presidential Address at the Maharashtra Provincial Conference, Poona, 3 May 1928, in *The Essential Writings of Netaji Subhas Chandra Bose*, op. cit., p. 86.
93. Bose, Presidential Address, Haripura, February 1938, *The Essential Writings of Netaji Subhas Chandra Bose*, op. cit., p. 203.
94. Bose, Speech at all-India Naujawan Bharat Sabha, Karachi, 5 April 1931, ibid., p. 111.
95. Bose, Presidential Address, Haripura, February 1938, ibid., p. 205.
96. Read in absentia, London, 10 June 1933, ibid., p. 145.
97. Bose, Presidential Address at the Maharashtra Provincial Conference, Poona, 3 May 1928, in *The Essential Writings of Netaji Subhas Chandra Bose*, op. cit., p. 90.
98. Read in absentia, London, 10 June 1933, ibid., p. 144.
99. Bose, *The Indian Struggle, 1920–42, Netaji Collected Works*, vol. 2, Calcutta: Netaji Research Bureau, 1981, p. 351.
100. Report of interview with R.P. Dutt, 24 January 1938, ibid., p. 398.

101. Bose, February 1938, Haripura Address, ibid., pp. 205–06.
102. Lothar Frank, 'India's Ambassador Abroad 1933–1936', in *A Beacon Across Asia: A Biography of Subhas Chandra Bose*, edited by Sisir K. Bose, New Delhi: Orient Longman, 1996, p. 55.
103. Bose, February 1938, The Haripura Address, *Netaji Collected Works*, vol. 9, New Delhi: OUP, 1995, pp. 10–11.
104. Bose, Presidential Address at Tripuri Congress, March 1939, ibid., p. 226.
105. Bose, Speech at All-India Naujawan Bharat Sabha, Karachi, 5 April 1931, ibid., p. 111.
106. Bose, Free India and its Problems, August 1942, ibid., p. 290.
107. Prem Sahgal, Oral History Project, NMML, New Delhi.
108. Ibid., p. 306.
109. Address to Tokyo University, November 1944, ibid., p. 320.check
110. Subhas Bose to Anil Biswas, Mandalay Jail, 1925, in *Netaji Collected Works*, vol. 3, Calcutta: Netaji Research Bureau, 1981, pp. 178–82.
111. Subhas Bose to Santosh Kumar Basu, Mandalay Jail, Burma, 26 April 1926, ibid., pp. 279–82.
112. *Calcutta Municipal Gazette*, 27 September 1930, p. 873.
113. 'Municipal Socialism', Address to the Bombay Corporation, 10 May 1938, in *Netaji Collected Works*, vol. 9, edited by Sisir Bose and Sugata Bose, New Delhi: OUP, 1995, p. 31.
114. Subhas Bose to Santosh Kumar Basu, Mayor of Calcutta, 18 June 1933, in *Netaji Collected Works*, vol. 8, edited by Sisir and Sugata Bose, New Delhi: OUP, 1994, pp. 16–17.
115. Bose to United Press, 30 March 1936, in *Netaji Collected Works*, vol. 8, p. 352.
116. N.G. Ganpuley, *Netaji in Germany: A little known chapter*, Bombay: Bharatiya Vidya Bhavan, 1989, p. 136.
117. Answers to questions posed by Meghnad Saha at The Indian Science News Association, 21 August 1938, in *Netaji Collected Works*, vol. 9, edited by Sisir Bose and Sugata Bose, op. cit., p. 45.
118. Message to Sarat Bose, May 1941, *Netaji Collected Works*, vol. 11, Netaji Research Bureau, 2002, p. 54.
119. Bose, Address at the Industries Ministers' Conference, Delhi, 2 October 1938, ibid., p. 50.
120. Bose, February 1938, The Haripura Address, *Netaji Collected Works*, vol. 9, New Delhi: OUP, 1995, p. 14.

121. Answers to questions posed by Meghnad Saha at The Indian Science News Association, 21 August 1938, ibid., p. 47.
122. Ibid.
123. Bose, February 1938, The Haripura Address, *Netaji Collected Works*, vol. 9, op. cit., p. 15.
124. Bose, February 1938, The Haripura Address, *Netaji Collected Works*, vol. 9, op. cit., p. 15.
125. Nehru, *An Autobiography*, pp. 451–52.
126. Subhas Bose at All Bengal Youngmen's Conference, 1922, in Hemendranath Das Gupta, *Subhas Chandra*, Calcutta: Jyoti Prokasalaya, 1946, p. 53.
127. Subhas Bose, 'Presidential Address at Surma Valley Student Conference, Sylhet, April 1929', in Subhas Chandra Bose, *The Mission of Life*, Calcutta, 1949, pp. 126–67.
128. Bose, February 1938, The Haripura Address, *Netaji Collected Works*, vol. 9, op. cit., p. 15.
129. Subhas to Sita Dharmavir, 7 July 1937, in *Netaji Collected Works*, vol. 8, op. cit., p. 210.
130. Gandhi with his creed of non-violence could not stomach the brash martial display, and the clicking of heels and the marching of boots provoked him to compare the Congress with the Bertram Mills' Circus. See Nirad C. Chaudhuri, *The Continent of Circe: Being an Essay on the Peoples of India*, London, 1965, pp. 103–04.
131. Subhas Bose to Amita Purakayastha (Guha), 3 September 1938, in *Netaji Collected Works*, vol. 9, op. cit., pp. 270–71.
132. See Alexander Werth, 'Planning for Revolution 1941–43', in *A Beacon Across Asia: A Biography of Subhas Chandra Bose*, edited by Sisir K. Bose, New Delhi: Orient Longman, 1996, pp. 106–07.
133. Iqbal Shidei, an Indian Muslim who had left India after World War I, made his way to Italy in 1940 and tried to raise a force from among the Indian prisoners of war captured by the Italians in north Africa.
134. N.G. Ganpuley, *Netaji in Germany: A little known chapter*, Bombay: Bharatiya Vidya Bhavan, 1959.
135. See Alexander Werth, 'Planning for Revolution 1941–43', in *A Beacon Across Asia: A Biography of Subhas Chandra Bose*, edited by Sisir K. Bose, New Delhi: Orient Longman, 1996, pp. 106–07.
136. Pramode Sengupta, Oral History Transcript, NMML.
137. The close colleagues of Bose at the Free India Centre who worked for

the radio programmes included Girija Mookerjee, M.R.Vyas, Pramode Sengupta, Ambique Majumdar, J.K. Banerjee, Sultan, Moorthy, Hakim and Ahuja. See Alexander Werth, 'Planning for Revolution 1941–43', in *A Beacon across Asia: A Biography of Subhas Chandra Bose*, edited by Sisir K. Bose, New Delhi: Orient Longman, 1996, p. 111.

138. Ibid., p. 112.

139. See Abid Hasan Safrani, *The Men from Imphal*, Calcutta: Netaji Research Bureau, 1971.

140. See Fred Saito and Tatsuo Hayashida, 'To Delhi, To Delhi!', in *A Beacon across Asia: A Biography of Subhas Chandra Bose*, edited by Sisir K. Bose, New Delhi: Orient Longman, 1996, p. 139.

141. It was ironical, however, that despite Japanese promises, during the actual combat in Kohima in 1944 the INA found itself being merely a supply wing of the army.

142. Lakshmi Sahgal, *A Revolutionary Life*, p. 169.

143. Ibid.

144. INA Papers, File No. 802, INA, NAI.

145. Prem Sahgal, when asked by the German military attaché at a party in Singapore what the Hindustani equivalent of 'cheers' was, replied off the top of his head 'Chakta', which was actually a war cry. Subsequently, when Subhas, confronted by the German officer, had to down several stiff toasts to the cries of 'Chakta', he got to the bottom of the story. Not amused, Subhas reprimanded Sahgal saying, 'The next time you decide to commit India to something, will you please consult me first?' Recounted in Peter Ward Fay, *The Forgotten Army: India's Armed Struggle for Independence 1942–1945*, New Delhi: Rupa & Co., 1994, p. 208.

146. Ibid.

147. Lakshmi Sahgal, *A Revolutionary Life*, p. 64.

148. '*Subh sukh chain ki barkha barse Bharat bhag hai jaga*', which translates as 'May there be showers of welfare and happiness now that India has awoken to her destiny'.

149. Lakshmi Sahgal, *A Revolutionary Life*, p. 156.

150. Abid Hasan (Major in the INA), 'Netaji and the Indian Communal Question', *Oracle*, vol. 1, no. 1, January 1979, p. 44.

151. M.K. Durrani, 'Muslim Image of Bose', in *Forgotten Images: Reflections and Reminiscences of Subhas Chandra Bose*, edited by T.R. Sareen, Delhi: S.S. Publishers, 1997, p. 181.

152. General J.K. Bhonsle, 'Reminiscences of Netaji', ibid., p. 226.

153. Abid Hasan Safrani, *The Men from Imphal*, Calcutta: Netaji Research Bureau, 1971, p. 14.

154. Observation of A.C. Chatterjee, in Peter Ward Fay, *The Forgotten Army: India's Armed Struggle for Independence 1942–1945*, New Delhi: Rupa & Co., 1994, p. 235.

155. Subhas's instructions to INA dated 11 February 1944, INA Papers, File No. 199, INA, NAI.

156. Fay, op. cit., p. 258.

157. Speech to INA, 10 June 1944, INA Papers, File No. 199, INA, NAI.

158. Speech to officers of Azad Hind Fauj at Bidadari camp, 22 July 1943, INA Papers, File No. 199, INA, NAI.

159. Lakshmi Sahgal, *A Revolutionary Life: Memoirs of a Political Activist*, New Delhi: Kali for Women, 1997, p. 64.

160. Radio talk, 21 October 1944, INA Papers, File No. 199, INA, NAI.

161. Broadcast, 31 August 1942, in *Netaji Collected Works, Volume 11, Azad Hind Writings and Speeches 1941–43*, edited by Sisir Bose and Sugata Bose, New Delhi: Permanent Black, 2002, p. 142.

162. Broadcast, 15 October 1942, in *Netaji Collected Works, Volume 11, Azad Hind Writings and Speeches 1941–43*, op. cit., p. 164.

163. 'The anti-imperialist struggle and Samyavada', Presidential Address at the 3rd Indian Political Conference, London, 10 June 1933, in *Essential Writings of Netaji Subhas Chandra Bose*, edited by Sisir Bose and Sugata Bose, New Delhi: OUP, 1998, pp. 139–40.

INDEX

pacifism, 177, 179
Palestine, 157; Jewish problem, 131
Panchayati raj, 11
Pant, G.B., 71–72
Patel, V.J., 52–53
Patel, Vallabhbhai, 40, 46, 48, 49–50, 52, 53, 56, 60–61, 63, 68, 72
patriotism, 8, 25, 96, 160, 175, 176
Patwardhan, Achyut, 59
Pearl Harbour: Japanese victory, 152
peasant distress, 49, 57
perseverance, 214
personal law, 3–4, 18
Planning Commission, 83, 206
planning process, 2, 186–88, 190, 200, 205
plurality, pluralism, 7, 10, 11, 21, 194–95
political bargaining, 42
politics, 6, 56, 62, 162, 190; and religion, 13
Poona Pact, 66
Port William, 90
post-colonial reconstruction, 205
post-Depression retrenchments, 57
poverty, 21
power brokering, 12, 196
pragmatism, 168
Prasad, Rajendra, See Rajendra Prasad
prejudices, 16, 18, 183
Presidency College, Calcutta, 86
Presidency Jail, Calcutta, 128
private sector, 6
progressiveness, 3, 95
prostitutes, 176
Provincial Legislative Assembly, 58, 62
provincialism, 173
Provisional Government, 215
public sector, 2
purdah, 171, 202
purna swaraj, see complete independence

Quaroni, Alberto, xii, 24
Quit India movement, 25, 83, 140, 154–55, 206

racial arrogance, racism, 77, 87, 146, 147
racial equality, 104
radicalism, 34, 58
Rajagopalachari, C., 61, 152
Rajendra Prasad, 56, 60, 63, 70, 74
Rajputs, 171
Ramakrishna, 96
Ramgarh Congress, **1940**, 152
Ramrajya, 14, 110, 117, 179, 184
Rangoon: Japanese victory, 152
Rani Jhansi regiment, 18–19, 95, 99, 141, 210–11, 213, 215
Rao, P.V. Narasimha, 5–6
Ray, Acharya Prafulla, 175
Raychandbhai, 106
reformism, 34
religion, religious, 10, 20, 93, 111, 113, 127, 132, 177, 179, 181; barriers/ divide, 13, 129, 136, 183; consciousness, 14; identity, 213; and state, 3, 130
reservation issue/ system, 5, 15–16
Rolland, Romain, 79, 119, 133, 137, 139, 149, 162
Roosevelt, Franklin, 152–53, 217
Round Table Conference, 41, 49, 81
Rowlatt Act, 111
Rowlatt satyagraha, 115
Roy, Bidhan Chandra, 33, 67, 74
Roy, Dilip Kumar, 51–52, 90–91, 96, 122, 129, 132, 133, 163–64, 166, 168
Roy, Kiron Shankar, 154
Roy, M.N., 65, 70, 74
Roy, Ram Mohan, 172
ruling classes, 3
rural indebtedness, 57, 184
Ruskin, John, 106